FROM
TO

Answers to Questions

In the same 'Answers to Questions' series:

FROM MAMMOTHS TO MEDIUMS...

Answers to Questions

RUDOLF STEINER

Sixteen discussions with workers at the Goetheanum in Dornach between 30 May and 22 September 1923

English by A.R. Meuss, FIL, MTA

RUDOLF STEINER PRESS

Rudolf Steiner Press
Hillside House, The Square
Forest Row, E. Sussex, RH18 5ES

www.rudolfsteinerpress.com

Published by Rudolf Steiner Press 2000
Reprinted 2009

Originally published in German under the title *Rhythmen im Kosmos und
im Menschenwesen, Wie kommt man zum Schauen der geistigen Welt?*
(volume 350 in the *Rudolf Steiner Gesamtausgabe* or Collected Works) by
Rudolf Steiner Verlag, Dornach. This authorized translation is based on
the 3rd edition, edited by Paul Gerhard Bellman, and is published by
kind permission of the Rudolf Steiner Nachlassverwaltung, Dornach.
All drawings in the text are by Leonore Uhlig and are based on Rudolf
Steiner's original blackboard drawings

A catalogue record for this book is available from the British Library

ISBN 978 1 85584 078 2

Cover by Andrew Morgan Design
Typeset by DP Photosetting, Aylesbury, Bucks.
Printed and bound in Great Britain by
Cromwell Press Group Limited, Trowbridge, Wilts.

Contents

Main Contents of the Discussions

see the outside world if everything in the eye is transparent, and we can gain inner sight if something is deliberately made opaque. The right and wrong kinds of movement. Anything to do with machines must take its orientation from man.

4   *Discussion of 9 June 1923*
Effects of light and colour in earthly matter and in cosmic bodies
The colour of a body is connected with the whole way in which it exists in this world. The seven colours of the rainbow. The prismatic colours. Gaseous flames. Spectral analysis. How do colours develop? Sodium flame. Radiant matter. Iron in the blood. Mars and Saturn as opposites.

5   *Discussion of 13 June 1923*
The way our guardian angel works
Examples of the way a spirit who guides a human being from one earth life to another works and gives warnings. Stephenson and academic prejudices in his day. Schleich's experiences with patients who had premonitions of death. Sir Oliver Lodge seeking contact with his son who was killed in the First World War by consulting mediums.

6   *Discussion of 16 June 1923*
The deeper reasons for the disastrous World War
How the inner strength of one individual can have a tremendous influence on the soul of someone else who is rather weak. Examples to show that we are all of us much cleverer in our ether body than in our astral body and I. Julius Robert Mayer and his observations as a ship's doctor. People did not want to know about things of the spirit until 1914, and world destiny has chastised them for this.

7   *Discussion of 25 June 1923*
Effects of relative star positions on the earth and on human beings
The extraordinary weather conditions of recent years. About the mammoths found in Siberia. Periods of great cold, volcanic eruptions and earthquakes are due to unusual relative positions of the

Publisher's Foreword

The truly remarkable lectures—or, more accurately, question and answer sessions—contained in this book, form part of a series (published in eight volumes in the original German)* dating from August 1922 to September 1924. This series features talks given to people involved in various kinds of building work on Rudolf Steiner's architectural masterpieces, the first and second Goetheanums in Dornach, Switzerland. (The destruction by fire of the first Goetheanum necessitated the building of a replacement.) A vivid description of the different types of workers present, as well as the context and atmosphere of these talks, is given by a witness in the Appendix to the first volume of this English series, *From Elephants to Einstein* (1998).

The sessions arose out of explanatory tours of the Goetheanum which one of Steiner's pupils, Dr Roman Boos, had offered. When this came to an end, and the workers still wished to know more about the 'temple' they were involved with and the philosophy behind it, Dr Steiner agreed to take part in question and answer sessions himself. These took place during the working day, after the mid-morning break. Apart from the workmen, only a few other people were present: those working in the building office and some of Steiner's closest colleagues. The subject-matter of the talks was chosen by the workers at the encouragement of Rudolf Steiner, who took their questions and usually gave immediate answers.

After Rudolf Steiner's death, some of the lectures—on the

---

* 347–354 in the collected works of Rudolf Steiner, published by Rudolf Steiner Verlag, Dornach, Switzerland. For information on English translations, see the list on page xvi.

subject of bees — were published. However, as Marie Steiner writes in her original Preface to the German edition: 'Gradually more and more people felt a wish to study these lectures.' It was therefore decided to publish them in full. However, Marie Steiner's words about the nature of the lectures remain relevant to the present publication:

> They had, however, been intended for a particular group of people and Rudolf Steiner spoke off the cuff, in accord with the given situation and the mood of the workmen at the time. There was no intention to publish at the time. But the very way in which he spoke had a freshness and directness that one would not wish to destroy, taking away the special atmosphere that arose in the souls of those who asked the questions and him who gave the answers. It would be a pity to take away the special colour of it by pedantically rearranging the sentences. We are therefore taking the risk of leaving them as far as possible untouched. Perhaps it will not always be in the accustomed literary style, but on the other hand it has directness and vitality.

In this spirit, the translator has been asked also to preserve as much of the original style, or flavour, as possible. This might necessitate that readers study a passage again, trying to bring to mind the live situation in which the talks were given, before the whole can be fully appreciated.

S G

Rudolf Steiner's Lectures to Workers at the Goetheanum

GA (*Gesamtausgabe*) number

347 *From Crystals to Crocodiles, Answers to Questions* (Rudolf Steiner Press 2002)

348 *From Comets to Cocaine, Answers to Questions* (Rudolf Steiner Press 2000)

349 *From Limestone to Lucifer, Answers to Questions* (Rudolf Steiner Press 1999)

350 *From Mammoths to Mediums, Answers to Questions* (Rudolf Steiner Press 2000)

351 Nine of the 15 lectures in the German edition are published in *Bees, Nine lectures on the Nature of Bees* (Anthroposophic Press 1998)

352 *From Elephants to Einstein, Answers to Questions* (Rudolf Steiner Press 1998)

353 *From Beetroot to Buddhism, Answers to Questions* (Rudolf Steiner Press 1999)

354 *From Sunspots to Strawberries, Answers to Questions* (Rudolf Steiner Press 2002)

1 *Dornach, 30 May 1923*

About repeated lives on earth. Physical exercises, dancing and sport

Good morning, gentlemen. As not all of you are here today I think I'll talk about things in such a way that the people who are not here won't miss much. Would you have any questions?

Mr Burle asked about reincarnation. Surely there are a lot more people on earth today than there were before.

Another question was that he had often noted people liking to go round and round – dancing, maybe, or in other ways. And a running dog would always come back to the same spot. Also, if one got lost in the woods or if there was a fog, one would find oneself in the same place again.

Rudolf Steiner: That is indeed a most interesting question.

First, then, the question about incarnations. As you know, if we take account of the anthroposophical science of the spirit, we realize that everyone who is living today has a whole number of earth lives behind him and also ahead of him, and that the human soul therefore returns again and again. Now you should not think that this has anything to do with the belief, which was also quite common in earlier times, that human beings have lived in animal bodies and things like that. This is something our enemies pretend we say. There can be no question of this. But there are two objections that may be raised against the idea of human beings always coming back. The first of these is the one Mr Burle means.

The general view is that the earth's population is always growing, so that we have very many more people in Europe today, for example, than there were about 150 years ago. Is that right? Is this what you mean? That the figures would be too high if we were to trace the earlier lives of all the people who are part of today's large population? One would then have to say that there were fewer people in earlier times and many more people live on earth today. So how can it be that those people from earlier times appear in present-day bodies? That is the question. It is asked very often, the idea being that there are too many people on earth today for us to be able to say that they have all existed before.

Now there are a number of things that have to be taken into account. In the first place, statistics are always only produced for particular areas where the population happens to be increasing to an extraordinary degree, and this gives the idea that the population of the whole earth has always been growing. It would seem as if 3,000 or 4,000 years ago, let us say, there were only few people on earth, whereas today they are here in enormous numbers. People do sums of this kind. They say, for example, that the population of Europe has more or less doubled over the last 150 years. Continuing their calculations on this basis, they then say that there must have been terribly few people on earth 2,000 or 3,000 years ago.

But, gentlemen, this goes completely against the facts as we generally know them. Let me just mention the following. You see, if we go back to before the birth of Christ, let us say, 2,000 years back, that was a time when the most enormous pyramids were being built in the Nile region in Africa, in Egypt; the whole river was being regulated. And if you consider the masses of people needed to erect those vast buildings, even just to build the sphinxes, for instance, which are gigantic in size, in the large numbers in which they were built, you realize that it is quite wrong to say that Egypt's population was small at the time. No, the population must have been dense in Egypt then, much denser than the population of Saxony or of Belgium is today, for example. The historical facts thus definitely contradict the view that going further and further back in earth evolution one would find fewer and fewer people.

Also, if we go much further across into Asia we find vast canal systems. You know, if this is Europe [*drawing on the board*] – I've drawn this for you before – then Africa would be here. That would have been the Nile and Egypt, and over here this would be Asia. That is a vast continent which goes further. And here we have the teeming population who built the pyramids and so on. Over there in Asia was ancient Chaldea. As you know, the Bible says Abraham came from Ur in Chaldea. The land Chaldea existed in those times. And in that country vast canal systems were built in earlier times, remnants of which can still be found. This, too, needed vast numbers of people. So you have to see that the facts prove, quite simply, that vast masses of people existed in Africa and Asia some thousands and thousands of years before Christ's birth.

You also have to consider the following. When the Europeans went to America they settled there. But America was not empty of people at that time. The ancient Indian population that I told you about,[1] the people with copper-coloured skins, has now died out completely. Looking at the things they left behind, some of them buried by now, you realize that a vast population existed there, but the Europeans did not have contact with them.

So this is simply something that is not true, that there were far fewer people on earth in the past. Just think about it – exact figures are not known about the present population; it is only possible to give figures for specific areas. What do European statisticians of today know about the Chinese population now and a thousand years ago? All the things travellers tell us suggest that the population does not always decrease when one goes back in time as is generally assumed but that there certainly have been times when the earth was very highly populated. Then, of course, there have also been times when some areas in particular were less densely populated, but we shall see in a minute that this was nothing special. Generally speaking, and with reference to the things it is possible to know at a superficial level today, the objection that too many people exist today to be reincarnations from earlier times can definitely be shown to be untrue.

But there's something else to be considered as well. You see, looking at people today one comes to realize that one person may have gone through 1,000 years between death and his present birth, someone else perhaps only 500 years, and yet another may have been in the world of the spirit for 1,500 years before he came down again. The people who live today thus have definitely not all been here before at the same time but at different times. If the earth's population was smaller at some time, the souls would wait up above until it had grown larger again.

The things we are able to say about incarnation and reincarnation do therefore agree completely with the facts. I have often said — for this objection has been raised again and again over the years that I have been lecturing — it's just a matter of arithmetic. Let us assume someone lived in AD 800 — somewhere or other. Someone else lived in AD 1000 [*drawing and writing on the board*]. It is now the year 1923. It is perfectly possible that the one I've drawn there meets the one you see here, because the second one had a shorter distance to cover. So now, in 1923, you have two people, but at those earlier times it was always only one. They do not all of them need to be here at the same time in order to return at the same time. It therefore is perfectly true also for times when the earth is less densely populated; it is just that fewer souls come down at such times.

So you see, if one is not thinking in fantasies but in real terms one has to understand that it simply was not the case that there would be two people, later four, then six, and so on. As we go back further in looking at the earth's population we realize that this is completely rhythmical. There are times when there are many people on earth and times when fewer people are on earth. And we shall never get back to a single pair, as it is says in the Bible. That is not what it means. There can be no question of 'one pair', the way it says there. For if we assume that there were just two people at one time we would have to say that there would always have to be just two, and none at all in between times. But that is not the way it is. Here true knowledge contradicts the beliefs of knowledge based on fantasy today.

But there's something else as well. You see, we have to understand clearly that some time must pass before a human being comes down to earth again. And so you may ask: 'Yes, but when does he come down?' Investigating the matter right through to the end one finds that one of them gave much thought to the world of the spirit when on earth, and he'd then grow into that world more easily after his death. Having given much thought to the world of the spirit, he'd need a relatively long time between death and rebirth. He could stay in the world of the spirit for a long time because he had already learnt a great deal about it here. People like that, who've given much thought to the world of the spirit, are able to develop better there, stay longer and return to earth later. Someone who has only given thought to the material world will come back relatively soon. So this is another way in which things shift and change.

That would be one objection. Then there is also another one. I have talked to you about this before.[2] It is this: 'Why do we not remember our earlier incarnations?' Well you see, gentlemen, it's like this. If someone says human beings are able to do sums, that is beyond doubt. They can do sums. But then someone will come and say: 'I'll prove to you that man cannot do sums.' 'Oh, how'll you do that?' And he'll bring along a young child who cannot do sums. 'He's a human being, too,' he'll say.

That is how it is with earlier lives on earth. Human beings can learn this, and they will learn to remember their earlier lives on earth as they continue to evolve on this earth. This is one of the things we hear of in the science of the spirit, that at the present time human beings are not yet able to remember their experiences from the previous life. But what we have to say on this in the science of the spirit is in complete agreement with it. You see, gentlemen, you are in the waking state from morning till evening. You gain living experience from everything around you. And when you remember things, you'll only remember things you have known like this, in the waking state. Just think how quickly we forget even our dreams—which have no particular significance, as I've told you. Human beings therefore remember the things they have come across in the waking state. But there's something else which they do not remember, even here on earth. These are the things they experience in the sleeping state. And we actually experience a great deal more in our sleep than we do in the waking state, only at our present level of conscious awareness we are not yet able to take them in. Once we have gained the ability to do this—and human beings can gain this—we'll know that we experience a tremendous amount in our sleep. As a rule, however, people do not know this, and when they die the things they experienced in their waking life go away after two or three days. It then seems as if all the thoughts one has experienced in the waking state simply go away after two, three or four days. And then all the things we have experienced in our sleep will come up. As I have told you,[3] they'll take a length of time equal to a third of our whole life on earth. Here on earth we therefore also do not yet know about the things that are wholly inward experiences. We shall know them if we enter more and more deeply into the science of the spirit.

So we also need not be surprised if things that happened in our previous life on earth do not come to conscious awareness in our present life. The other day[4] I told you about the difference if I put down a collar stud unthinkingly — I'll then be running about, looking and looking for it in the morning — and about the situation where I specifically recall: that's where I put the stud; in that case I'll not run around but go straight to it. It all depends on whether we give thought to something.

In earlier times people knew that they lived on earth several times over, but as the millennia passed they did not think of this at all as something that was of the spirit. This is why they cannot remember it in their present life on earth. But a time will come when they will remember, just as a time will come for the 4-year-old child when he will be able to do sums.

Now to your other question. People have a desire to go round in a circle. That is a perfectly true statement. Here I have to remind you of the following. We have to learn to stand and walk when we are young children, something we have spoken of before.[5] Imagine now you are lying asleep in your bed, waking up again with a dream, and the dream may not just be one where you are turning round and round — this, of course, would be in your dream — but actually flying. Dreams of flying, in the first place only in one's soul, of course, are not that uncommon. The reason why someone flies in his dreams is usually this. He wakes up; he is used to having the ground under his feet or the seat of a chair or something under him when sitting up in the waking state, in short, always to have something under him. When he is lying down, it is quite uncommon to touch the bottom of the bedstead with the soles of his feet, and the soles are usually free. The individual will thus wake up in a position he is not used to. He'll think he is in the air and flying. This is what he'll think at first.

But now you have to consider the following. If we first have to learn to walk and to stand, that is, to be upright, as children, this means being upright is not something we have in us from birth; we have to learn it. But if we ask ourselves: Where does it come from, this being upright? What is it that we do when we walk upright? Now you have to consider this carefully. Imagine this is the surface of the earth [Fig. 1]. If you loosen a stone here it will fall to the ground. Why? We say because the earth attracts it. If it is really just like that, so that the earth pulls it towards it as if it were on a string, this is something we need to think about. We might talk about it another time. But in any case, a force exists that pulls it down, otherwise it would not fall to the ground. And wherever the stone may be, it will always drop to the ground straight down.

We, too, must learn to take the direction of this line. We must learn to stand in the vertical when we are earthly human beings. And so we adapt ourselves to this vertical line. The whole of our physical body would serve no purpose if we did not assume the vertical position. Look at animals that do not walk upright but on all fours—their toes are quite different in form from our fingers. If our physical

Fig. 1

body is to have meaning, therefore, we must take up the vertical position. This is absolutely necessary.

But does the ether body also need what the physical body needs? You know I've told you that we do not only have this physical body which we see with our eyes when we look at someone, which we can touch with our hands, but we also have a subtle ether body. Now this ether body does not need to adapt. It keeps different habits. What habits? Well, gentlemen, you know that the earth is round and that night and day alternate. What makes night and day alternate? You know, the sun is here [*drawing on the board*], and when its rays come to the earth like this, it is daytime on this side. It would always be day if the earth did not rotate. So when this half, which I've made red, gets to over here, it will be night on this half and day on the other half, which then comes over here.

Night and day therefore arise because the earth rotates. Just think now, the human ether body, this subtle body which we also have, does not get so used to the vertical position as a child does, but always wants to follow this rotation of the earth. This ether body always wants to move around the earth; *this* is how it wants to be; *this* is the movement it always makes. If the ether body did not want to make this movement, you would want to rotate all the time when you are just walking in the direction of the earth, wanting to go round and round all the time because you'd hurt all over from the shove you are given. There has to be something in you that always goes with the movement of the earth; otherwise you'd be hurting all over all the time.

You can also see from this how little thought is given to things in modern science. People know very well that the earth is rotating and not just making the movement the physical body makes when it has adapted to the vertical position. But they do not know of any body that follows *this* movement. That is the situation.

Now imagine you faint. When you faint something departs from your physical and ether body. It is the I and the astral body, that is, the part of you that is the actual element of spirit and soul. And you'll then be aware that the astral body wants to rotate. You will first of all rotate in soul and spirit just as you do with that dream in the morning when you sensed that you had no ground under your feet. When you faint, therefore, you first of all rotate in the mind. When someone feels dizzy, for instance, only the soul part wants to rotate. But imagine now you walk on without giving it a thought. Now, if you walk without giving it a thought you are moving the physical body mechanically. You then do not think about your walking, and especially if there's a mist in the woods you won't be able to give thought to your walking. You don't know which way to turn — where should I go? For you normally aim towards a particular point when you walk with your physical body. You may not always be aware of it, but the path directs you towards a particular point. But if there's a mist you don't see anything, and then your physical body does not know its way about. Along comes your ether body; it only wants to follow its own movement, which is circular. It will follow its own circular motion and take the physical body along with it! When you are merely dreaming or feeling dizzy, the astral body makes the movement. But once you've got going, the ether body brings the physical movement into the physical body and you go along with that. You can see from this that the ether body is not at all earthbound. The human ether body thus does not go along with the way things are on earth.

Now consider this. Between birth and death man is a creature of this earth. He has to work. But as you know, you can't work all the time. The physical body would be worn down, and so on. The person then wants to move his physical body, but not the way it has adapted to the earth;

he wants to follow the ether body. The ether body wants to make circular movements, however, and so the person dances. Dancing is usually a matter of someone not wanting to follow his physical body but his ether body. The desire to dance actually exists so that a person may forget his physical body and can feel himself to be a spirit that belongs to the cosmos.

The problem would be, however, that people would always want to follow their inner feeling and belong far too much to the cosmos, going with their ether bodies. People do not usually want to move the way the earth wants them to move, they'd really like to follow their ether bodies. And it might suit them very well to move as much as possible in circles, the way the ether body wants to move. People must therefore get used to the kind of movements that belong to the earth. And we have also adopted those movements in education, doing physical exercises. Why do people do physical exercises? It means that they adapt even more to the earth than they would otherwise be able to do. People do physical exercises so that they let go more of the ether body, do not always follow the ether body. But if they are not to be completely estranged from the big world, the outer world, people must also make movements that do not tie them to the earth.

Now you see, we live in the age of materialism today. The people who have the greatest longing for materialism live in the West. The Orientals, who once had an ancient culture, the people of Asia, have no great desire to belong to the earth. They see the earth very much as a vale of tears, much more so than Christians do, and the people who live in the Orient, in Asia, want to be off again as quickly as possible.

But Western people like the earth so much, terribly much. It is not that they admit this to themselves, but they'd really like to stay on earth for ever. And here I must tell you something. The ether body wants to move towards the heavens. The planets move in orbits, and so the earth, too, moves in an orbit. The ether body wants to be in orbit, the physical body wants to get out of this orbit. It does get out of it when it has much work to do; but let us consider how it is for people of the upper classes in the West who do not have to do any work. It feels a bit strange to them, for the ether body is always tormenting them. When such a steak-eating individual moves around in the world his ether body is teasing and tormenting him all the time, and he wants to go round in circles. This steak-eater then wants to follow the circular movements of the ether body. Wow! This is extremely uncomfortable! The ether body always wants to dance, to make nice round movements, and the steak-eater cannot keep up. He therefore wants to get his physical body in a condition where it is strong enough not to let itself be pulled into circular motion by the ether body all the time. The individual therefore takes up sport—not just physical exercise but sport. And the result is that the individual comes completely out of the ether body and only follows the physical movements of the earth. He makes friends with the earth more and more and leaves the world of the spirit aside.

You must not think that we merely leave the world of the spirit aside by not thinking about it. We do it also by such means as being so active in sport that we separate the physical body completely from the ether body. This is a terrible thing for the human being; I'd say it is a matter for serious concern. The more they get involved in sport the more do people forget about things of the spirit. After their death they will then come back immediately from the world of the spirit, within a very short time. If it were not the case that everything in the West does receive a little of the spirit, the earth would gradually be populated only by people who do not at all want to go back to the world of the spirit. And you would then have nothing but people on earth who gradually bring the earth to utter ruin. We are beginning to do this a little bit even now. This little bit is already quite serious for present-day humanity. But once people start to give no more consideration to their ether body but only their physical body, this will bring about horrific conditions on earth. And so one must once again intervene by means of the science of the spirit. The only possible way is to oppose movements that are entirely designed to drive man into his physical body, making him wholly earth-man, using other movements that are in opposition.

People's minds are already turned towards becoming earthly human beings. You'll understand, now that I have given you so many talks, that without being a philistine, such things do make one's heart ache.

You see, I also went to England last summer. When we were just about to leave, all England was full of excitement, waiting for the evening papers to read about the most important event. Everyone was eagerly waiting for the evening papers. What were they waiting for? The football results!

Now we've just come from Norway. Many people were there when we left. The station platform was full of people. And when the train started to move people shouted hurrah, hurrah. At the next station they were shouting: 'Three cheers for him!' Well, this was not for us, of course, and the question is, who was it for? I just managed to find out that it was for football players who'd come to Norway from Central Europe and were on their way home again.

So what does interest people today? Well, they are much more interested in these things which gradually draw the physical body away from the ether body, making the human being wholly into a creature of the earth, than in any event connected with the weal and woe of millions of people.

Because of this, other movements have to be made to

oppose the movements that are now being made all over the world, spreading more and more. These are the eurythmic movements. They take their orientation from the ether body. When you see eurythmy being done, you'll see all the movements which the etheric body makes. When you see sport being done, you'll see all the movements which the physical body makes.

Yes, gentlemen, this is extraordinarily important, for it also means a longing for sport. I do not want to say anything against sport in general. Sport is of course quite a good thing if it is done by people who also work, for one has to get used to more unnatural movements at work; if one then does natural movements in sport, movements that are more adapted to the physical body, then recreation in sport is a good thing. But the way people are active in sports today, with many of them having no need for recreation, what is this, really? You see there are sports people today who may perhaps — not all of them, of course, but there are certainly some — quickly go to church in the morning, where they pray: 'I believe in a god in heaven,' and so on. Then they go to the sports field. Now they are not putting it in words, but if we put what they do in words it is this: 'I do not believe in a god in heaven, of course. I believe in flesh and bones, for this alone makes life worth living.' You see, that is the inevitable, unconscious consequence of the things people do today. You are a materialist not only if you say you do not want to know about things of the spirit but also with things like these, where the whole human being is torn away from the spiritual element.

Concerning your question one is therefore able to say this. When someone walks in the woods and there's a mist and he loses his way, it'll happen on occasion that he runs after his ether body. That is not so bad, for he'll come back to the same place again. When you turn around yourself — that is not so bad, it means a lot of swinging to and fro like a pendulum, now to the ether body and now to the physical body. This is because human beings have both of them and should also develop both. That is the way the situation is. But in the Western world there is a general tendency today to leave the ether body out completely and care only for the physical body, and this causes the terrible materialism which is the truly harmful materialism. For materialism in thought is not the most harmful. The most harmful kind of materialism is the one where the whole human being descends to the animal level. This is what we have to consider.

It happens only too easily that people say: 'Oh, he's a philistine, for he rants and raves against sport. Sport is something extremely useful!' But I do not rant and rave against sport. People are free to indulge in sport, they are free human beings. But they will completely ruin themselves as human beings if they devote themselves only to things to do with sport.

Here it is necessary to understand clearly that the things I said in the first chapter of *Towards Social Renewal*[6] apply in the widest possible sense. When I wrote the book I did of course think I'd write in a way that would make people think about the subject. Well, they've not cared a rap about it. They did not reflect at all and the book has not been understood. I said that whilst we do have a large democratic proletarian movement, one finds, on taking a closer look, that most proletarians today are copying everything middle-class people have done before, they follow the academic line, and they believe in the things that are said at the universities. Sometimes the proletarian parties are the first to agree to legislation — remember freedom of choice in medical treatment? — and the socialists are generally the first to say, 'Yes, that calls for an expert committee,' and so on. And when it comes to sport — sport is of course a middle-class invention which they try to copy as well. It won't always quite work; but they certainly copy it as far as attitude goes, considering sport to be the only beneficial thing. But in fact the proletarian movement will only come to be something if they do not copy what the other classes did before. I therefore specially wrote that first chapter. One could see the proletarian movement everywhere getting under the influence of belief in authority. That is why I wrote that first chapter of *Towards Social Renewal*, thinking that people would give thought to the matter.

But of course, giving thought to things is something people who do sports do not like at all. For when someone is very active in sport this will get him out of the way of thinking things over. For we can only think with the ether body. You may try as hard as you like — you can't think with your physical body. And when someone asks if they should eat meat or only vegetables in order to be able to think better, all one can say is: 'You can't cultivate your thinking by eating; you have to do it with the ether body. You have to enter into the ether body there.'

So you see, the ether body reveals its presence in the human being in the circular movements which people want to make, in the longing to dance, or in people losing their way and walking in a circle.

Yes, gentlemen, if you've ever lived in Vienna, for example, you'll know that the Viennese like to enjoy life. They are quite frivolous; they have warmth of heart, but they are frivolous. In Vienna you have the Prater, large pleasure gardens, vast pleasure gardens. It is a place where people usually go on a Sunday, unless they are the kind of ne'er-do-well who goes there every day. You get hot dogs there, clowns and all kinds of things. But the paths in the Prater are laid out in a peculiar way. They are laid out in such a way that you will always end up in the same place. You walk down a long avenue, entering the woods some-where, and after some time you'll be back in the place where you were before! If you started from a hot dog stand, you'll be back there again. That is how the paths are laid out. You see, they did not of course say to themselves, 'Let's encourage the people of Vienna to come out here and enjoy themselves,' but they had an inner feeling for this, and so they made the paths run in such a way that people don't even need a mist to find themselves back at the beginning again. They made the paths go round the way the ether body likes them, so that people feel quite taken out of their physical bodies. For you can feel taken out of yourself there, and this will really make you feel good. You'll go around in circles unless you have a direction. And if the paths are already made in such a way that you'll walk in circles willy-nilly, you'll also feel good. And that was what the people who designed the Prater wanted the Viennese to feel — that their ether body would feel really good as they found themselves back at the hot dog stall again and again. It is very cleverly done. You can go and look how the paths run. When you give yourself up to this — you'll always come back again, but you go round. And it is this turning round which makes people feel really good, especially if they do it all Sunday afternoon.

This is of course a much more innocent feeling of well-being than in many other cases. You know that one can also lose one's bearings in other ways. I've told you the story before. Coming home late at night and not quite knowing if you're drunk or not, you put your top hat on your bed. If you see one, you're not drunk, if you see two, you're drunk. This is because it is going round. You see, in that case, something is also turning. It is the astral body. When someone lies in bed who is drunk, his astral body is going round. But when someone brings the ether body into it in a more mental way, by following paths that go round, it is the ether body which goes round. That is the more innocent way of going round and round.

Drinking goes to the astral body; turning round oneself

more to the ether body. There you can also see the difference. For when I look at someone who is drunk, well, he does not turn round like someone following circular paths, for everything is going round and round for him, as if his astral body itself had now become the earth's globe. He goes round and round the way the earth goes round. That is the astral body which is going round.

But when people are dancing or going round and round in Vienna's Prater, the ether body is going round. It takes the physical body along with it; it is the more innocent way. We may say that when someone is dancing the ether body is going round, and when someone is drunk it is the astral body which is going round.

You see, these things are not considered in modern science and because of this the big questions relating to our civilization cannot be answered, for people do not know how to arrange things so that human beings will not become utterly inhuman. Humanity will get more and more animal-like if today's sports craze continues.

Something of the spirit must come to humanity. And I am convinced that people who on the one hand get to know the earth through work will on the other hand also feel a longing to enter into things of the spirit and will gradually come to understand that we must also take care of the spiritual side of things, that this is necessary.

This, then, is what I wanted to say to you for the moment. We'll be talking a lot more about these things, so that they will be clear to everyone.

How the etheric and astral principles work in man and earth

Good morning! I'd really like to add something today to what I said last time. I believe we shall have better and better knowledge of what man really is within the whole scheme of things if we study exactly this kind of thing. So I'd like to add to what we discussed the last time by considering how things really are when people develop conditions such as grey or black cataract. The eye becomes useless in that case. At first it seems to a person as if something was flickering before his eyes, and then he will no longer be able to see the things which he was able to see before.

The question is, what causes this eye condition? It develops because something which should be as transparent as glass in the eye becomes non-transparent. If you have some kind of non-transparent paper or cardboard in your window instead of transparent glass, you'll no longer be able to see through the window. And that is how it is when an eye develops cataract. Something that should be transparent has become non-transparent.

Let us be really clear about this. I have drawn the eye for you on several occasions. It grows out from the brain like this [Fig. 2], from the skull; this is looking at it from the side. It projects a little in front, and inside the eye you have blood vessels spreading and the optic nerve. Blood vessels and optic nerve thus come together there.

Then there is something else in the eye, a kind of muscular attachment. It holds the part we call the lens in position. The muscle in the eye thus holds a very small,

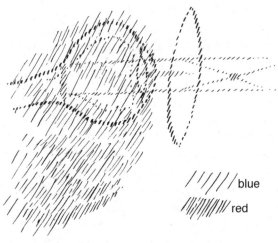

///// blue

/////// red

Fig. 2

transparent, lentil-shaped body in position. Think of a
small lentil, but transparent — this is suspended in the eye.
And we have to look straight across and through this lens.
Seen from in front, the lens looks like this [*drawing on the
board*], and we must be able to see through it. This alone
will show you that we have to have a transparent eye if we
are to be able to see. The eye must be transparent. And of
course if you think about it you have to say: 'It cannot be
the eye itself which sees, for the eye must actually get itself
out of the way, make itself transparent, so that it may see.'
If you smear something on these window panes, for
instance, so that you cannot see through them, then you'll
no longer be able to look out. Yes, it is you who looks
through the panes. The panes cannot see; it is you yourself
who sees. In the same way it is not the eye which sees but
there is something in the human being that sees through
the transparent eye.

What, then, happens when someone develops a cataract?
When someone develops a cataract, the lens in the eye loses

its transparency. It is very small, this lens, but if you take it out of the eye and look through it, it is transparent. A lens taken from someone with cataract, however, is white, milky, non-transparent. I would then have to draw the lens, which is so beautifully transparent in a healthy eye, like this [*drawing on the board*]. It has become milky and is no longer transparent.

You see, we always have the benefit of the human body being elastic in its individual parts, elastic in many respects. So if you have an eye affected by cataract and cut into it in a particular direction, this muscle here brings its elasticity into play, and the lens, which is normally held by the muscle, will pop out if you make a hole here. The operations are relatively simple, because the body always comes to your aid. The lens pops out. You hold it in your hand and put it in a glass dish, this lens which has grown opaque. The individual will of course be quite unable to see clearly once the lens has been removed, for he needs the lens to be able to see. I'll show you in a minute why he needs a lens to be able to see.

When one has done this operation on someone, having removed the lens, the world around him will light up again where before he saw nothing at all. He will now be able to look out, but, having had the operation to remove the lens, he'll only be able to see objects that are far away. His power of vision will not be adequate. We then have a useless eye. The power of vision is not enough to be able to see things which we might have been able to see, still have been able to see, with the lens that has been taken out. The eye has become useless.

You then give the person who has had the operation a pair of glasses. You see, they are actually artificial lenses. Before he had the lens in his eye, and now he has an artificial one. The artificial lens now makes the visual rays— which went like this before the lens was removed [Fig. 2], so that he would only have been able to see things a long way off — go in such a way that he can see nearby things again. This is the effect of the glass put in front of his eye. The lens he had inside his eye can therefore be replaced with a transparent glass lens. It will of course be less perfect, because there's no life in it. The lens in the eye has life; it can be moved, and that does have its advantages. But at least one will be able to see if need be, if the lens which has grown opaque is simply taken out and replaced with glasses, cataract glasses. The individual will then be able to see again.

This makes it possible for us to see exactly how things are with our seeing — that in the eye we have an apparatus, a tool that allows us to see, for it is actually possible to replace a small part of the eye with an external tool, the cataract glasses. You will realize that the living tool, that is the lens, has an advantage over the cataract glasses used to replace it, for if one wants to see something that is a long way off one has to make the lens, which looks like this [drawing on the board], a bit thinner. You'll then see something that is further away. So when a hunter takes aim and wants to shoot something that is further away, he has to make his lens thin. This is done by the muscle here [pointing to the drawing]; this makes it thinner. If one wants to see something close by, reading small print from close-up, one has to make the lens thicker. Again it is the muscle which does it. This is something you can't do with cataract glasses, of course; all one could do would be to use a different pair. People sometimes do this. There certainly are people today who have to have two kinds of glasses, one for things nearby and one for distant things. But the lens in the eye is a living thing and can be changed inside so that one sees both near and far.

You'll now also realize why someone will only see distant objects when I've taken out the lens, for that is as if I'd made the lens quite flat, having taken it out. I then see things again that are a long way off. But the ability to see is not adequate.

Behind the lens is a body that is quite slimy, the 'vitreous body'. This can also grow opaque. In that case no operation is possible, for it cannot be replaced in some way or other. The eye is black if you look into it from outside. The lens lies behind this black pupil, which looks black because you are looking at the background of the eye, looking through the whole of the lens and through all this.

Now we have to ask ourselves what actually happens when the lens grows opaque. Think of glass once more. When glass is transparent the light goes through it. If you have something that is not transparent, this means that the light does not go through; it is stopped. Now the situation with the eye is that light must go in and out through the lens. You see, the light belongs to the ether. It does not belong to matter, to the stuff of gravity, which is outside. Light belongs to the ether.

Now I've told you that apart from his physical body man also has an ether body. And what does it mean that the lens is transparent? The fact that the lens is transparent means that the human ether body, which goes through every-thing—I'll make it red here—can simply pass through the lens. If the lens is nice and transparent, the ether body is able to pass through it. This means that the human being has a little piece of ether body in the place where the lens is. When the lens grows opaque, this is because the lens gets all stuffed up with matter. If salt or something like it settles in the lens it grows opaque. It is just like having salt dissolved in a glass of water. For as long as the salt is in solution you have an almost transparent salt solution. If the salt settles down at the bottom [*drawing on the board*], the glass of water is not transparent down here. The matter will not let the light through. And the lens grows opaque when salty matter settles in it. Salty matter will settle like that in old age, and the transparent parts of the human being then lose their transparency.

With a cataract, therefore, a transparent lens grows opaque. What is the result of this? It is that the human ether body is no longer able to get into the opaque lens. So then there's a small hole here. The human being has his ether body everywhere, and when he's in good health the ether body fills the whole of him. If the lens gets sick, grows opaque, the ether body cannot get into the place where the lens is. So then you don't have ether body in the place where the lens is. We therefore have to say: What kind of condition is this cataract? Cataract means that the person has no ether body in the place where the lens has grown opaque.

You can't, of course, see with just the ether body. If we were able to see with the ether body, we would also see all night, for we have our ether body when we lie in bed at night; only the astral body is outside. We therefore do not see with the ether body. We see with the soul. But we need the ether body to be able to see. The astral body is there as well — it is the third thing a human being has, and it also fills up everything. When the astral body wants to see here in the place where there is no ether body, it cannot do it, for the ether body is missing there. And so we are able to say: What makes it possible for us to see? The fact that our astral body is inside our ether body. But if the ether body has been eliminated somewhere, pushed aside because the lens, the eye, is opaque, we are unable to see. Then the astral body cannot see. Can you understand this?

Agreement — yes!

Our astral body is therefore able to see because the ether body is able to get in everywhere where we have the lens, where it is most needed. So if one really knows what a cataract is, one can truly see that the human being has an ether body and an astral body.

When someone is just beginning to have such a cataract, we can say that the cataract is developing because the salts which settle in the eye, in the lens, do not let the ether body into the eye. And one would have to do something to make the lens transparent. When matters have gone a long way and the lens has salts in it everywhere, one cannot do anything but remove it and replace it with cataract glasses. But the situation is that one can still do something if the cataract is only beginning to develop. And on this occasion I think I can show you how human beings are completely bound up with the world around them.

Let us assume this is the earth [Fig. 3]. Plants grow in the soil. You see, such a plant does of course have a physical body. We can touch it, look at it. But the plant also has an ether body, for it lives, and everything that lives has an ether body. The plant is not able to feel, however, to respond to things inwardly. It does not have an astral body. But there is astral substance everywhere around the earth. Let me tell you how one can discover the fact that the astral is everywhere. To do this we'll need to bring in something that seems rather remote and does not appear to belong here.

You know that volcanoes will now and then—well, they'll start spewing, as we may put it, so that red hot

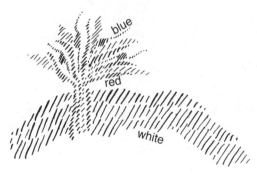

Fig. 3

masses fly out from them. Let me describe such a mountain a little bit for you. First of all there is the ground, filled up with ordinary rock material. And if we look at Vesuvius, for example, which is in Italy, the ground, the basic ground, is Apennine rock, as it is called. So we have ordinary rock down there, which you also have everywhere else in that region. But then somewhat different layers pile up here [Fig. 4]. The layers go like this. And in the place where Vesuvius erupts there is a cleft. When there is an eruption, particles of ash will first of all come up from the cleft, mixed with water; then come rocks like bombs. All this is flung to the surface. It is sometimes liquid, sometimes like bombs. It then runs down, runs further down. And the rocks which are thrown out like bombs are everywhere. They flow down. In between comes a rain mixed with mud. All this will really pile up to make such a mountain, create such a mountain. So the first thing thrown out from the inner earth is hot water mixed with ash. It makes a very sticky sludge as it runs down. Then, a bit later, these bomblike lumps come,

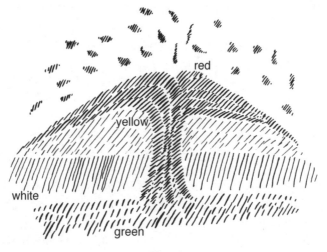

Fig. 4

rushing upwards and flung all over the place. So that is how such fiery mountains are made.

Now let me tell you, gentlemen, how a phenomenon like fire-spewing mountains is usually considered in science. It is said that all kinds of things that are under the earth rush up and out. Fire-spewing mountains are normally near water, it is said. And that is, of course, true. You have few volcanoes in the middle of a land mass; they are usually close to the shore, to water. As there is a cleft in the ground, the water can get in, they say, and the heat inside the earth brings the water to the boil. And this boiling water then pushes out all the matter which is down below. This is what a learned person will say, writing a book about it, and people will then say he has explained how volcanoes develop.

Then someone else comes along and says: 'Yes, but we have reason to believe that these clefts are not big enough for water to get in. We cannot assume that the water gets in through those clefts in the earth, even if the volcanoes are close to water.' It therefore does not appear to be quite right what the first expert said, and the matter will have to be explained in another way.

The next person will say: 'Well, in the inner earth, things are not the way they are on the outside; metals are liquid in the inner earth. As iron is liquid when you work it in a smelter, so are the metals liquid in the inner earth. You have liquid metals in there.' Well—and it is easy to put a name to things—these liquid metals are called magma. So you have magma in there, well and good, liquid metals. And when this liquid metal, this magma, gets to a place where it can escape more easily—everywhere here it is too hard for it to escape, or it would spew forth everywhere—when it gets a place where it can escape more easily, then it will get out just there, and that is how it comes out.' That is what this person has to say. He is saying, therefore, that it happens because of irregularities in the density of the earth; the magma then shoots out in one direction or another.

Then a third person comes along, or a fourth, and he'll say: 'Yes, but the magma cannot have the enormous energy needed to throw out those bombs! So this cannot be the explanation either.' Other people will say something else again. And this then ends up in the ordinary books produced for the general population.

So that is more or less the situation as it is today. You will usually find that one person says one thing and another says something else, but people do not really know where the cause lies. These things are enormously important, but they do not know where the cause lies.

But now let me tell you something. The matter is this. When you come to a region where Vesuvius is not far away, into the neighbourhood of a volcano,[7] you'll see something that is rather nice. If you take a piece of paper and set it alight, the ground will suddenly begin to smoke. You see, if this is the ground [Fig. 5], and you light a piece of paper here, so that it burns (red), the ground will start to smoke, quite by itself, everywhere here beneath the burning paper, and if you burn a large piece of paper you may gradually be completely enveloped in the smoke. This is really a most

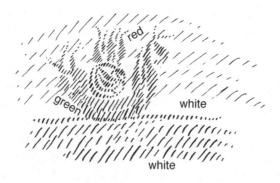

Fig. 5

interesting phenomenon. Guides will show visitors to Italy how the smoke comes up from the ground if one just burns a piece of paper.

Now what does this really mean? Well you see, gentlemen, some water vapour has collected in there, in that place. It has collected in there in the soil, where this vapour will then rise. It cannot get out if the air that is above has a certain density. The air keeps the vapour in. Now you all know that air gets thinner if you warm it up. The air in a room also gets thinner if you heat it. The thinner air can then no longer keep the vapour in and it will stream out. It has to be there in the first place, of course. There has to be something down there which can stream out. Yes, but think, gentlemen, what you have been doing there! You have not been down below to blow the vapour up and out. No, you did not do that. You have coaxed the vapour out by lighting a piece of paper. You can coax the vapour out by setting something on fire up here, above ground. You do so by making the air thinner.

You see the learned gentlemen are always looking for the reasons why water vapour rises from a volcano and even bombs fly out; they look for the reasons—yes, they look for them below ground. But that is not where they are, just as the reasons for water vapour coming out when you light a piece of paper are not below ground but outside, outside and not in it.

You really must be able to understand the facts rightly, and then you find out how things are. But just as you are not in here [*pointing to the drawing*], blowing vapour out of the ground, but coax it out with the help of thin, hot air, so something there is coaxing out something from down below. And you see, you won't get solid rocks coming out if you just light a piece of paper, otherwise the curious English tourists would not just be enveloped in vapour but also get all kinds of rocks hitting them in the face when they light the paper. No, you don't get that; it is only that the air is thinned and vapour rises. But here above Vesuvius, when it begins to spew, to erupt, everything that is astral above it is thinned down. And this astral element is thinned down by forces that come from the stars, the planets, forces that are a long way off. So if the stars above Vesuvius are in a particular position relative to each other, which happens often — it does not happen elsewhere but just in that place — then it is just as it is with the paper here, in this case through the position of the stars, with the astral element above thinning out, and things are forcibly pulled up from below.

You thus produce a small volcanic eruption by making the sulphurous vapours — it is not only water vapour but also a sulphurous vapour — come out. These places are called *solfatara*, volatiles. So wherever you have these tremendous volcanic eruptions, the activity lies not in the matter which is below ground, but in something which is outside, coming from the relative position of the stars.

Now you'll sometimes also get — what shall I call it? — busybody activity, officiousness. Someone did once realize that some such things come from the positions of the stars, the relative positions of sun and moon, for instance. His name was Rudolf Falb.[8] Some of the older ones among you may have heard something about his famous theory. Mr Falb said that not only earthquakes but volcanic eruptions, too, were due to the positions of the stars. And that was quite right. But he was also an extremely vain man who liked to show off.

He discovered something else as well, which is equally important. You know about the firedamp explosions which are a terrible problem in mines. Something happens down the mines because gases ignite, rushing through the mines with great vehemence. Mr Falb said that this particular quality of the gases also did not come from below ground but from the positions of sun and moon, for example.

Having thought this up, he actually forecast earthquakes and firedamp explosions in mines. Well, his forecasts would sometimes come true and often they would not. The thing is that unexpected elements often play into natural events, and then the matter won't be as expected. Mr Falb would however publish forecasts every year that gave you the critical days. When the stars were in particular relative positions, when sun and moon were in particular relative positions, he would say that firedamp explosions would occur on such days or that there would be an earthquake.

I once went to a lecture by Falb — it's a long time ago now, much more than 30 years ago. He was a tall, slender man and very convincing as he presented his theories. So he said — he knew nothing about the astral but thought it all just came from this dilution of heat — that heat was diluted and this would coax up gases from below in the mines — just as in the *solfataras* — which would then result in firedamp explosions or the like. It was a large hall. Mr Falb was standing up high. He explained it, explained it well. Much of what he said was correct. Suddenly, as he was in the middle of his explanation, saying: 'So a particular relative position of sun and moon causes a change in the air, firedamp must develop, and the gases are coaxed up' — bang! a knock on the door. A boy from the *Neue Freie Presse* came in and brought a telegram, putting it on the desk. Mr Falb was not exactly subtle. Saying, 'Must be something important,' he opened the telegram in the middle of his lecture and read: 'Major firedamp explosions have just occurred in such and such a mine.' Now he'd just forecast those firedamp explosions in his lecture. He had previously contacted the paper and asked them to send any news of this kind to the lecture hall as soon as it came in. He did such things on several occasions; he was a bit vain. But it did happen, gentlemen. Just when Mr Falb had said that something like a firedamp explosion was due to happen, the boy brought in the telegram. And he actually said: 'You see, ladies and gentlemen, that is how proof is put straight on the table!'

Well, that was a case of showing off, of course. But there was something behind it all that was extraordinarily true, especially in the case of Mr Falb. The situation is such that one has to say that even the dense, heavy masses thrown up into the air are not pushed up from below but coaxed up from above, by the relative positions of the stars. Only I'd say that the air has thinned down a little if you get vapour rising with a burning piece of paper and you are quite enveloped in the vapour. When solid masses are thrown up into the air, this cannot be just due to the air thinning down; the ether must be thinned down in that case and also the astral. So in finding the right explanation for our volcanic eruptions we also discover that the earth is enveloped all around not only in earthly matter but also in the astral. In modern science, people do not have the courage to explain these things exactly as they are. There is a lack of courage there.

So if we imagine this is the earth [*drawing on the board*], we have to think of it being surrounded everywhere firstly by the ether, and then also by the astral. But the astral also penetrates into everything. Plants, however, do not generally take in the astral. They only have an ether body. But some plants do take in the astral and these are poisonous plants. The difference between non-poisonous plants and poisonous plants is that non-poisonous plants do not have anything astral in them and poisonous plants do.

What does this mean, however? You see, deadly nightshade is one of the most poisonous plants. If you have a deadly nightshade berry, it is as black as it is because the astral has been taken up into it. Deadly nightshade thus takes in the astral. And because deadly nightshade takes in the astral—it does not really destroy itself completely—it has the power to destroy physical matter all the time. A deadly nightshade berry is quite acrid inside; it wants to destroy physical matter. And if we eat one, the juice begins to destroy our inner substance as soon as it is inside us. We then have to perish under the deadly nightshade influence. Deadly nightshade has the power inside it to destroy physical matter.

Just imagine we now bring deadly nightshade extract into a person's blood in the right way by inoculating it in a highly diluted form. If the lens begins to have salts in it, to get dark, we can fight this cataract exactly by using deadly nightshade extract, if properly diluted, having been made so thin that it is no longer poisonous but destroys the deposits that have formed. I have drawn the sediment on the board for you. And if we have done the right kind of inoculation to bring the destructive deadly nightshade extract, which always makes everything else go apart, to the lens here, it will also drive apart the salts that have settled there, and it may be possible to cure the lens.

Of course, you won't be able to depend too much on this if the cataract has already developed too far. But if you have someone whose cataract has not yet gone far and this is noticed in good time, it will still be possible to fight the cataract and not have to remove the lens later on.

This is why it usually does not get one very far to do it the way homoeopathic physicians do it. They give diluted deadly nightshade by mouth. It will have an effect, but not a very powerful one, and the problem will keep coming back. So it is not usually possible to achieve anything in this way. But you can do a great deal if you inoculate it into the blood. The blood goes everywhere, also into the eye.

Now this also shows you something else. It is this. If we have a poison like that of deadly nightshade, if we eat a lot of deadly nightshade berries—a little would be a lot, of course, in this case—but if we eat relatively much of the deadly nightshade, it will destroy our physical substance, starting from the stomach and even the gullet. We'd no longer be able to live. If we dilute this deadly nightshade extract more and more, it will no longer attack the physical parts but will be digested and still attack the head very strongly. You can thus use deadly nightshade extract when people have grown nervy, when they are all at sixes and sevens; you can put them to rights again by giving them highly diluted deadly nightshade extract to eat. It will drive out the stuff that has become deposited. But if you take it so highly diluted that it will no longer attack the head, it will still act on the eye. The eye is the organ which is sensitive to the most dilute quantities of deadly nightshade. It is called belladonna, 'beautiful lady', because of its lustrous black eyes. The eye is therefore able to react even to very small amounts of deadly nightshade extract. And it is strange that our human nature is sensitive to different substances from the world around us in so very different ways. As I said, too much deadly nightshade extract destroys the whole eye, but the eye is sensitive to deadly nightshade extract in high dilution. Other organs are sensitive to other extracts. So there is always something in our body that is particularly sensitive to a particular substance and one gets different effects.

Take the human liver, for instance. Now the situation is that the human liver really has an awful lot to do. I have told you before that it is an internal observer.[9] It has an awful lot of things to do in our digestion. Above all the liver has to perform a major function in processing fats in the human organism. If the liver is unable to function properly, all the fat in a human being gathers itself up and wanders about in the body in all kinds of different ways. Fat migrations happen instead of the fat being processed in the liver. The fat we eat therefore has a special relationship to the liver. And just as good substances have a relationship to different parts of the body, so poisons, too, have a particular relationship to all parts of the human being.

And so we can say that it is possible, in a way, to lighten the lens in the eye again when it has darkened, thus sending the astral body back into this small part of the human being by inoculating the individual with something from the outside world that will specifically attack the eye. And that is deadly nightshade extract in suitable dilution. So you see, deadly nightshade extract is something which will draw the astral back into the eye, so that the person is able to see again, thanks to the astral principle. It draws in the astral, and the astral in turn will draw in the ether principle.

I'd therefore also like to say that deadly nightshade also attracts the astral when it grows out there. The etheric is in it already, it does not need to be attracted. But if we are able to do a proper study of the subtle process involved in curing eyes affected by cataract with deadly nightshade, we shall also understand what happens in the plant outside. The extract attracts the astral principle which has been excluded. And the sap of the plant therefore also attracts the astral principle from the world. Deadly nightshade sap is something that attracts the astral. And when we are poisoned by the plant, with too much of the astral drawn to us, this astral element comes to a boil and this boiling process destroys our physical substance.

And when too much of the physical has been destroyed — in an eye affected with cataract it is destroyed because deposits form in it — we must get rid of those deposits. Get rid of them! One might thus also hope, gentlemen, to cure situations where salts or similar substances have settled elsewhere in the body with belladonna, deadly nightshade. When someone develops gallstones, for example, or stones in the bladder, something solid is deposited that should not be there. One would hope, therefore, that if we can cure the problem in the lens of an eye affected by cataract with belladonna we might also cure gallstones and stones in the bladder with belladonna. And one can do this, if things are done the right way. One can do it!

We can see, therefore, that it all goes together, and if we gain the right understanding of nature we can also gain a right understanding of the human being. Once again we have arrived at the ether and the astral body, just as we did the last time when we talked about people going round and round. If one finds the right way of looking at things, one always comes to these higher bodies of the human being. This is not something thought up but something that has been discovered in a science that goes further than ordinary science does in every respect.

Next Wednesday we'll talk more about these things, unless you'll have some other questions you have prepared.

3 Discussion of 6 June 1923

Blood circulation and movement of the heart. Perceiving things of the spirit through the lens of the eye

Good morning, gentlemen.
Does anyone have a question?

A question is asked regarding grey cataract. The individual says he was in hospital in Basel in 1916 with an inflammation of the iris, and he had been given injections in the head. He now wanted to know if these injections might not have done harm.

Rudolf Steiner: Why, did you notice something? You must not think, of course, that those injections could play a role in developing grey cataract. The spots before your eyes you mention need not indicate any form of cataract; they are due to something else. Now you see, injections have the peculiarity that they sometimes make the muscles in the area a bit weaker, and one can then no longer bring the muscles freely into play; the eye becomes a little bit rigid. If you then direct your eye to something it will not focus properly right away, and that causes these 'flies and midges'. But this is often only due, I'd say, to a minor weakness of accommodation. Why did you have those iris injections?

They thought it was the vitreous body.

Rudolf Steiner: The thing is, it is always better to fight such things by other means, that is, for as long as possible with medicines taken by mouth. Some things cannot be treated with medicines taken by mouth; then one tries inoculation. But you need not feel concern over this. There's no need for that.

Is there perhaps some other question to be asked, so that we may answer it?

Questioner: I'd like to go back once more to the business of going round and round. I have noticed, and so have my colleagues, that some things are not clear when we are discussing the heart. I have been thinking about the way Dr Steiner once did a drawing for us of how the earth is connected with the moon and there is that aura — I'm not sure I'm getting this right — around the sun. The heart is on the left side of the body. Now I wanted to ask if the heart is also connected with all the things that go on in the world at large.

Rudolf Steiner: Here we need to remember a number of things we have been discussing before. I once said that the ideas people have about the heart in modern science are wrong. They imagine the heart to be a kind of pump, and that the heart pumps the blood through all parts of the body. They see it like this. The heart contracts. When the heart contracts it gets smaller, has less blood in it. It therefore pushes the blood out through the arteries, the blood gets pushed into the body, and being elastic — that is what people think — the heart then expands again. The heart is therefore said to act as a pump today, pumping blood through the body.

You see, that is quite the wrong idea. It is altogether an idea which only comes from the age of materialism, reducing everything to mechanics, therefore, with people thinking the heart is a proper mechanical pumping station which pumps the blood through the whole body. No account is taken of the way in which the whole of life really goes in a living creature. Let me draw your attention to one thing here.

There is a very small lower animal which is really just a kind of tube. If I were to draw it [Fig. 6], it would be something like this. There you'd have a skin. The creature is such a tube. Inside it is hollow, and there it is simply like a small bowl, a small dish. There it has little trapping hairs, and hairs it can move around with. It lives in water, this

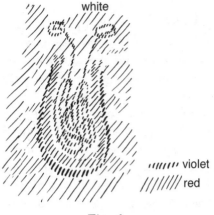

white

ⅰⅰⅰⅰⅰⅰⅰ violet

//////// red

Fig. 6

creature. It is called a hydra, because it lives in water. This creature, the hydra, has the peculiarity that compared to higher animals or human beings it is really nothing but a stomach. And this tube really does nothing but take in all kinds of little granules, all kinds of foods that come near it, and digest them in there. The creature lives in the water, as I said; and all kinds of food float around in the water. The creature swims about, swims up to the bits of food, takes them in and so does just what our stomach does, for that, too, takes things in. The creature does not of course have a gullet, a mouth, for preparing the foods. The hydra simply takes in the foods and digests them. Now the odd thing is that its mouth is also its organ of elimination, its anus. It also eliminates things through the mouth. So you have everything together in this creature.

Now of course to be a form of life, and especially an animal, it must not only eat—eating is something it has to do—but also breathe. And this creature breathes with the outer side of its skin. Everywhere there you have tiny little holes. You always have such little holes where there is organic matter, living matter. And it absorbs the air it needs from the water through these little holes. So we can say this tiny creature, the hydra, has an inner side, a hollow space, which it uses to eat. On the outside it has its breathing organs. The creature draws in air, and the air also gets in there, into the hollow space in the middle. The creature is able to feed, to breathe. Those are its main occupations. It floats about everywhere in the water, eating and breathing in air, which is of course also present in the water.

Now what would a materialistic person say? He would say: 'Ah well, this creature simply consists of this skin. This skin has grown in such a way that it is a feeding apparatus inside and a breathing apparatus on the outside.' That's what a materialist would say. But we cannot say that, for we have to consider this to be a highly superficial way of looking at it. We have to say: 'No, this creature also has an ether body, and it is inside this, and it also has an astral body, being inside that as well. These it has as well, these are its invisible parts.'

Well now, gentleman, is there some way in which we can prove that the creature has something invisible to it as well as the visible part? A materialist will say: 'The visible is of interest to me, the invisible is not. The visible creature shows me a kind of stomach inside, and a kind of lung on the outside. And I am content with that.'

Now there is something you can do with this creature. You know, gentlemen, people like us don't wear gloves, but we know what that looks like. If you have a glove you can turn it inside out. So imagine the glove is brown on the outside, let us say, and has a grey lining inside. If you turn it inside out so that the grey part is on the outside and the brown part inside, you have turned it round completely; now the inside is outside and the outside inside. You could cut off a finger and do the same thing with just a finger of the glove. And if you cut off a finger of the glove and turn it inside out, you get something like this hydra. The hydra looks like the finger of a glove. And the odd thing is that just as you can turn the finger of the glove inside out so that the inside is outside and the outside inside, so you can also turn the hydra inside out. The part I have made red in the drawing will then be on the outside, and the part I have made violet on the inside. But the hollow space is now also on the outside, and whatever was outside before is now inside. And the strange thing is that the hydra suddenly starts to swim about again. It is not at all bothered. It will swim about in the water again, feeding and breathing. It will now take little grains into the hollow space inside, which has been newly created, just as before, and it will now breathe with what was the lining of its stomach before. So the hydra does not mind at all. It takes no harm at all. It begins to feed with the part it had used to breathe before, and to breathe with the part it used to feed before [Fig. 7].

Well, gentlemen, if the situation was that it had grown just so that you had the stomach inside there and the breathing organs on the outside, all the hydra could do in that case would be to breathe in there and start to feed on the outside. But it does not do this. The moment it is turned

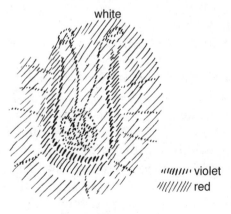

Fig. 7

inside out it makes its stomach into a lung and its lung into a stomach. I'd like to know how that could be done if you had nothing there but a stomach and a lung! If you have a tool, a glove or whatever, you can turn it inside out if it is something physical. If it is something inner you'll of course not be able simply to turn it inside out. The part of it which is ether body and astral body, therefore, the invisible part, still remains. And it is because that part is there that the hydra can simply be turned inside out. So you see that if one just takes a clear look at the things that happen in the natural world, you will immediately find that the materialistic view simply has to be wrong. We are therefore able to say that the actual feeding and breathing is done by something which is invisible. And because the body of a hydra is not made as firm as ours, does not have bones and muscles but is all one kind of material, the hydra is in fact able to use this material for everything.

You see, don't you, that we cannot turn our stomach outside in simply because it is made in a particular way, because we do not consist of the same material all the way through the way the hydra does but of different materials. But our stomach must also breathe inside, and the air we have in it is also taken in from outside. Our stomach is therefore also a kind of hydra.

We can see from all these things, and much more could be added, that it is possible to show in even the smallest of creatures that there is something invisible on which this creature is based.

Well now, gentlemen, you can see from this that even if we talk about the principle which really moves the whole human being, we find that it is something invisible. If you take the external movement of walking, you'll not at all think it is your big toe which takes a step. Instead you say to yourself: 'I am walking; it is my will which make me walk.' When the organs inside us are moving — and that is not only the heart, our intestines are also moving all the time, for instance — when the organs inside us are moving, therefore, these movements are not brought about by the physical matter in us; they are brought about by the part in us that is invisible. We therefore have to say: 'The heart is not a pump, for the heart is moved by our astral body.' So we have an astral body and this moves the heart, or rather, seeing that our I is actually also in the astral body, we also move our heart with our I, and we do so in a quite specific way.

If you look at the heart, it is a bit to the left in a normal person, as Mr Burle said, quite rightly. Not as much as people generally think, but it is a bit to the left. And then these large vessels come from the heart [*drawing on the board*]. The aorta and the other blood vessels really come from the heart.

Now it is like this. When I breathe in, for example, I feed myself oxygen, as it were. When I breathe out, I give out carbon dioxide. As soon as I have given out the carbon dioxide I hunger for oxygen. I want to breathe in again. In the first place, this has nothing at all to do with my heart but with my whole body. My whole body hungers for oxygen. Because it develops this hunger for oxygen, the instinct arises to get all the blood moving, for the blood has to have oxygen. Using its astral body, the physical body sends the blood to a place where it can get oxygen.

Or let us assume I walk, or I work. The food in me is burned up then. I have discussed this with you before. The blood then has few nutrients left. If you work, the blood always loses most of its nutrients. And what does the blood want now? It wants more food again. The blood grabs the food for itself, as it were, which the stomach and intestines have taken up. All this, the hunger for air, the hunger for food, sets the blood in motion. It is the blood which moves in the first place, and the blood takes the heart along with it.

And so it is not the heart which pumps the blood through the body, but the blood moves because of its hunger for air, hunger for food, and this moves the heart. We therefore have to say that it is the invisible human being in us which moves the heart.

Well, gentlemen, hearing this you may well raise a question. You see, the situation with our anthroposophy is always such that our opponents believe that they are raising the objections. But we've already known the objections long before that. You raise them yourself in the first place. This is why I am also always drawing your attention to the objections. You may object: 'Yes, but why do we have a heart if it does not pump the blood through the body? If the blood moves by itself, maybe we don't even need a heart that needs to be taken along in the movement.'

Now you see, that is the kind of thing people will say who have no real idea of the whole human body. There is a big difference between the human head and the rest of the human being. I have spoken of this difference before. Just think you are walking or working. Well, the head does not join in the effort. The head sits on the rest of the body, more or less the way we would sit in a carriage. You sit there without moving. The carriage has to move its wheels, the horses must pull it along. But it is our hands and our feet that have to work like this, and the head sits in there and does not join in the effort, you see? Otherwise we'd need ropes or something on our ears and we'd have to set the wheels of the machines in motion with these. We don't do that. The head does not join in the effort. Just imagine one might fix such ropes to one's head of hair — most people can no longer do this today, having gone bald. Doing this will not do people any good. The head does not really share in the effort; it sits calmly on top of the rest of the organism. The question is, why does it do this? Well, you see, the head is something completely different from the rest of us. The rest of us is a movement apparatus. The head is only a movement apparatus in so far as it goes along with the movements, and so on; the movements thus act up into the head. But the head is not the part of us which moves of its own accord.

The head has sense organs on its outside. There it perceives what exists outside. But the head also perceives what goes on inside, though unconsciously so in most people. If I want to look outside, so that I'll know what goes on out there, I use my eyes. If I want to look inside, at the blood circulation, I use my heart. The heart does not exist to pump blood through the body; it is a sense organ which perceives everything, just as the whole of the head does. We would not be able to know anything about our blood circulation — of course, we know nothing about it directly in our brainbox, but there has to be a knowing in the head — if the head did not perceive the whole of our blood circulation through the heart.

I have told you that the liver is an organ with sensory functions. It perceives the lower movements, for example. But the movements of the whole human being are perceived by the heart. It is this which sets the heart in motion. The movements caused by the hunger for air and the hunger for food set the heart in motion. And the movements of the heart show you if something is out of order in the body or if it is in order.

You can easily see this, gentlemen. For what do we do when someone gets sick? The first thing to do is to check the pulse. Someone who has developed the habit of checking the pulse can tell an enormous amount from the pulse beat. The pulse beat truly is a barometer for the whole state of health and sickness. The pulse beat is nothing but the movement of the blood, however. The head is all the time doing what we do when we feel the pulse of a sick person. It is continually sensing the whole blood circulation and it does so through the heart. And indeed, the head senses everything that goes on in the body, doing so through the heart.

Imagine someone has drunk a lot of alcohol one night, getting thoroughly drunk, as we say. This will upset the whole of his blood circulation. The next day the head will know, from the heart: the whole blood circulation is upset. It develops a hangover, the well-known thick head. But why does the head feel like that? You see, if I go for a walk on a beautiful day, using my eyes, I am impressed by the beauty. If the weather out there is terrible, I get a bad impression. Yes, gentlemen, if everything moves the way it should in the blood, the head gets a good impression, and all is in its proper order in the head. But if there's a thunderstorm in the blood—which is the situation when someone got drunk the night before—the head gets a thunderous impression through the heart, with everything going topsy-turvy.

We can therefore only understand what the heart really is if we know that it is in fact the inner sense organ through which the head perceives everything that is going on in the body.

When we look about us in the world we find that man is related to the whole world through his invisible part, the part I have called his astral body. Sun and moon are the most important stars to which we relate. Now the situation is that the head relates mainly to the sun and the rest of the human being actually relates to the moon. And we can say that it is of course a terrible superstition when people think they can do something with today's moon phases. But there is a rhythm in the human being that is also reflected in the blood. This is similar to the moon rhythm. Man does indeed take his orientation from the whole world. And so it is also the case that the internal movement of the blood does not only depend on the food we eat. When someone is in good health—in a way he is an independent creature—he makes himself in a sense independent of the influences of outer nature, and in a sense also makes himself independent of the whole world. But the moment a person begins to be a little bit sick, he becomes dependent on the whole world.

Let us assume someone is sick and you notice this when you check his pulse. Someone able to read the pulse will find an enormous difference in the pulse between morning and evening. Much can be learned from the difference between the morning and evening pulses. With some sick people there is also a big difference between the pulse at full moon and the pulse at new moon. The individual is dependent. He may be able to make himself independent when in health, but some dependence remains, and this shows itself particularly in the case of sickness. We thus have to say that with regard to the influences on the heart we certainly have a relationship to the movements of cosmic bodies, especially the moon. We relate to the movements of the moon. This is something where many, many observations still need to be made.

As I said earlier, the heart is a little to the left in a normal human being. But just as there are left-handed people though most people are right-handed, so, oddly enough, there are also people with the heart on the right. There are people whose hearts are on the right and not the left side. This is not noticed, as a rule, for the difference is an internal one, of course. You soon notice it if someone is left-handed, but you'll not notice so easily if his heart is a little to the right rather than the left. It would, however, be interesting to follow up people who have their heart on the right side and see if they are a bit different in life from people whose hearts are on the left. People whose heart is on the right, that is, placed more to the right, are people who must always do certain things they do at a particular time of the year or of the day. A right-hearted person is much more dependent on the environment than a left-hearted person. And if the heart is just a little bit to the right—after all, it's not in the same place in every person but a little bit different in each individual—if it is still to the left but just a little bit to the right, he'll have a longing to take his orientation more from the outer environment. He'll want to do something special in spring, let us say, and something special in autumn. He won't always be able to do that, of course, and this will then have a bad effect on him. People have no idea of the things that can have a bad effect on them.

If children have their hearts a bit to the right, one needs to do things slightly differently for them at school—this need not be at all noticeable—than for children who have their hearts in the right place. Someone whose heart is more to the right is led to make many more demands on his astral body.

You see, gentlemen, that's how it is. If someone operates a machine for a long time you'll realize that as a general rule his work will become mechanical. It gets more unpleasant because one is oneself becoming a piece of machinery, and if you operate a machine for a long time your actions and so on become mechanical. Now imagine you're a completely normal person with the heart properly to the left. Your father also had his heart to the left, and your grandfather and your great grandfather. So there's been a gradual development, and when you are born as the son, you will of course make the same movement inwardly that your father and grandfather and great grandfather have made. That happens as easily as if one had been operating a machine for a long time.

Someone whose heart is to the right has not inherited the position of his heart from his father. The father will not generally be a right-hearted person. It is not a hereditary trait. In this case one has to do everything afresh again, as it were, out of the astral body. You do not then have all the heredity in you. And the result is that such a person, who is a right-hearted person, needs to use much more inner strength to have his blood circulation in proper order. And it is because of this that such a right-hearted person takes his orientation much more from the outside.

The following may actually happen. Let us assume that you are not at all right-hearted, but quite normally left-hearted. But if you become a ballet dancer—this is something that also happens to men, but even more so to women—the dancing will also affect the heart. At present ballet is very materialistic. But in earlier times, when people were asked to dance, in ancient Greece, for example, they would follow movements that imitated those of the stars and this would actually move the heart a little bit to the right, in their lifetime. Dancing, even though it has grown materialistic today, does have a powerful effect on the heart, for it does move it a little to the right. And if people were to pay more attention to such things they would certainly see, if they dissect the body after death, that certain vessels in the heart are enlarged. Because the individual concerned was a dancer, the heart—and one can see this even after death—has moved a little to the right.

This answers the question Mr Burle has asked. It is answered because we see that someone who is given more to his astral body, does not want to follow his normal blood circulation but wants to control it more. He therefore gives himself up to movements that are more like those that occur beyond the earth, like those of the moon. Can you understand this? [*Answer: Yes.*]

So the matter you asked about today, that one easily notices that people have a certain longing to do this, has to do with the fact that human beings control the whole movement of the heart from their invisible part, and that they then, I'd say, slip over a little in the direction of the invisible, and then really take their orientation from the outside world and not only the internal movement of the blood which takes its orientation from the breathing and the blood. All these things can be explained if one really understands the human being.

I'd now like to talk about something that still has a little bit to do with what we discussed the last time. The last time we met we saw that there is this small lens in the eye [*drawing on the board*]. When someone has normal vision, this small lens is transparent. When someone develops cataract the lens grows opaque. Salts are deposited in it. We are thus able to say that in a healthy person, we have the lens here — if this is the front part of the eye. It is transparent. In someone with cataract, the lens is opaque, with salts deposited in it. If the lens is transparent, the human astral body is able to see the world with that transparent lens. He'll see everything in the world.

If the things I have written about in my little book *Knowledge of the Higher Worlds* get one in the habit of very, very intensive thinking, a moment will come when one is able to do something quite special. But people are not easily prepared to get in the habit of very intensive thinking today. They'll not do such a thing as withdrawing completely into their thinking, for they say everything should be given to them from outside; the secrets of the world must be investigated from the outside. Of course, it is not at all easy, for one has to pay very careful attention with this thinking. If one is very much alive in one's thinking, one must of course be terribly careful. But a moment will come in life where one is able to do something quite special.

You see, anyone will understand it if I use my hand to lift up a chair, for it is something that is done all the time. But I can also keep my hand still and not use it to do the things it usually does. The work done by the lens in one's eye is not in our power like that. When an impression comes from outside, well, you simply look in the direction of it through your lens. When there's no impression coming in, the lens is at rest.

But just think, gentlemen, that someone has really worked very hard to make his thinking very strong. He then lives wholly within his inner thinking. He does not look at the outside world, keeping his lens still just as we keep a hand still when not using it to do something. What happens then is that the whole of the starry heavens is reflected in the place where one otherwise has the transparent lens that enables one to see. This is the truly wonderful thing, I'd say, that if one uses the method I have given in *Knowledge of the Higher Worlds* one learns to use one's individual organs not for the earth but indeed for the other world. Now if salts have become deposited, of course, the lens develops cataract and becomes non-transparent whether you want it or not. When someone thinks very deeply, it will stay transparent, of course, but the person is not looking through the lens, he is not looking at the outside world. And then it begins to illumine the whole world from the lens. But it is the spiritual element one then sees, the whole of the starry heavens in their true inner significance. This small area in the human being where the lens is located can teach us about all the things one then takes heart to say about the stars and so on. You see, that is how magnificent things are with the human being, that tremendous insights are gained in the smallest place.

Someone who has cataract — we won't wish it on anyone, of course — actually has it easier with the whole of this, he need not make quite such an effort with his thinking. He only needs to concentrate just a little and he can reach the point where he sees inwardly, having lost the ability to see in an outer way. But this is something we always need to emphasize when speaking of such higher insights. However, speaking of such higher insights, it is obvious that one may also make too much of an effort and then something like a disorder of the lens may develop instead of higher insight. With this powerful inner concentration the lens may grow a bit less transparent, even if one does not get cataract. Because of this everything in my book *Knowledge of the Higher Worlds* is written in such a way that a person can achieve the things that are described but will not get sick in doing so. No exercise should be described in such a way that people may also get sick from it. But the lens is the place in the human being where the whole spirit world can indeed be revealed in the inner eye. And we may therefore say that we can see in an outer way if everything is transparent in the eye. We can see in an inner way if something is deliberately made opaque.

Yes, gentlemen, this is something which will show you how insight into worlds of spirit comes about. Insight into worlds of spirit arises if one first of all finds the individual points in the head, points which are then not used for ordinary activities by keeping them at rest. The lens will in the first place give us insight into the outside world. But one can get the whole body to a point where all kinds of things inside are not needed for the moment. If one does not use the heart, for instance—the circulation may continue, but you do not use the heart as a sense organ—you actually begin to perceive the whole of your blood circulation. But you'll not only perceive the blood circulation in that case. If you make your heart such that you look at your blood circulation through your body, as it were, and do not have inner sensation of the heart, nor of your pulse beat, but look through them, as you look out into the world through your lens with your head, that is, if you learn to see through yourselves—then, gentlemen you will see not just the blood circulation but you'll see the whole movement of the moon, everything the moon does, and you'll see how the moon relates to the sun. And you will then see the relationship which the heart has to sun and moon.

You see, in earlier times people had it easier with all this. They had not been taught at school to gain all their knowledge from the outside world only. They simply did not want to see only the things in front of them. If you had taken a Greek who may have lived 2,700 or 2,800 years ago to a cinema he would not have looked at the film for long, for he would have fainted. The moment the ancient Greek would have looked at the film, something would have happened in him — not just in a limb but in the whole human being — which happens to you if a limb goes to sleep because there is some pressure on it. He would not have had a real sleep, but this going to sleep of the whole person would have happened if you had made an ancient Greek sit down and watch a film. He would of course have fainted. The ancient Greek could not have looked at this at all because his head would have suffered such disorder through the heart in his whole blood system that his whole body, not just individual limbs, would have gone to sleep and the head would not have had anything under control. He would have fainted. People are very different now from the way they were in the past. Today people's blood circulation is already so disordered because of our modern civilization that they'll not faint at the pictures.

When one has really inwardly worked a bit with the science of the spirit and goes to a cinema, one has to make quite an effort, or one may pass out even today. But of course we're all human beings, and the one takes up the characteristics of the other. And the situation is that people no longer have the blood circulation system they had in earlier times, like the people of old. Those people of old therefore found it easier to see through to the blood circulation system and to speak of sun and moon than we do. We are cut off from that and have to get back to it first by doing exercises. We must first really make our organs such again that we'll be able to see.

You see, the ancient Greek would still have been able to understand the things earlier people told him about what really happens on earth. You should not think that everything that has come down from antiquity is superstition, it is only that later people often changed it so much that it has turned into superstition. It is really strange how things that were quite sensible to begin with later on simply become superstition. If one no longer knows how things actually should be presented, they will of course become superstition. The ancient Jews would not eat pork, for example. Yes, they knew that, being of that particular race and living in the area they did, pork would make them weak. Later this became a superstition. Things that later on are superstition will always come from things that originally were quite sensible. So we must not think that all the knowledge of ancient times is always nonsense, but you can't always rely on the old things because they have often been falsified later on. We must therefore investigate everything afresh again.

It is nonsensical therefore for people to say that anthroposophy is a collection of things that have been known before. Nothing is taken up as it is; everything is investigated again. And when someone says to you, gentlemen: 'In anthroposophy they're just putting together all kinds of ancient teachings of the Gnostics,' ask him if he can show you where the business of the lens may be found that I have told you about this time and the last time, if this can be found in a book anywhere. It can't, of course, for the business had been completely forgotten. You can therefore say to anyone who says the things have been collected up: 'You're lying, for you simply do not know what is being said there,' meaning all the things about the heart and so on, where a new look is being taken.

The truth is that everything here comes from original investigation, and concerns the whole human being. Such simple things like people dancing, turning round and round, which I referred to the last time and today, in answer to Mr Burle's question, can show one a great deal. And one can understand it.

But, gentlemen, something else will then show itself, something of which humanity is most afraid. For you see, when anthroposophy wins through — today you can't do a thing; if you want to do anything practical, all hell is let loose immediately; and even if you just say things, opposition will immediately arise, as you know only too well — but when anthroposophy will have reached the point of entering into our schools, putting things into effect everywhere, something else will come. People will then know which movements are good for a person's health and the whole development of metabolic activity, and which are wrong. A time will then come when work will be adapted to the human being. Today work is determined by the machines. Today one has to move the way the people who discovered the machine think appropriate. Later people will find that what matters is not what comes from the machines but that what matters is the human being. Because of this all machines must be made for human beings. This is something that will only be possible once anthroposophy has been fully accepted. Then one will be able to say: everything mechanical must take its orientation from the human being.

Something else is needed for this, however. First we have to understand that the heart is not mechanical but takes its orientation from the human being. Then people will also find the basic principles for external machines, making them such that they take their orientation from the human being. But in a science which has so much taken the easy way that the heart is described as if the human being had just a pump there in his blood circulation, in such a science people will feel no compunction to make machines where the human being has to take his orientation from the machine. All the problems in our social situation are due to this wrong view that is taken in science. And so one really has to understand that a proper way of thinking must first of all come upon people, for only then will it be possible to begin a proper social life. For as long as people think the heart is a pump, they will also not be able to relate to outer life in the right way. It is only when people know that the invisible human being is greater than his heart, that it is he who moves the heart, that they will also design their machines to be in accord with human nature. One first has to begin to see this.

People make things much too easy for themselves today. They really make things much too easy for themselves. What is the most international thing today? Football. I explained this to you the other day.[10] But the things which are of the spirit are more and more limited to small groups and so on. It is all split up. You know, in Norway you'll hear them sing 'For he's a jolly good fellow', or you'll hear them sing a German song if the players come from Germany. But otherwise people go their own ways.

What we have to take hold of is the spirit, but in such a way that we take hold of it in detail. One should not speak of the spirit in general terms, but take hold of it in every detail.

We'll say more about this next Saturday.

Effects of light and colour in earthly matter and in cosmic bodies

Well, gentlemen, what have you in mind?

Question: Various chemical substances have the property that they produce specific colours in a flame, for example. On the other hand many stars also have a bit of colour. Mars, for example. When iron oxidizes, rusts, you also get a reddish colour. Would these things be connected?

Rudolf Steiner: That is of course a very difficult question. One would first of all have to remember the things we have already discussed about colours.[11] We have talked about a number of things relating to colours. You have to consider that the colour of the solid has to do with the whole way in which it exists in the world. Imagine, therefore, that we have some substance or other. This substance has a particular colour. Now I believe you're thinking this colour may look completely different in a given situation, for instance if we put it in a flame, so that the flame will then have a particular colour? We have to remember that the flame already has its own colour when it develops. If we put some material into the flame, the two colours interact, the colour of the substance and the colour of the flame. But it is altogether most peculiar how colours behave in the world. Let me tell you a few things about this.

You know the ordinary rainbow. It has a band of red, then the colour changes to orange and yellow, then it is green, blue, a somewhat darker blue, indigo blue, and finally the band is violet. We thus have more or less seven colours in the rainbow [Fig. 8]. People have always observed these seven colours which one gets in the rain-

Fig. 8

bow, the most beautiful colours ever to be seen in nature. And you must also know that these colours are such by nature that they are floating freely. As you know, they develop when the sun shines somewhere and there is rainy weather between you and the sun. The rainbow will then appear in the sky on the other side. So if you see a rainbow somewhere you have to say: 'Where's the rainy weather? Yes, the sun must be on the other side of the rain, the side facing away from it.' That is how things have to be. That is how the seven colours of the rainbow develop.

But these seven colours also appear elsewhere. Imagine we are burning a metallic body, heating it more and more so that this metallic body gets very hot. As you know, it will first turn red hot, and finally white hot, as one says. Imagine therefore that we have created a kind of flame by having what is really, I'd say, a metal flame. But it is not a real flame, it is glowing metal, metal that is wholly aglow. If you look at a metal which is thus wholly aglow through a prism, as it is called, you do not see a white hot mass but you see the same seven colours as in a rainbow.

Let me draw you a diagram [Fig. 9]. Imagine this to be the glowing metal, and I then have such a prism here. You know what a prism is. Here it is shown from the side, such a triangular piece of glass. There's my eye. I now look through this. And then I do not see a white body but the

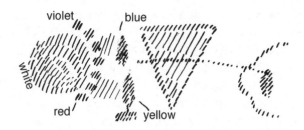

Fig. 9

seven colours of the rainbow in the order red, orange, yellow, green, blue, indigo, violet. Looking through the prism I see something that is really white, white hot, in seven colours. You see from this that it is possible to see something that is white hot shimmering in the colours of the rainbow.

Now we can also do something else that is most extraordinarily interesting. You see, we can only produce such a white hot mass if we heat a metal, or any solid body. But if I have a gas and burn up the gas, I do not get the seven colours looking through my prism, not such a band of seven colours, but something quite different.

Now you may say: 'How do we get such a glowing gas?' Well, it is quite easy to get a glowing gas. Imagine, for example, I have some ordinary table salt. There are two substances in it—a metallic substance called sodium, and then also chlorine. Chlorine is a gas and if you let it spread anywhere, if it is present anywhere, it'll immediately rush up your nose and it is biting. It is the same gas which people use to bleach their linen, for example. The linen is bleached if you let chlorine pass over it.

So if you have sodium and chlorine together, as a solid, this is the ordinary salt we use to season our food. If you take the chlorine away and put the sodium, which will then be whitish, into a flame, the flame will turn quite yellow.

Why does this happen? Well, gentlemen, it happens because sodium turns into gas if the flame is hot enough, and the sodium gas will burn yellow, giving you a yellow flame. So now we have not only a glowing metal but also a gaseous flame. If I look at this through my prism, it'll not show seven colours but on the whole stay yellow. It is just at the side—and you have to take a very good look for this—that you see something a bit blue and a bit red [Fig. 10]. But one generally does not notice this but only sees the yellow.

But all of this is not yet the really interesting thing. The most interesting thing is this. If I set the whole thing up [Fig. 9],[12] and then put the yellow flame in here and again look through my prism—what do you think? You'll say: 'Looking through there I'll get red, orange, yellow, green and so on. And yellow, too.' 'It'll be a particularly strong yellow here,' you'll say, 'a particularly bright and luminous yellow.' But you see, that is not true. What happens is that no yellow appears at all, the yellow is completely eliminated, extinguished, and you get a black bit there.

Just as you can have a yellow gas flame so you can also have a blue one. One can find other substances, lithium, for example, that have a red flame. Potassium and similar substances give a blue flame. If you put a blue flame in here, for instance, the blue will not come up more strongly, but you'll again have a black spot. So the peculiar thing is that

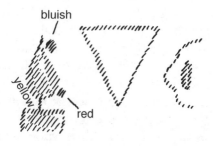

Fig. 10

when you make something glow, if a solid body is completely aglow and is not a gas, you get this band of seven
colours. But if you only have a burning gas, you get more or
less a single colour, and this single colour then extinguishes
its own colour in the band of seven colours.

These things I am telling you are something people have
not known all that long; they were only discovered in
1859.[13] It was not until 1859 that it was found that if you
have a band of seven colours coming from a glowing solid,
then individual colours coming from glowing gases, burning gases, will extinguish the corresponding colours. You
can see the highly complex way in which one colour
influences another. And it is because of this that if one looks
at the sun in the ordinary way, it looks as if it were a white
hot body. It is really like this. If you look superficially
through a prism, you'll also see the sequence of colours —
red, orange, yellow, green, blue, indigo, violet — in the sun.
But if you look more carefully, then you'll not have those
seven colours in the sun's disc. The seven colours will
merely be near each other, with lots of black lines in
between, a whole lot of black lines. If you look very carefully at the sun you do not have a band of seven colours;
you'll have the seven colours, but always interrupted by
lots of black lines.

What does one have to say to oneself in that case? If it is
not the usual, continuous band of colours that shines out
from the sun but a band of colours with lots of black lines
in between, well, then one has to say to oneself: 'There are
lots of burning gases between us and the sun and these are
always extinguishing their particular colours between us
and the sun.' If I do not look at glowing metal, therefore,
but at the sun, and see those black lines, I have to say to
myself: 'There, always in the corresponding place, the yellow is extinguished by sodium, for instance. Looking into
the sun and seeing a black line in the yellow, I have to say

that there is sodium between me and the sun.' And I get such black lines for all the metals in the sunlight. So all kinds of metals exist as gases in cosmic space between me and the sun.

What does this tell us? Gentlemen, it tells us that cosmic space, or at least, in the first place, the area surrounding the earth, is filled with lots of metals that are not just glowing but burning. If one thinks about this one must altogether understand that basically we can never just say that we are standing here on the earth and up there is the glowing sun, for anything we see actually depends on what is there between us and the sun. And physicists would be most surprised if they ever actually managed to get into the sun, for it would not be as they expect. What we see actually comes from the things that are between the human being and the sun. So there you can see from just one example how complex the connection between substances and colours really is.

So if you have a flame somewhere and the flame, say a candle flame, has a particular colour, you must first of all ask: 'What does the candle contain?' Solids from the candle exist as gases in the flame; they are usually made into gases by the heat of the flame. If we then look through a prism, as I did here [pointing to the drawing]: when a substance is a gas it colours the whole flame. Sodium will colour the flame yellow, for example. If you had a flame somewhere, in this room, for example, and looked through a prism—the sodium is almost always black. You don't actually have to put it in first. If the apparatus is very exactly set up, so that you can see things properly, you'll always find these black lines that should really be yellow and basically develop because very small traces of sodium are present everywhere. This proves to you that sodium is altogether necessary in the natural world. We cannot live unless it is there. We must also always have a quite specific amount of sodium in us and have to process the sodium in us. Its presence is really only betrayed because it always extinguishes the yellow lines and makes them into black lines.

Now you need to remember what I have told you before.[14] How do blue and violet colours arise? And reds and yellows? Well, blue, as I told you, is the colour of vast cosmic space, for there is nothing out there where we see the blue firmament. It is vast, black cosmic space. We thus see vast, black cosmic space. But we do not see it, though it is there right in front of our eyes. Water vapours are rising all the time between us and that vast, black cosmic space. Even if the air is pure, you always have water vapours in the air. So if this is the earth [*drawing on the board*], these are the water vapours, and all around is black cosmic space, the sun will shine through those water vapours. If you stand down here and look up, you do not see black but blue. You look through something that is illumined and therefore see dark space as blue. It means that if I see something that is dark through something that is illuminated, I see it in blue.

The red sky at dawn and dusk is, as you know, yellowy or a yellowy reddish colour. If this here [*drawing on the board*] is the earth, and there are the vapours all around, and now the sun comes up here, I see this illuminated. I see something that is lit up, but I see it through the dark vapours. This makes it yellow for me. When I see something bright through something dark it will be yellow. When I see something dark through something that is lit up, it will be blue. Blue is darkness seen through something that is lit up, yellow is the brightness seen through something dark. I am sure you can understand this.

If I have the yellow produced by the yellow sodium flame, this yellow colour of the sodium flame means that sodium is a substance that gets very bright when it evaporates but at the same time also creates something dark

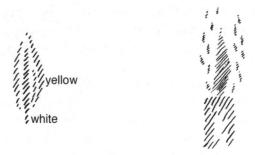

Fig. 11

around itself. Sodium therefore really burns like this. If the sodium is burning here, the white light shoots up in the middle [Fig. 11, left] and I therefore see the whole as yellow. The sodium radiates light, but creates darkness all around it because it radiates light so powerfully.

It need not surprise you that sodium creates darkness around it by radiating such a powerful light. If you are a fast runner and run really fast, someone who wants to keep up with you will inevitably lag behind. The light spraying out is a fast runner; it therefore shows itself as shining in the darkness—it appears yellow to me.

With an ordinary candle flame the situation is that the particles go apart like this [Fig. 11, right]. This makes it light all around here and dark at the centre. So if you have an ordinary candle flame you see the darkness through the light. Here the bright little dots scatter; here at the centre it stays dark and therefore appears blue. If you have a yellow flame, therefore, as in the case of sodium, it means that it sprays out with tremendous power. If you have a blue flame this means that it does not spray out very much but goes apart and scatters.

That is the difference you always get in the world with the effects substances have. Imagine I have a glass tube here; I fuse it so that it is closed at both ends. I then also pump out the air so that I have a glass tube that has a vacuum inside.[15] I then do the following. I let an electric current go in here, letting it go this far, and another current on the other side. This gives me a closed circuit. So the two poles of electricity are opposite each other here. Between them is a vacuum. And now something very strange happens. On the one side the electricity sprays out and on the other side, where it looks bluish, you get such waves [Fig. 12]. And that then goes together. Light is all the time spraying into the darkness, we might say, bright electricity into the darkness. So there you have the two flames I have shown you separately. You have this one at the one pole of the electricity and that one at the other pole. Here on one side you have the same thing as in the sodium flame, and here on the other side the same thing as in an ordinary candle flame. If one does this properly, one gets different kinds of rays here, including X-rays, which, as you know, can be used to see solid parts such as bones and so on, or foreign bodies in the body.

So the thing is that there are substances in the world that are radiant. Others are not radiant but, we might say, give off a faint light and cover themselves with such waves on the surface. Substances that cover themselves with such waves are bluish; substances that are radiant are yellowy. If a dark body then comes in front of the yellow the yellow will turn reddish. So if you make the yellowy light darker again it may turn reddish.

Fig. 12

So you see, gentlemen, solid bodies in the world are such that some are radiant and therefore have the bright colours we see on one side of the rainbow; others are not radiant but send out those waves. This gives us the bluish colours from the other side of the rainbow.

If you know this you will say to yourself: 'There are many stars such as Mars, for instance, which is yellowy or reddish, or like Saturn which has a bluish light.' You are then able to see from this what the star is like, how it behaves. Mars is simply a star that radiates a great deal and therefore it has to appear yellowy or reddish. It is a star that radiates a lot. Saturn is a body that stays quieter and covers itself with waves. You can almost see the waves around it. When you have Saturn you can also see the waves as rings around it. It appears to be blue because it surrounds itself with waves.

So the things we observe on solids here on earth tell us, if we are not dull in our minds but observe correctly, what the bodies are like out there in the universe. Only one has to know, of course, that the whole of cosmic space is filled with all kinds of substances, as I've told you, and these are really always in a state where they'll burn.

Take just one solid, iron for example. It rusts. I think that is what you meant with your question, isn't it? The iron rusts and therefore grows redder than it usually is. So we have a solid that is relatively dark, which rusts and then turns reddish. Having studied the colours we'll be able to tell ourselves what it really means that iron turns reddish when it rusts, which means when it is continually exposed to the air. Let us see clearly what this means. I don't have chalk in all the colours to hand, but you'll see what I mean. Let us assume, then, that we have blue iron. Now it is exposed to the air. And because it is exposed to the air it turns reddish as it rusts.

Now you can say to yourself that the reddish colour develops because something light is seen through darkness.

If I look at iron in its usual state it is dark at first, which means it produces waves. But if I expose it to the air for a long time, if the iron is in contact with air for a long time, the air gets to the iron; and the iron gradually changes in the air for it begins to defend itself against the air. It defends itself against the air and begins to grow radiant. And something that radiates like our sodium flame here, so that you get darkness all around, will be yellowy or reddish. You are therefore able to say that the relationship between iron and air is such that the iron begins to be all on edge inside and grows radiant. The iron gets all on edge and grows radiant.

Now you know that iron is also present in the human body, where it is a very important substance. Iron is in the blood and it is a very important part of human blood. If we have too little iron in the blood we are people who cannot walk properly, getting tired quickly, people who grow lethargic. If we have too much iron in the blood we get excited and smash everything to pieces. We therefore have to have just the right amount of iron in the blood, otherwise we don't do well. Well, gentlemen, people do not pay much attention to these things today, but I have mentioned this to you before: if you investigate how the human being is connected with the whole world you find that in man the blood is connected with influences that come from Mars. Mars, which always moves, of course, really always stimulates the blood activity in us. This is because of its relationship to iron. Scholars of earlier times who knew this would therefore say that Mars had the same nature as iron. So in a sense we can regard Mars as something that is like our iron. But it also has a reddish yellow shimmer, which means it is all the time growing radiant inside. Mars we thus see as a body that is all the time growing radiant inside.

We only understand the whole of this if having made these studies we say to ourselves: Mars is iron-like by nature, is a substance rather like iron; but it is always on edge, wanting to grow radiant all the time. As iron does under the influence of air, so does Mars want to be radiant all the time under the influence of its environment. By nature it is therefore inwardly on edge all the time, wanting to come alive. Mars constantly wants to come alive. We can see this from the whole of its colouring and the way it behaves. With Mars we have to know that it is a cosmic body which really wants to come alive all the time.

It is different with Saturn. Saturn has a bluish light, that is, it is not radiant but surrounds itself with a wave element. It is exactly the opposite of Mars. Saturn all the time wants to go dead, become a dead body. One can see that Saturn is surrounding itself with brightness, as it were, so that we then see its darkness as a bluish colour through the brightness.

Now let me draw your attention to something. You can see something really interesting if you walk through a willow wood on a night that is not really dark but rather dusky — walking through a wood where willows grow. Every now and then you may see something that'll make you ask: 'Goodness, what's that light there?' You come close to it and the light can be seen to be coming from rotting wood. Something that is rotting down thus becomes luminous. If you then walk a long way off and look at it again, with something dark behind this luminous stuff, it would no longer appear to be luminous but blue. And that is how it is with Saturn. Saturn is decomposing. Saturn is really decomposing all the time. Because of this there is something of a brightness all around it, but the star itself is dark, and it looks blue to us because we are looking at its dark shape through the decomposing matter which is all around it. So we see that Mars wants to live all the time and Saturn wants to die all the time.

This is what is so interesting, that we can look at cosmic bodies and say: 'The cosmic bodies which appear to have a bluish shimmer are perishing, and those that appear to have a reddish, yellowy shimmer are only coming into existence.' And that is how it is in the world. In one place something is coming into existence, and in another something is passing away. Just as on earth you have a child in one place, and an old man in another, so it is also in space. Mars is still a young man who wants to be alive all the time. Saturn is already an old man.

You see, the ancients would study this. We'll have to study it again. But we'll only understand what the ancients meant if we find it again for ourselves. Because of this it is really silly — I spoke of this also the last time — for people to say that in anthroposophy we are simply writing up all the things that can be found in the ancient writings. For you cannot understand the things you find in ancient writings! You see, one only understands the things written in the ancient works, which are based on real wisdom, if one has first found them again for oneself. There was a verse known in medieval times, before America was discovered, that was most interesting.[16] Almost every single person would say it. In medieval times all kinds of people would say the verse, for they would learn it then the way people today learn — well, I don't know — an agitators' slogan perhaps.

The verse goes like this.

O Sun, a king of this world!
Luna keeps your generations going.

Luna is the moon.

Mercury soon couples you.
Without Venus you'd all be nothing,
Venus who chooses Mars to be her husband.

So the verse suggests that Venus, another young figure, has chosen Mars for her husband. It is suggested that Mars is a young man out there in the universe.

Without Jupiter's might you'd lack everything.

It is therefore suggested that Jupiter gets busy everywhere.
And then, in the end, we have:

So that Saturn, ancient and old
may show himself in many colours.

Just think how beautifully this medieval verse contrasts
Mars' youth with Saturn's age.

O Sun, a king of this world!
Luna keeps your generations going.
Mercury soon couples you.
Without Venus you'd all be nothing,
Venus who chooses Mars to be her husband.
Without Jupiter's might you'd lack everything.
So that Saturn, ancient and old
may show himself in many colours.

So you see it is something one can't understand, and
people show this. For a present-day academic reading such
a verse would say: 'Well, that's just silly superstition.' He'll
laugh about it. And when one rediscovers the truths that lie
in such a verse, he'll say one has copied it. Yes, well, you
know, it is quite unbelievable how stupidly people behave
really, for they cannot understand it, of course. No academic today understands what is said in such a verse. But if
you are able to do spiritual research, you'll discover it
again, and then you'll finally understand it. One has to find
these things out for oneself again, otherwise the ancient
verses, which are popular wisdom, really have no value at
all. But it is also a wonderful thing when one discovers
these things through spiritual research, and then finds this
tremendous wisdom in simple popular verses. It shows that
the old popular verses were taken from things taught in the
ancient schools of wisdom. That is where the verses come

from. Today people can no longer go to their academic scholars in that way, for today's knowledge does not give us any verses! You won't find much that is of use in life. But there was a time when people did know things like these, which I have also told you again today. They then put them into such nice verses. And then all kinds of things came of this, of course, and sometimes also misunderstandings. Now the verse about all the planets that I've just recited for you has been forgotten. But other verses later came to be distorted.

Now it is of course also true that it means something when animals do something or other. They are connected with the universe. We can know that something is happening with the weather if we look at a tree frog. You know, tree frogs are used as weather prophets when they move up or down their ladder. This is because all that lives is connected with the whole universe. Only it came to be distorted later, and then there is perhaps also some justification in having verses to amuse oneself, having listened to some that have been taken hold of by silly minds. So if someone says, for example: 'When the cock on the dunghill does crow, the weather will change or it'll stay as it's now,' well, it just shows that one should not mix everything up together, and not mix in silly things with wisdom.

The verse I cited does of course point to secrets in the universe that have to do with light and colour. The things people often say about a cockerel or the like are, of course, something we can laugh about, like the saying I have just quoted. But on the other hand old country maxims sometimes still have something extraordinarily deep to them, something most wise, even today. And it is not for nothing that a countryman is unhappy if it snows in March, for there simply are connections between seed grain and March snows.

We thus truly see from such things that we can understand the whole world in the light of the things we observe on earth. It would perhaps be better if one stuck more to what the tree frog is able to do as it climbs up and down, depending on the weather, rather than to what a dormouse does when it sleeps and sleeps, so that one sleeps through all the secrets of the universe.

I hope you've been able to understand what I have been talking about in answer to your questions. It is of course quite complicated and one cannot put it in just a few words. I therefore had to say all those things, but you'll be able to put it together. It really is quite interesting, isn't it, to see how things go together in this way.

We'll continue on Wednesday.

The way our guardian angel works

Does anyone have a question?

Mr Burle: I'd like to tell you something that happened when I was young, something connected with destiny. Religious people will say, for example, that it is because we have a guardian angel. I was a skittle boy once, setting up the skittles, I'd have been 9 or 10 then, and as I was busy setting them up a voice called 'Move!' with such intensity that I quickly jumped aside. And a moment later the big skittles ball came to the place where I'd just been, it was tremendously powerful. I asked who'd called out to me. But everyone said it was not them, and it was also that the voice could not have come from there.

The other occasion was in a smithy where people sharpened their ploughshares. There was a big wheel there. We were five or six boys amusing ourselves in the place. I was about 11 then. I got up on a spoke to force the wheel down. I liked that. I then said to the other boys, pull out the rebound stopper because then I can get from one spoke to the next. They all pulled as hard as they could but did not manage it. I was the smallest, but I went to take a look. The wheel had gone round very fast, and it clearly would have been my death if they'd managed to raise the rebound stopper.

I'd be pleased to hear if Dr Steiner has anything to say about whether a higher power can show itself in such situations.

Rudolf Steiner: Well, gentlemen, I'd like to talk to you about such things, but we always have to discuss them in a way that is properly scientific. Things like this are not simply accepted in the anthroposophical science of the spirit, the way people often do accept them, but they must of course be considered scientifically, for they are much more important in life than people think. I'll start by telling you one thing, as a kind of preparation.

You see, people really only give thought to a very small part of life. There is a great deal they do not consider, and because they do not consider it they also think it does not exist. Let us assume, for example, someone walks past a house somewhere and at that moment a tile drops down from the roof and kills him. This will get a lot of attention, and a lot will be made of it of course among the man's friends and acquaintances. People will talk about it. It is something they have observed and so they'll talk about it.

But now assume the following. Someone wants to go out in the morning. At the last minute, just as he is about to leave the house, he realizes he has forgotten to do something that absolutely has to be done. He is therefore five minutes late. He now leaves the house. The tile fell off the roof five minutes before he went past, and therefore did him no harm. If he had gone that way five minutes earlier the tile would have stove in his head. Nobody can possibly know about it — he himself forgets, of course, and no one pays attention to what would have happened if he'd not been delayed by a few minutes. Now you see, no note is taken of these things, but they are just as much part of life. Countless such things, where destiny prevents disaster, happen, but no note is taken of them. They are not considered because it is not so easy to track them down. You can only track them down if the situation is really noticeable in some way, drawing your attention. Then one does take note of such things.

There was someone once[17] who spent a lot of time at his desk, with the rest of the family living below. One day he dreamt that something terrible was going to happen to him on a particular day and that he would be shot. What did the man do? He told the others about it; people said he should be very careful, for he might be shot dead one of these days.

So he did not leave the house but stayed in his room all day. But the dream had made such an uncanny impression on him and he knew from a number of earlier experiences that such dreams might come true—this happened some time ago, when people still paid more attention to such things. He had an unpleasant feeling. Because it all felt so unpleasant he became aware of himself. And it then happened that he grew restless at a particular moment and because of this inner restlessness had to get up from his chair. At that moment a shot went very close to his chair! The situation was that an old gun from much earlier times hung in the ante-room. The door stood open and his servant had taken the gun in his hands. He did not think it was loaded and rather carelessly held the gun in such a way that it went off and the bullet went just where the man had been sitting.

So you see a double destiny link here. First a banal dream. On the other hand, because his destiny was not yet fulfilled and he was meant to live on, he was driven away by an inner urge at just the right moment. But now there is also something else to be considered. You see, he might just as well have heard the word 'Move!' at that moment, as you did [turning to Mr Burle]. He might equally well have heard that. How would that have come about? You see, when we speak of a world of the spirit we must clearly understand that one must not talk about it in a stupid way. But we would always be talking about it in a stupid way if we were to believe—and many people do believe it, at least those who are spiritualists—that there are Germans and French people and English people and Spaniards and Chinese people in the world of the spirit. They would have to be there, of course, if one were to hear the word 'Move' from the world of the spirit, for in that case some spirit or other would have to be speaking German. It would speak in French to a French person, for if it were to speak English or

German the person would think it was an unarticulated sound and might even think it was something quite evil. So it would be rather silly to think that a spirit had said 'Move!', for a spirit cannot be a German or a French or an English person. That is the silly thing with spiritualists that people think they connect with the dead through a medium and get answers, believing that spirits talk like that. They don't, of course. They are there, but they don't do that.

The situation is like this. This kind of connection with the spiritual world, which also makes it possible for us to speak of the spiritual world in a scientific way, requires us first of all to get out of the habit of thinking that the spirits talk in some kind of earthly language. You must first get to know the world of the spirit and then be able to translate what the spirits are saying in a supersensible language into an ordinary language. If the man sitting at his desk had heard the word 'Move!' that might have been quite good, too. But the thing is like this, gentlemen. You have heard me say that the whole human being is filled with good sound sense. I once told you how the liver perceives processes in the human abdomen, the lung perceives things, the whole human being is a sense organ. The heart perceives; through the heart we perceive the blood circulation. But in ordinary life we don't use those other organs for our sensory perceptions. We use our eyes and nose, but we do not use those other organs for sensory perception. These organs have a quite specific peculiarity. Take the liver, for example, gentlemen. You see if the liver is removed from the body it is this organ which you know from animals, because you've probably all seen a liver some time or other—a goose liver if nothing else. But this organ has an ether body which is connected with the rest of the ether body [Fig. 13, yellow], and it also has an astral body [violet], and then there is also the I in it. This liver therefore has something that is of the spirit. You can be aware of things that are of the spirit in

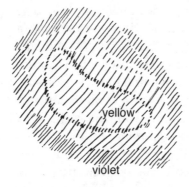

Fig. 13

your head, but you do not perceive them consciously in your liver. The way you are made in ordinary life you cannot gain a view of anything there, just as I explained to you the other day that you do not perceive the spiritual element in the small lens in your eye. But it is possible to perceive the whole of the heavens with the small lens in the eye. Spirits hardly ever speak through any of the organs in the head. The whole world speaks there; the stars in their motions and so on; they speak through the organs in the head. But spiritual entities do indeed also speak to us, and they do so through the other organs, such as the liver. The stomach speaks to the liver, but so do spirits, and also to the lung. Spiritual entities speak to all the organs which we do not use for our ordinary life in the conscious mind.

Now, gentlemen, as the head really has to depend on perceiving only the things it sees there in the outside world, the inner part of the human being, the lower organs, are actually designed to perceive things in the world of the spirit. These organs are, however, extraordinarily subtle. They are really quite subtle. And you can see that they are subtle even if you just consider the conditions that some-times arise from those organs. People don't usually pay attention to those conditions, and they don't pay attention to them because our medicine is so imperfect. You see, I'm sure you'll have known someone get diarrhoea because he was terribly afraid. No attention is paid to this because people can't think that diarrhoea may come from fear. But it does. An influence is there from the outside world, but the influence may also be from the realm of mind and spirit. And it does come from that world in such a way that those organs do indeed perceive things, but things that are quite different from those that exist in the outside world.

I have told you a few times now that we human beings go through different lives on earth. Now if until now people had been expected to go through different lives on earth without much ado, they would not have been able to do it. If a human being is to develop from infancy here on earth he must have a guide, someone to bring him up and teach him, or someone like that, otherwise he'd always be quite stupid. And the human being actually has such a guide in the world of the spirit, who guides him from earth life to earth life and really looks out in the individual life on earth not for things where we are acting freely, things we can think about sensibly ourselves, but for things we cannot think about, though our human organization depends on them. And so it happens that if someone is sitting there and feels a certain anxiety he grows particularly sensitive to something that lies ahead. This sensitivity must be considered in the right way. We have to distinguish quite clearly: does the sensitivity relate to the spiritual side or is it after all something for which a physical explanation can be found? It is impossible to talk about these things properly unless one takes a critical view.

Let me give you another example. A sick woman lived on the fourth floor of a house and the doctor had to come and see her daily, even when she was getting better, for it was a fairly dangerous condition. The doctor would not come at the same time each day but at different times, but the woman up on the fourth floor would always know he was coming, even if he was still down below. He'd still be at the front gate, but she'd know: The doctor's coming. Above all she'd be sure of it when he was in the hall on the ground floor, though he had not yet taken one step up the stairs. People told the doctor, saying she was clairvoyant. Well, the doctor was a bit edgy about this at first. Doctors don't believe such things straight off. But when the people went on and on at him, saying their daughter was clairvoyant for she'd know when he was there downstairs, he decided to put the matter to the test. He quietly took off his boots before he went in through the gate. And then she did not know! So you see, there are also such cases, and one needs to put them to the test. The patient's hearing had simply grown very acute from lying in bed for so long and she had heard steps down below which one normally does not hear. If you always say right away that all of it is clairvoyance, you have no right, of course, to speak of spiritual worlds. You must learn to distinguish carefully between things the senses are still just able to perceive and things that cannot be perceived with the senses.

Developments like these show us that the senses may grow extraordinarily acute. In ordinary life one is of course unable to hear someone's steps below if one is on the fourth floor. But just as the senses in the head and elsewhere may grow acute, so our internal organs, also being senses, may grow more sensitive to spiritual elements. And if the liver, for instance, has the impression that it might be shot that day, it will be particularly sensitive, with the result that the liver is able to hear the warning given by the spiritual entity which really does exist, but not, of course, in Italian, German or some other language.

But just think, now something amazing happens. The liver must first pass this on to the head, otherwise the human being cannot be aware of it. And on the way from the liver to the head the matter is translated into the language which the person speaks. This is the remarkable thing, something truly mysterious. And it is only here that you can really say what a remarkable creature man is. Not only is he able to have premonitions but, and this is much more to be marvelled at, he unconsciously translates something that comes to him in the language of the spirit into his own language.

You can see from this that everything people in various spiritualist organizations record in writing is something that is said to the abdomens. People would prefer not to admit this. They believe the spirits speak Italian or French, but it all comes from the human being himself. And yet, there is a connection with the spiritual world even in those seances, but it is something very bad. This is then translated into all kinds of things.

But you'll realize that when there's something like this 'Move!' one has to understand that the actual connection with the world of the spirit would still not be clear to one. It is not the right idea to imagine that the guardian spirit has murmured something in one's ear. Instead we must know the roundabout route that is taken. You then also understand something else. You understand that people can easily refute such things. For an ordinary person the business of the man who took off his shoes is equal to a refutation. He'll say: 'People believe it to be clairvoyance, clairaudience, but it was not a case of clairaudience but of ordinary hearing. And that is also how it must have been in the other situation.'

Well, gentlemen, this is exactly what needs to be investigated first. And one will then see, proceeding with the necessary caution, that human destinies are indeed being worked on all the time out of the spiritual world, using these roundabout routes—most of all, of course, in childhood. Why in childhood? Well, the astral body is much more active in childhood, working with much greater intensity. Later on it no longer works with the same intensity. When the liver is still soft in the child, the astral body is able to transmit the things it hears in the world of the spirit to the liver. Later, when the liver has grown harder, it can no longer transmit things.

Now you have to consider the significance of an event like the one Mr Burle has known, when death is really about to come and then the event, perfectly well arranged for in terms of the outer nature of things, does not happen. For it might have been your death at that time, when you heard the word 'Move!'? [*Affirmed*] So it would have been your death. There are many such instances in human life. It is merely that many go unnoticed. But that was one you certainly took note of.

However, you went through many other lives on earth before you came to this one. Yes, gentlemen, the things one has gone through in earlier lives on earth now want to come into their own in the right way. They want to come into their own in such a way, for example, that one may have a long life this time, so that everything laid down in earlier lives can develop fully in this one. Outer nature may actually go against this. External circumstances may put me in danger of having an accident one day, so that I'd have to die, and the matter might turn out in such a way that if I were to die, let us say, I'd really die disproportionately early as far as my earlier life on earth is concerned. According to my earlier life it is not right that I should die so soon, because I still have something to do on this earth. Now I might indeed die. Don't think there is any absolute certainty that I won't die. I might indeed die, the accident might happen. I might die, and this would change the whole of my destiny. The spiritual entity that guides the human being from earth life to earth life intervenes at this point. It is able to warn the person. There is always a reason why it is able to warn him. But the situation is of course extremely complex, and on some occasion it may also be that this entity which wants to protect the individual, if we want to use the term, has to obey other spirits which will prevent it, stop it. Such conflicts can certainly also arise in the world of the spirit. But when evil spirits do not have a special interest, if I may put it like this, the warning will come through. And it does happen on countless occasions that quite unusual things may happen, even externally.

You were wondering, weren't you, why the wheel did not go on turning in the second event you told us from your life. For if it had gone on turning you would have perished. The others could not make the water run, only you could. So what was the reason? You were quite unable to see any outer reason why this should happen? [*Mr Burle: No.*] It happened because the spiritual entity wanting to warn you or keep you alive paralysed the other boys' will at that moment. This always works through the person concerned, not in an external way, not through another person. The others' will was paralysed at that moment; they did not manage to move their muscles.

So that is how things are, that's how they are connected. And whenever one wants to speak of the world of the spirit one must realize that the spiritual world works through the human being. Just as you cannot see a colour unless you have an eye, so one cannot perceive the spiritual world without this inner activity of the human being. This is something we must always take into account if we want to be truly scientific and not fall into superstition. For the fact is that the different languages we have on earth are no longer valid in the world of the spirit. We first have to learn the languages that can be used there. To penetrate into the world of the spirit—I have spoken of the exercises that need to be done to enter into the world of the spirit—one must above all be able to get out of the habit of thinking. Not all the time, that would be a bad thing, but for the moments when one wants to enter into the world of the spirit. For human thinking belongs to this earthly world. This is also why thinking relates so closely to talking. We really think in words in the physical world, and it is only by gradually learning not to think in words that one gets close to the world of the spirit.

Now let me explain to you what it is like when one looks directly into the world of the spirit. Imagine Mr Burle had been a clairvoyant, a proper clairvoyant, at the moment when he was told to 'move'. What would have happened then? If Mr Burle had been a clairvoyant he would not have had to do the terribly ingenious work inside of translating what a spiritual entity told him into his own language. Something else would have happened instead. For he would have known that spirits can indicate the same thing by gestures, signs. For the spirits do not use words, they make gestures. Not the kind of signs deaf and dumb people use, but they make gestures. It is just that people do not usually find the gestures enough; they want to hear something, like the spiritualists. But it is not like that in the real world of the spirit. There things cannot be heard with the physical ear. It is impossible to see why a reasonable human being would imagine he can hear spirits with his physical ears, for physical ears cannot hear things there. It is nonsense to think that physical ears can hear the spirits. It has to be the astral body of some organ, of course, which hears the spirits. But then that also is not a real, external way of seeing and hearing. It is knowing how to take the signs the spirits make. And if Mr Burle had been clairvoyant he would not have heard the word 'Move!', but he would have seen a spiritual image, you know, as if someone were pushing him aside. And if he had truly perceived it in the spirit he would not have needed to translate it into 'Move!' But all of this happens calmly and quietly, and people are not in the habit of taking in the world of the spirit calmly and quietly, in silence. And of course if there was danger threatening somewhere one would never think of wanting to be particularly quiet. You're excited then, but it is exactly because of your excitement that you'll not perceive the world of the spirit. And if destiny has to speak after all, it will speak in such a way that the person then translates it inwardly.

You see, there are people, as you know, who find it easy to think mathematically, and others who cannot think mathematically at all; people who are good at doing sums and others who can't do sums at all. People have different abilities. But it is easier to get into real clairvoyance if one makes a real effort to think mathematically than if one has no idea at all of mathematical thinking. And there we already have the reason why people find it so hard today to gain insight into the world of the spirit. For those who seek to develop inwardly are after all mostly people who have gone through Greek and Latin and all kinds of things, everything that makes for sloppy thinking. Yes, most of the people we call educated and learned have really only learned to think in a sloppy way, for their thinking moves within the thinking of the ancient Romans or Greeks, and other people then learn it from them. Today's thinking is terribly sloppy, therefore; it is not a thinking that has real power to it. Because of this, people are not at all able to have a proper understanding of things brought to them from the world of the spirit. If they were able to think really clearly they would find it much easier to understand what is going on in the world of the spirit. You can see from events that have happened in recent centuries that people are actually trying very hard not to consider the world of the spirit. I'll explain this to you by means of an example.

You see, when a man called Stephenson[18] said one could make carriages with iron wheels that would move on iron rails, the matter was presented to the academics of his day. This was not all that long ago. The academics started to make calculations, quite correct calculations. What did they find? They found that if you have a rail here [*drawing on the board*] and a wheel here, a carriage would never move if the wheel was meant to run on a rail like this. They did further calculations and found that the wheel would only move along the rail if the rail had teeth cut into it, like this [*drawing*]. So they worked out that if the carriages had cogwheels and the rails had teeth cut into them for the cogs to engage in, that would be the only way for trains to move on rails. Well, gentlemen, you can see it works fine today, with no need for cogwheels and teeth cut in the rails! What did those people do? This wasn't all that long ago. Well, they did their sums. But they only kept those sums in their heads and did not let the rest of the human being play a part in them. With this, the sums lost their edge. Doing sums is actually something that can make you bright. But in the last century people actually went against doing sums. This then also threw all the rest of their thinking into confusion. And in 1835, when people were no longer debating about 'cogwheels' but the first railway line from Fürth to Nürnberg was about to be built, the authorities consulted the Bavarian Medical Council[19] and asked them if the railways should be built, if it would be a healthy thing to do. The document about this is extraordinarily interesting. It is much more recent than you'd think — less than a hundred years. The body of learned gentlemen produced a document saying that it would be better not to build railways, for people sitting in the trains would grow very nervy. But if people were to insist on having them built, wanting to go that fast, one would at least have to put high wooden walls on either side of the track, so that farmers would not suffer concussion of the brain as the trains rushed past. This is what the document issued by the learned gentlemen says.

Yes, that was the opinion then. But don't think people form different opinions today about things that really point the way ahead as they come into this world. We may laugh about what happened in 1835, but that is after the event, and people will also only be able to laugh later on about what is happening today, when it will be almost 100 years in the past. It was not all that easy with the railways because it really went against people's way of thinking. When the first railway line from Berlin to Potsdam was to be built, the postmaster general had to be consulted,[20] for he had been in charge of the four mail coaches that went from Berlin to Potsdam and back again every week and he had to be asked to give his professional opinion about building a railway. His professional opinion was that he had four coaches going from Berlin to Potsdam every week and hardly anyone ever travelled in them. So why build a railway when no one ever travelled in the mail coaches? Today, 10 or 12 trains go from Berlin to Potsdam every day and they are always full. Not just now, at this moment, but they were always full. You see, that is how hard people have been finding it for some centuries now to relate to what is really going on in the world. They therefore do not notice what is really happening and will at most only believe someone who's an authority in an outer way, I'd say. People will sometimes believe him.

Let me tell you a story. Not long ago, it's about 40 years now, a very famous engineer lived in England, I think he was called Varley,[21] and no one doubted his intelligence. The following thing happened to this very famous man. He went from London into the country with his wife, for his sister-in-law, his wife's sister, was very ill; she was practically dying. They were going to stay in the country for a few days. The first night this gentleman, who was such a famous engineer, suddenly had a nightmare, as it is called, and found himself lying in his bed unable to move a muscle.

Now you know, it's not so bad if such a nightmare passes quickly, but if it goes on a long time and a person is unable to move a muscle and stays awake, he may die from lack of breath. So he lay there, quite benumbed already, and was still just able to think: I'm going to suffocate. Well, you know, someone was there in the house who, it was believed, would die within a few days. And the house had to be kept quiet. He therefore tried to pull himself together, but he could not. Suddenly he saw the sick woman standing by his bedside, and she addressed him by his first name, saying: 'Get up!' This gave him such a fright that the shock enabled him to move again. Being an intelligent man he knew that this had saved him. He was glad, of course, that such a thing had been possible.

You can understand this, for such things happen in the world. People who have been dumb for 15 or 20 years would suffer a sudden major shock and be able to talk again. A big shock can thus have a terrible effect on a person, but it may also be beneficial. And in the morning, when the gentleman had got up, he went to see his sister-in-law, who had been lying in her bed all night. But the first thing she told him, without him having made any reference to it first — wanting to spare her he did not want to mention the dream to her — was that she said: 'You know, I had the most peculiar dream last night. I dreamt I had to go to you and give you a fright so that you would not die from want of breath. And I went therefore and gave you a fright so that you would not suffocate. That was my dream.' Her room was quite some distance from his.

You see, this is a story about which there can be no doubt. I am telling it to you merely because it was told by someone who was otherwise very factual in his thinking, being an electrical engineer and famous in his field. I don't want to tell you any old story, but this one is confirmed to be true, just like something someone reports from a laboratory.

What was going on here? I have told you, gentleman, that the human I and the astral body go out of every human being at night. So when the sick woman was asleep, her I and astral body were not in her body. Now the principle which is known as the guardian spirit was unable to reach the man, for his thinking was of the factual kind that has become a habit over the centuries. If Mr Burle had had that kind of factual thinking—he definitely did not have it as a young boy, of course, for he'll have been no more of an academic at that age than he is now—he would not have heard what he did, for factual thinking drowns it out, blows it away. Mr Varley was a factual thinker. His guardian spirit could not have given him a fright just like that. And so this guardian spirit chose a roundabout way, using the astral body of his sick sister-in-law as she lay asleep, guiding that astral body to his bedside, so that he did get a fright. His sister-in-law would never have known about this, would not have been able to speak of it, if she'd been in good health. She died a few days later, which is when the astral body goes into the world of the spirit anyway. At the time, the astral body was already prepared. Because of this the sick woman found it easier to recall something she perceived a few days before she died, for it was something she was soon to experience. And the result was that she also knew about the matter.

So you see that if one observes these things properly one is able to talk about them exactly the way one talks about situations of the kind where you have a flask in a laboratory somewhere, a flame beneath it, and put in sulphur, let's say; the sulphur will be yellow at first and then turn brown and later red. One can describe it. And one can also describe how things are with phenomena in the spirit, providing one is really sound in one's thinking. And that must, of course, be the basic requirement. It is just that in our time everything is thrown into confusion, and the confused thinking I have mentioned predominates. And I did not describe this confused thinking for you just in order to describe it, but because I wanted to make you see how the roundabout way involving the sick woman was chosen in order to intervene in the destiny of someone who still had something more to do on this physical earth. But you have to see the matter in the right way.

I think I have told you before about what happened to me with Dr Schleich, the medical man who died recently in Berlin.[22] He was quite a famous man in Berlin, a famous surgeon, but he also had a tendency — he was more intelligent than his colleagues — to understand such things. The following once happened to him. Someone came to him one evening and told him: 'I just stuck a steel pen into my hand in the office, and some ink got in. You must remove that hand right away, amputate it, or I'll die of blood-poisoning.' Schleich said: 'But sir, I have to look at the wound first.' 'No,' said the man, 'it must be done right away!' 'It won't do,' said Dr Schleich, 'I am not permitted to do this!' He then looked at the wound and said: 'It will be quite easy to remove the stuff from the wound by suction.' And he did so. The patient insisted on having his hand removed. 'I can't amputate your hand,' the surgeon said. And the man replied: 'In that case I must die!' He did not believe that the wound was harmless and said he must die.

Dr Schleich had an uneasy feeling. Later on another medical man telephoned to say that the patient had told him he'd seen Dr Schleich who'd refused to amputate his hand and that the man was now with him. But he, too, could not amputate the hand because of a small puncture wound. Dr Schleich could not sleep all that night, for the whole thing seemed most uncanny to him.

The next day he went to the house where the man lived. He'd died in the night! A post-mortem examination showed no signs of blood poisoning. But the man had to die. Well,

Schleich simply said to himself that his death had been due to suggestion—it is known nowadays, of course, that such a thing as suggestion exists. All kinds of things are done under suggestion. One can make all kinds of things happen due to suggestion.

To give you an idea of what can be done by means of suggestion, let me tell you the following. You can say to someone, for instance: 'I'm applying a blistering plaster, a Spanish fly plaster.' But in fact you are only applying a little piece of blotting paper, yet the man will develop a huge blister! There the soul principle is entering into the physical. One can do such things. Today everyone who studies such things knows that it is possible to do this. Schleich said to himself that the man had imagined he'd die and he did die. The idea had a suggestive effect on him, hence death by suggestion.

He simply did not want to believe me that that is nonsense. But it was nonsense in this case to say the man died by suggestion, for something quite different was going on. You see, the stress he had suffered in more recent times as an office worker and business man had completely destroyed the man's nerves; blood had got into the nerves. The blood in his veins could be examined quite easily, and it was all right. And when the nerves were examined, the amount of blood that had got in was so small that it could not be detected by external means; but the nerves had been destroyed due to blood getting in. The man had therefore grown nervy and irritable and stuck the pen into his hand because he'd grown clumsy. And without anything much being apparent on the outside, he was already a marked man—for the following night. He had to die for internal reasons, because blood had got into his nervous system. And he had a premonition and grew anxious, so that the psychological effect was exactly the opposite. Schleich thought he had suggested his own death. He did not suggest his death, however; death had come because of his physical organization, but he had an inner premonition that death would come.

You see, this is a striking example of how one has to think in the right way if one wants to see into the world of spirit. One has to know exactly where the problem lies, or you can be a great and learned man and still get the wrong idea.

This is exactly what happened to Sir Oliver Lodge,[23] one of the greatest physicists in England. For he put entirely the wrong interpretation on the world of the spirit. His son had been killed in one of the battles fought in the recent [First] World War. He mourned his son, Raymond Lodge, deeply, and then got himself embroiled with a whole tissue of mediums. A very clever medium was brought to his house and arrangements were made for his son to speak to him after death. In view of the fact that his son had died on a German battlefield, this did of course make a tremendous impression, and it was also a consolation to him.

But Sir Oliver Lodge is an extraordinarily great scientist who does not believe anything just like that. But then something else happened which meant he could hardly do anything but believe. What happened is the following. The medium had gone into a trance, which is a half-conscious state, and told him that his son had his photo taken a few days before he died, saying that there were two photos, however.

Now it is quite common for several shots to be taken when photographing someone, and people will usually be asked to sit in a slightly different way for the second photo. The medium therefore said that Raymond Lodge was sitting in a slightly different way in the second photo, and gave a perfectly correct description of the difference. Oliver Lodge immediately said to himself: 'Wow, if only that were true what she is saying — photos taken a few days before his death, in two different positions!' At the time, no one in

England would as yet have been able to know if this was true, for it had only happened a few days before the death. And lo and behold! A week later the two photographs arrived by post in London—the mails were very slow then—and it was correct, absolutely correct. He then could not think anything else, from his point of view, but that his son had told him this from the other world.

And yet that was not the case, for the medium had already gone into a trance and had a prophetic vision, which is something that does happen. The people sitting around the medium only knew about the photographs a week later, when they arrived, but the medium had a prophetic vision and saw them a week earlier. So there was no link with the other world, but it all happened on earth. The medium just had a prophetic vision, and Oliver Lodge was deceived after all. That's how careful one has to be! So it is all true, that human beings live on beyond death, and they can also tell us things, but one has to be sure. If Raymond Lodge was telling them in English: 'I've had two photos taken just before my death, and the positions were different,' one has to ask oneself if that did in fact come from him. For after death this is no longer conveyed in the English language; otherwise the spirit would also have to know English. The information must have come from the medium's subconscious, from something that does not come to conscious awareness in ordinary life.

Mr Burle's question has made me discuss some rather difficult things today, but I also wanted to tell you how careful one has to be, for we are responsible for the things we say. I wanted to show that one cannot simply accept some idea or other, but has to follow everything up. And it is only after thinking about it for a long time that one is able to say: 'Yes, in that case a guardian spirit was indeed speaking.' But that the words were in German, that could only happen through human mediation. And when people are not able to do something somewhere sometime, their muscles have to be paralysed first out of the world of the spirit. Everything has to come through the human being.

Having gained these basic insights, one is then able to go further. We'll talk more about this next Saturday.

The deeper reasons for the disastrous World War

Have you thought of something, gentlemen?

Mr Dollinger: I wanted to ask about human destinies. Millions of people have died in the Great War. Did they bring this with them into the world as their destiny? How does this look in the world of the spirit and in relation to world evolution?

Rudolf Steiner: This is something we can also discuss in connection with other things, for in anthroposophy it is certainly necessary for us not to explain things the way other people sometimes do. The things we say have to be scientific. I'd like to tell you something especially in connection with this that will then guide us to understand how the disastrous situation we have now, this terrible misery so many people are going through in the world today, has actually been possible. People usually no longer pay much attention to the way one individual is connected with another. The situation is that people are really isolated individuals in the world today. Even when people know about the kind of things I spoke of the last time we met, knowing them from habit or as some remnant of superstition, they'll generally give a wrong explanation.

Now let me tell you a simple story[24] to show you that people no longer remember at all that one person is in some way connected with another. The following once happened, its truth is pretty well assured, like a scientific fact. One of the younger members of a family, a girl aged 18 or 19, was sick, not so sick as to have to stay in bed, but she had to lie down every now and again. She was lying on the sofa, with her mother looking after her, and once, when she'd pretty well gone to sleep, her mother went to another room, where she read something from a book to her husband and other members of the family. This was in a room that was quite a long way from the one where the sick girl was.

The sick girl was then aware of the following. When her mother had left the room, she suddenly felt the urge to get up. She got up and followed her mother through two other rooms into the third, where she found her reading to the others. She was greatly surprised that they were not at all amazed. The sick girl, hardly able to walk and sleeping when her mother left her just a moment ago, had now appeared in the room where her mother only intended to be for a time, because she wanted to do something for the others as well. The girl thought it a bit strange that they remained so calm. Then her mother, who was reading, suddenly said: 'Now I must go and see how our daughter is!' and left the room. The daughter followed her, however. Her mother went through those other two rooms again and found her daughter lying on the sofa, looking very pale. She did not address her immediately. But when she did, the girl did not answer, but lay there looking quite pale. The daughter herself had followed her mother all the way and saw now how her mother went into her room where she saw herself lying on the sofa. And the daughter was again very surprised, firstly to see herself lying on the sofa, and secondly to hear her mother address her. At that moment the daughter felt as if she was struck with great force, and then the form lying on the sofa gained a somewhat better colour and things were as they had been before.

This is a story we can pretty well rely on; the thing did happen. But now there are all kinds of people wanting to explain it. They'll explain it as follows, for example. 'Well, apart from having a physical body the daughter also has an astral body.' The astral body is something people used to talk about up to the sixteenth century, which is now about 400 years ago, the way we talk about a nose or an ear. But it is not something that has survived to this day; it has been generally forgotten. So people would talk about the astral body in the past and say: 'Ah well, the astral body went out, walked through those rooms, took in what the others were reading, and so on, went back again and slipped in again the moment the mother addressed the girl.'

But, gentlemen, you have to be clear in your minds that when someone explains the matter like this, he's explaining it as if there were a second physical person inside one, as if there was a circle around one, and this circle would be large, and as if one slipped out and walked around like a physical human being. Today it is a powerful superstition to explain it like that. This superstition is widespread among academics today, otherwise things like those with Oliver Lodge that I've told you about would not happen. It is always important to know exactly what went on.

Now what really went on is the following. The mother had been sitting by her daughter, nursing her. You know, this is a case of what we call 'tender loving care', and the daughter found it most pleasant to be cared for by her mother. She experienced her mother's love. At such a moment, gentlemen, when someone feels the love of another so strongly and at the same time is also rather weak, the strange thing happens that he no longer thinks with his own astral body. This grows dull and the astral body of the other person gains power over one's own astral body. Then it can actually happen that one begins to think with the thoughts of the other person who is beside one. Now the situation was that whilst the mother was still nursing her daughter, the feeling which arose in her transferred to her daughter in such a way that the daughter felt and thought just as her mother did. Then the mother went away. Just as a ball will keep rolling if I give it a push, so the daughter was then not thinking with her own thoughts but with those of her mother. And as the mother went through those two rooms, the daughter was all the time thinking her mother's thoughts. And when the mother was reading aloud, the daughter was thinking her mother's thoughts.

The daughter did of course continue to rest on the sofa, but she was all the time thinking her mother's thoughts. And when the mother grew concerned and went back again, the daughter thought she, too, was walking back. And now you need not be surprised that the daughter grew pale. You'd be pale, too, if you were to lie as though in a deep swoon for a time. For a situation like that, where one thinks with the thoughts of someone else, does of course create a condition similar to a faint. And when the mother returned, the effect on the daughter was that she was deeply shaken and therefore able to have her own thoughts again. So you see that in this case, the right explanation is that one person has a most powerful influence on another, particularly in mind and spirit. This will happen particularly if the one who is influenced is in a greatly weakened condition, that is, if he is unable to develop inner strength, then the inner strength of the other person will easily influence him.

But that is how it is in life quite generally. One often does not consider the great influence people have on one another. Do you think that if someone tells you something and you then believe it, you actually always have reasons, sensible reasons, to be convinced of the truth of it? That is not at all true. If you like someone you believe that person more than you do someone you hate. The thing is that the one person's soul has an extraordinarily strong influence on the soul of another. I therefore have to know very exactly how things are in the realm of the spirit if I am to talk about them at all.

Let me give you another example, which I'm telling you for a particular purpose. For someone might now say: 'Well, Dr Steiner clearly does not believe at all that a human being can go out of himself; he only believes that one person is able to influence another.' No, I was only giving you an example that would clearly show you how one individual influenced another, in this case the mother the daughter.

Now another example, where one cannot in the least say that someone was influenced. Two students were sharing a room. This happens all the time with students. One was studying mathematics, the other was studying philology and knew nothing, absolutely nothing, about mathematics. One evening they were swotting terribly hard, which is the term students use, one of them his Latin grammar, the other a mathematical problem which he wanted to solve but simply could not get right. He was quite unable to do anything with it. The one managed reasonably well with his language studies and went to bed feeling reasonably satisfied. But the mathematics student did not feel satisfied on going to bed, for he could not solve his problem. With a language you usually don't know if you've got it right or not. At most you get things wrong but may well think they are right. The situation with mathematics is that you'll not get any result if you can't do it. That is the difference. So they went to bed; the two of them went to bed somewhere about 11.30 or 12 o'clock.

At about 3 o'clock in the morning the mathematics student got up — the language student looked at the clock and noted the time — sat down again at his desk and started to calculate and calculate and calculate. The language student was really surprised at this, but he had sufficient sense to wait calmly to see what would happen. The other one went on calculating, then got up off his chair, went to bed and slept on.

At 8 in the morning they both got up. The mathematics student said: 'Wow, I've got a really thick head today, as if we'd been to the pub all night. But surely we stayed at home?' The other one then said: 'It does not surprise me in the least! Why did you get up during the night and work?' 'What, me? Work? That never came into my head! I was in my bed all night,' said the mathematics student. 'But you did get up,' the other one said, 'you picked up your pencil and worked on and on.' 'Well,' said he, 'absolutely not.' 'Well, let's look and see,' said the language student, 'the stuff you've written must be there.' The mathematics student went to look. The whole problem had been solved, everything he'd been unable to do the night before had now been done.

Now you see, here you have an example where there can be no question of the other student cheating, for he could not have solved the problem. He was a student of languages and he also watched everything that happened. The other student got up, knowing nothing about it, and solved the whole problem. But there was no question of one of them influencing the other in any way. The student did in fact get up in the night.

But when one explains it, something very odd comes out. You see, as you know, we have first of all our physical body, then the ether body, the astral body and the I-body. I call them all 'bodies'; they aren't, of course, bodies in any outer sense, but I call these four parts of the human being 'bodies'. Well now, gentlemen, when we are sleeping, only our physical body and ether body lie in the bed; the astral body and the I-body are outside. We see them around the physical body and ether body on the outside. I have explained all this to you before. And that is also what happened with our mathematics student. He went to bed. He was able to sleep, so that his astral body and I-body went outside, but he was upset because he had not solved his problem. Now if the astral body and the I-body had then slipped into his physical body and ether body, he would have woken up and again been unable to do anything, probably not solving the problem. But the astral body and the I-body did not do this. But the unrest which had developed made it nudge the student. The astral body can nudge one, it can even nudge the skin a little. But this can only happen by means of the air, not physically, for the astral body is not the least bit physical. It can, however, set the air in motion. And this has an effect especially on the eyes, a bit on the ears, and especially on the nose and the mouth. Wherever you have sense organs, the nudging breath of the astral body has quite an effect.

So our mathematics student had gone to bed, the astral body was nudging him from the outside all the time, but not coming in. But because of this nudging, the physical body with the ether body felt compelled to get up, quite automatically, like a machine. The astral body stayed outside, however, for if it had been inside the student would have become conscious. So he sat down. His astral body and his I were not prepared to go inside. So who was doing the sums? The physical body and the ether body were doing them, and the ether body was able to do all the calculations which the student could not do when the astral body and the I were inside him.

You see from this, gentlemen, that you're all a great deal more intelligent in your ether body than you are in your astral body and your I. If you were able to do and know everything you can do and know in your ether body, wow, what clever fellows you'd be! For all learning really consists in bringing up into the astral body something which we already have in our ether body.

So what really happened with our mathematics student? You know, in earlier times there were hardly any tee-totallers among students, and they really would drink rather a lot normally. And those two students did not swot every night but also went to the pub a lot, and because of this—with the blood under the influence of alcohol—the astral body was ruined. The ether body was not ruined so much. And the result was that the mathematics student could have solved his problem quite well if he had not gone to the pub so much; but because he had allowed his astral body to be greatly influenced he could not solve it when awake. He first had to get rid of his ruined astral body; then he could sit down at his desk, and his ether body, which was still quite clever, solved the problem. So the things the rational mind does we actually do with the ether body. We can't love someone with the ether body, that is something the astral body has to do, but everything the rational mind does is something the ether body is able to do, this is where the ether body has to do its job. We are therefore able to say that we can see quite clearly from this example that in this case there was no influence from somewhere else, but the mathematics student just had to do it by himself.

Let us have a clear picture of this. There [Fig. 14] we have

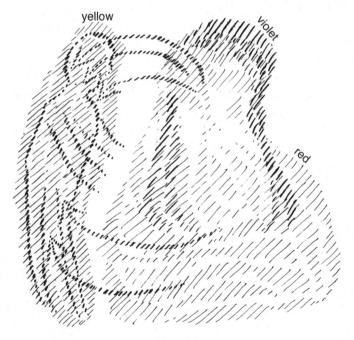

Fig. 14

the physical body; here the ether body [yellow] which goes through the physical body. And now, so that we get a better picture of the whole human being, I am going to draw the astral body outside, where it is during the night. It is quite small at the top and enormous, bulging out, down below. So at night we are really two people. You should not, of course, imagine that this is a second person who is also physical, for the part that is outside is entirely spiritual. If you were to fail to think of it as spiritual you'd fall too much into materialism again. But you can certainly take the view that in himself man really is this twofold creature, one part that is spirit and soul, and a physical part combined with the ether body. Someone who is awake is only the way he is because every morning the astral body and the I-body are brought into the physical and ether body [arrows].

But now imagine that this might not always happen in the proper way. There are some strange cases of this. There was a girl—if they happen of their own accord and not because of exercises, such things always happen when the individual gets a bit weak, in the case of young girls for instance when they have just reached maturity, when they have just entered into womanhood—so there was a girl of 19 or 20 and it was like this with her. There were days when she'd talk but the people in her family could not understand a thing she was saying, nothing at all. She would talk of completely unknown things. It was very strange. She might say, for example: 'Ah, good day, I am delighted at your visit. We met two days ago in . . .—yes, we went for a walk in those lovely woods. There was a spring there.' Then she'd wait. It was just like on the telephone; you did not hear the other person, but only her reply. It was as if she was replying to something: 'Yes, of course, you took the glass and drank.' And so one would always hear what she said in reply to something someone else was supposed to have said. The people around her could not see the other person. But she was in a very different world and having a conversation in it.

The following would happen, for instance. Now, you see, she could not move, she'd stay quite still on those days. But if she sat there and you nudged her, she'd not say: 'Why are you nudging me?' She'd say: 'The wind is terrible. Close the window, there's such a draught!' She had completely different ideas if one nudged her, for instance. She'd be like that for one or two days. Then there would be some days, or a longer period, when she was perfectly sensible, talking normally to people, and knew nothing about what had happened on those other days. She did not remember any of it. If people told her some of it, she'd say she knew nothing about it. It was just as if she'd been asleep. But something else would happen instead. When she was in this other condition, she'd remember everything that had to do with this condition, and nothing of what had happened when she was in her usual state. She was able to review the whole life she'd known in that other world which people said she'd dreamed up.

What was it with this girl? What I am telling you now does, of course, happen many, many times, and sometimes in a ghastly way. You see, I knew someone with whom I worked together for some time. He then became a professor at a German university, and one day he simply disappeared. No one knew where he'd gone. All enquiries ultimately led nowhere. The only thing people were able to find out was that he'd gone to the station from the place where he lived and bought a ticket. But quite a number of people had got on the train and so people did not know the destination to which he'd bought a ticket. He went away. And he did not come back for a very long time.

One day a stranger arrived at a hostel for the homeless in Berlin and asked to be admitted. When they asked for his papers it was found he was Professor XY from such and such a place. He had ended up in that hostel in Berlin. He came home again and was able to continue his work as a professor quite well. You know, things go on automatically; it does not matter if there is a bit of a break. But his family—he was actually married—made further enquiries as to what had happened in the meantime. And it was more or less that he'd bought a ticket to a station that was not that far away. He had been quite crafty about it all. He'd got off the train, bought another ticket—you did not yet need a passport at that time—and gone to another country, and then another country, then he'd taken a completely different route, to a town in southern Germany where he'd once been stationed, and on to Berlin where he lived in the hostel. He knew nothing, absolutely nothing of it all, being in a completely different state of consciousness.

What is going on in such a case? You see, with someone like that it is just as it was with that girl. When such a person is due to wake up, the astral body and the I-body do not come in fully, merely nudging the person from the outside, and then the physical body and the ether body go through all those things. Such people behave in a tremendously clever way. This story has also been fully confirmed. It is similar to the one I experienced with someone of my acquaintance.

Another story. Someone took a train ticket, did the same thing, going to a station that was not far away. He then had to think up all kinds of clever dodges; it was his ether body which did it all. He got all the way to India and stayed there for some years. And then, having forgotten all about it, he went on with his life as before.

Yes, you see these things really are such that one has to say: There one gains deep insight into the whole nature of the human being. For what happened later with the person I knew well, who'd travelled through two countries and ended up in a hostel? He returned to his university, and was even called to another university to take the place of a renowned professor. One day I happened to be in that town. We were no longer in touch, for it happened quite generally that when I gave anthroposophical lectures people I'd known well before would no longer have anything to do with me. One day people said Professor XY had gone off again. This time he did not reappear but his body was found. He had drowned himself.

What had happened? You see, what had happened was that he again returned to the state where the astral body would only nudge him. He then recalled the earlier events in his ether body and got such a fright that he committed suicide. So one is able to see deeply into human nature in that case, if one knows how the different bodies of the human being work together.

Now the matter is this. There was someone once who also got into such states, and then he'd talk in such a way as if he were someone quite different than he now was, so that other people did not understand any of it. He spoke — this was in the nineteenth century — of being involved in the French Revolution, describing whole scenes. What had happened to him? It was similar to the situation of the people I have just told you about. But what had happened in his case?

In their ordinary state of consciousness people know very little indeed about what is going on in the astral body and the I-body, but they do actually go through a lot in those bodies. Now imagine the following happens. You see, I want to describe to you what it is like when someone wakes up. As the person wakes up, his astral body first of all splits. It tears off here [Fig. 14], and one part goes into the head, whilst the other, the lower part, goes into the rest of the body. That is how it goes sometimes. Now consider this. If the head finds it easier to take in the astral body and the I than the lower part does, the astral body may be in the head sooner, before it gets to the lower part. In this case the person begins to talk as someone quite different. So what is happening? You see, for a moment the ability is there to look back into an earlier life. But the person is unable to understand or interpret this, and will therefore invent something based on history. The man who was in an altered state, because his astral body and I had entered into his head earlier, said he was a Frenchman involved in the French Revolution. This is something he had learned about and he simply reinterpreted the facts. He was actually finding himself in an earlier incarnation, an earlier life, and was unable to understand this right away; and so he interpreted it in his own way.

Now you have to understand that up to the sixteenth century—which would be four centuries ago—people would talk of such things, though in a rather silly and vague way. Wherever people forgathered—it was not that they would tell each other ghost stories, but the truth is that they took this just as seriously as other events in their lives—they told such things, knowing that they existed. It is certainly not true to say that they did not know about it. Today— well, I ask you, gentlemen, just try and tell stories like those I've told you at your party conferences and you'll be chucked out immediately—today there is no way of speaking of these things naturally or sensibly. People do not speak of them at all. And the academics have least to say about them. Let me prove to you that they know least of all about them.

Think of one of the most important scientific events in the nineteenth century. A citizen of Heilbronn had qualified as a medical practitioner. The people at Tübingen University thought he was not very gifted and so he did not have any real prospects. He therefore let himself be hired as a ship's doctor in 1839 and went to Indo-China on a ship that had quite a lot of people on it. The journey proved to be a fairly difficult one, with the seas fairly restless so that people got seasick. Practically the whole crew were sick when they arrived in Indo-China. The ship's doctor was kept very busy. At the time, it was still customary to let blood when people had one kind of sickness or another. That was the first thing.

People have two kinds of blood vessels. When one kind is opened, the blood that splashes out is reddish in colour. Another kind of blood vessel runs right alongside the first kind. If this is opened, the blood is bluish; bluish blood will come out. Ordinarily, when you bleed someone, you do not let the red blood flow out. The body needs this blood. You let the bluish blood flow out. Physicians know this very well. They also know where the blue blood vessels are and do not open the red ones. Dear Julius Robert Mayer,[25] who was that ship's doctor, therefore had to do a lot of blood-letting. But every time he opened a vein the blood that came out was not the proper bluish colour but pale red. Oh dear, he thought, I've opened the wrong one! But when he did it for the next person, taking special care, the blood was again a pale red. In the end all he could do was tell himself that when one gets to the tropics, the hot regions, things are not the way they usually are, and blue blood turns reddish because of the heat. Julius Robert Mayer thought this a most important discovery, quite rightly so. He had seen something that was extraordinarily important.

We now have to have a hypothesis, make an assumption. Imagine this had happened to someone in the twelfth rather than the nineteenth century. He would have travelled somewhere or other with people. Travels did not range far in those times, but it could certainly have happened that a whole crew fell sick. Let us assume, then, that a whole crew got sick, the physician bled them and found that the blood which should really be blue was reddish instead. Now in the twelfth century he would have said: 'What is it that causes the blood to turn blue?' And since he would have known all the things I have been talking about, though rather vaguely — for there was no anthroposophy then and things were rather vague — he would at least have had an inkling and would have said: 'Wow, yes, there the astral body does not enter as deeply into the physical body as it does in people whose blood is quite blue.' For he would have known that it is the astral body which makes the blood blue. The heat keeps the astral body out, however. The blood therefore grows less blue and looks similar to the red blood. He would have said: 'This is an important discovery, for now I understand why the ancient peoples of the East had such great wisdom. With them, the astral body did not enter so deeply into the physical body and ether body.' He would have had a profound respect for the wisdom of the ancient Orientals and he would have said to himself: 'Today the people of the Orient have merely been infected by the people who have a lot of bluish blood, and it therefore is no longer possible for them to bring their ancient wisdom to light.' That is what a twelfth-century ship's doctor would have said.

A ninteenth-century ship's doctor no longer knew anything of all the things I have been telling you. What did he say to himself? He'd say: 'Well, there's the heat. It burns things up. The blood therefore burns up more when one is in the hot zone.' He discovered the law of the transformation of heat into energy which plays such a big role in modern physics, a completely abstract law. The rest does not interest him at all. He found the law that plays a big role in the steam engine, for example, where heat is transformed into work. And he said: 'The fact that the blood flows red there shows that the organism works harder in the hot zone and therefore produces more heat.' Julius Robert Mayer thus found something that is wholly mechanical.

You see, that is the big difference. In the twelfth century, people would still have said: 'The blood is redder there because the astral body does not go in so deeply.' In the nineteenth century, people no longer knew anything of all this spiritual side and simply said: 'There the human being is like a machine, and the situation is that heat generates more work and because of this more heat is converted in the human organism.' Yes, gentlemen, what Julius Robert Mayer did there as a greatly learned man is more or less the way people generally think in our day. That is how it is. But because people are now only able to think and feel about things that are no longer of the spirit, they have lost their connection with other people. And it will at most be when they are sick and weak like the girl I spoke of that they'll enter so much into the other person that they actually go along with that person's thoughts into another room. That's an enormous difference, of course. Yes, we have made tremendous progress today, but our humanity has not progressed; it has grown less. We only speak of the human physical organism as if it were only a machine today. Even the greatest scientists now speak of it only as a machine, as Julius Robert Mayer did.

Yes, gentlemen, if things were to go on like this on earth, all thinking would fall into chaos. All horrors and disasters would come. People already no longer know what they should really do. They therefore go at things with might and main, saying: 'Yes, common sense no longer keeps us together, and so nationality must keep us together.' National states only arise because people no longer know how to keep together. And the fact, gentlemen, that people no longer know anything of the spiritual world has brought about the tremendous misery — all the rest are only external factors. It is this which has brought about the tremendous human misery. And to say that people deserve it because they've done bad things in their previous life is, of course, nonsense, for this is not the destiny of an individual person, it is the common destiny shared by each and every one. But every single individual knows it now in this life. Just think how much misery people know in this present life. That does not come from their previous life. But in the next life they will know the consequences of the present misery. The consequence will be that they'll be wiser, and the world of spirit will enter into them more easily. The wretched state they are in today is educating them for the future.

There is something else we can see from this. Just think that anthroposophy started as early as 1900 and has really got quite well known. But people have resisted it, not wanting to hear of the spiritual world. Well now, gentlemen, if you had a schoolboy in earlier times who did not want to learn – this has changed now; I'm not going to say if it was right or wrong – he'd be given a thorough beating. Some would then start to learn after all. It did help with some of them. Humanity has not been wanting to learn anything of the spirit until 1914. They have now had a beating for this from world destiny, their common destiny. We shall see now if it has done any good.

That is how it is, gentlemen, we have to see it as a common human destiny. For what did happen? You see, the girl I told you about thought her mother's thoughts. People have gradually got out of the habit of thinking altogether and now only think the thoughts of those whom they consider to have authority. People must start to think for themselves again, every single one of them, otherwise they will all the time be influenced by the world of the spirit, if they do not know anything about it, but in a bad sense. And it would then be fair to say that the misery which has come for humanity may be seen as a beating given by destiny, I'd say, and we can learn from this.

People can have as many congresses as they like; none of it will help. People who want to support the German mark, thinking the way they do today, will make it go down twice as much afterwards, for an understanding that is wholly of the earth is absolutely no use at all. If a body does not have enough fluid in it, it grows sclerotic, it calcifies. And if the soul does not know anything about the world of the spirit, it ends up with an understanding that is of no use at all. And that is the destiny humanity is moving towards, unless nourishment comes to them all the time from the world of the spirit.

So the only real way is for people to begin to take an interest in the world of the spirit. You see, that is how one has to answer the question put by Mr Dollinger. One has to put things in a fairly radical way, but that is how they hang together.

I have to go to Stuttgart next week, but I'll soon be back. I'll get them to tell you when our next session will be.

Effects of relative star positions on the earth and on human beings

Question concerning earthquakes.

Rudolf Steiner: You probably mean the earthquakes they have in America at the moment? With regard to questions like this, volcanic phenomena are especially important that are not so intense, I'd say, not so immediately powerful, but show in their details that something is also happening in the course of time from the cosmos that surrounds the world. And here I'd like to draw your attention to something else, something that may be less striking, but something that is much more of a personal experience for many people than those single events which have, of course, been terrible for the people in the area, but really are of less concern for the greater part of humanity. Just remember that in recent years one could really say that weather conditions have been unusual. We cannot deny that we have not had the proper, long summers, especially not in our part of the world. But this applies to a large part of Europe and beyond.

When the subject comes up, people will usually talk of vast icebergs in the northern oceans and of waves of cold coming from those mighty floating icebergs. You'll perhaps also remember that when there were such cold periods last year, mariners reported that these gigantic floating icebergs were to be found everywhere if they set their course just a little to the north in the Atlantic Ocean.

We have to understand that things like these certainly do not come from the earth only, but have to do with the whole of cosmic evolution. And so we have to ask ourselves what the situation really is with the distribution of heat and cold on our earth.

Here I'd like to draw your attention to something which I may well have mentioned before, but in a different context, something that may be important in considering this question. You'll probably have heard that above all in northern Siberia, that is over yonder in Asia, soil conditions are rather special. To put you in the picture, let me just say the following. If we have the map of Europe like this [*drawing on the board*], you get Norway here, then the north coast of Germany, and going on to Holland, and so on; this would be Ireland, England, and there, on the other side of this large peninsula, we'd already be in Asia. This is the border between Asia and Europe. This is Russia. Here we come to Asia and this would be Siberia. Over yonder is the Arctic Ocean, as it is called. I've merely drawn this to give you an orientation. A long time ago, animals rather like elephants[26] were found in the soil of Siberia. They no longer exist today, but they did exist on earth a very, very long time ago. And you know, of course, that there are no animals like elephants living by the Arctic Ocean today. Animals like elephants belong to much hotter regions. But the strange thing is that when these elephant-like creatures were found deep down in the soil, they were still so fresh that one could have eaten the meat even today, providing one likes elephant meat. The creatures were there in the icy ground as if people intended to eat the meat today and had kept it there to preserve it. So for millennia these animals have simply been preserved, as one says, there in northern Siberia, keeping the meat fresh.

Now you see, gentlemen, it is impossible for this ever to have been a slow process. For if the animals living up there had simply died and got into the soil, they would of course have rotted away long since, and the most one would find today would be bits of bones, the way one also does elsewhere. But there one finds whole fresh animals. The only possible way in which this could have happened was that a wave of ice came over the creatures that lived there with tremendous speed, enclosing them, so that they were preserved for millennia in just that state, with the meat still fresh. So you can see that there must have been a situation on earth at one time when a powerful push came from the south, throwing the water up into that region of ice. The water froze instantly, the creatures were instantly in that vast Siberian ice cellar, and were preserved there for millennia.

Now you'll all admit that the earth doesn't have any reason, of course, to do such a thing all of a sudden. For where in the earth would the energies to do such a thing come from? Such things can only happen under the influence of heavenly bodies beyond the earth. So if you imagine that this is the earth [drawing on the board], and these are the southern regions, the equatorial regions — southern only with reference to the north, of course — then the stars must have been in particular positions here at one time, and this simply threw the water up here. So it was due to the position of the stars that this water was thrown up there, freezing immediately and burying these creatures. You can really see from such things that the relative positions of the stars have a tremendous influence on the distribution of land and water and ice on earth.

Now the other day[27] I spoke of the way volcanoes, too, come from things beyond this earth, with matter that is below ground being fetched up from the inner earth. So we can also say that if, for example, there is now a tremendous eruption from Mt Etna, things are not thrown out from below, but the stars are in a position up above that will bring those fiery masses up from the inner earth.

We see from this that very many things act together today, and on the one hand that is the reason why we have these cold periods. The cold periods are therefore definitely caused by things outside this earth. And volcanic eruptions and earthquakes also come from there. But we can never wholly judge such a situation unless we understand that the human being himself is closely connected with all the conditions that exist beyond this earth.

You see, I'm sure you've heard of people having haemorrhages, with the blood no longer going the way it should inside them but coming out of their mouths instead. That's called a haemorrhage. Such haemorrhages happen particularly when people are at a particular time of life. We have to ask ourselves: 'What exactly is the connection between a haemorrhage and something that happens outside?' Now if you remember that the human being consists not just of a physical body, which we may touch with our hands, but of a physical body, ether body and an astral body and I-body, you'll have to say to yourself: 'Yes, of course, the physical body is something we can lay aside. It is heavy, a heavy mass, and is connected with the earth. But the ether body is connected with the surrounding world.'

Looking at things the way they are in the human being, we find that the moon in particular has a powerful influence on the human being. But the way things are now, the moon does not have such an influence on man, and we have to go back again to very early times. In early times, the moon had a tremendously powerful influence on man. People had to do something specific when the moon was waxing, and they had to do something specific when it was waning, and so on. And above all human procreation depended very much on the moon in those earlier times. It is so interesting to see how people who still preserve ancient traditions think about these things. And the moon then also influences the whole of human development, but in such a way that the human being has these moon influences inside himself. So it is not a direct influence when there's a full moon, or the like; but we see the moon wax, wane; at one time this had an influence on human beings, and this has remained and still continues. So it is not the present-day movements of the moon that have much of an influence, but something that is similar to the earlier movements of the moon. It is an old hereditary element that has a great influence. And so we can certainly say that the moon does have some influence.

But we would not have any blood at all in our head if this moon were not there. We'd all go about with absolutely pale faces, horribly pale faces, if it were not for the influence of the moon. The moon draws the blood in our body up to the head. That is the moon influence, that the blood actually consents to go up into the head. This is extraordinarily interesting. The blood only goes up into the human head because the influence of the moon is there. Otherwise it would always go down. When someone grows so weak in his whole body that he can no longer offer sufficient resistance to the powers of the moon that draw the blood up to the head, the blood rushes up into the head too powerfully, and this causes the haemorrhage. We always have to have that influence, but if it gets too strong, the blood rushes too strongly up into the human head and the blood then comes out.

And you see with this haemorrhage in the individual human being we have the same principle as with the kind of business, for instance, where water rushes up there [*pointing to Siberia*] or things come out of a volcano in the natural world outside. Only in that case it is not the influence of the moon, but of other heavenly bodies. You have to imagine that we are continually exposed to other influences simply in our development as human beings. Let me illustrate this for you. Once again imagine this to be the earth [*drawing on the board*]; here is the moon moving around the earth. I'll draw it the way it looks. So there the moon moves around the earth, and initially has a powerful influence on the human being. But beyond the moon are the other stars— Venus, Mercury, there's the sun, Mars, Jupiter and so on, and then the fixed stars. Now you have to understand that there's a difference when, let us say, Mars is behind the sun, or has already moved on and is beside the sun. When Mars is behind the sun, it has less influence on the earth, because the sun blocks out its influence. When Mars is in this position [beside the sun], it has a greater influence on the earth. And so it always depends on the positions of the stars how much the earth is influenced. This science of the positions of the stars has been very little developed today, and people therefore only consider what is happening on earth—icebergs and so on—and they do not look out at the stars.

Now it actually is not possible to explore these things from the earth, and we must understand that these things have to be explored by considering the human being. These things must definitely be investigated via the human being.

Now I'd like to tell you something. If you follow the evolution of humanity in more recent times, you'll see enormous changes in it. We won't go very far back, but let us go back, say, 600 years. Going back 600 years—it is now 1923—we come to 1323. Now you have to consider that if you had lived then, you'd have had no idea that places such as America, Australia exist. People did not know any of this. They only knew about Europe and Asia and a little bit of Africa, a very small bit of Africa. Six hundred years before our time, therefore, people only knew about a small part of the earth. And above this earth they saw the moon rise and go down, the sun rise and go down, the stars, and everything was such that the whole of life was lived within a small space. Yes, gentlemen, people knew little of the earth then, and they also had no idea of the movements of the heavenly bodies. But they did know something about the spiritual influences of the stars. This was because they lived in such a limited area. People were influenced by those limited conditions.

Now you know that not long after this, in 1492, Christopher Columbus of Genoa[28] set out with a number of ships, and he believed one could go right round the world. Christopher Columbus actually did not intend to discover America, but it was his opinion that the earth must be spherical. Before that, people had thought the earth was flat. In his opinion, the earth had to be spherical. And so he fitted out a number of ships. There was resistance, but he did get those ships from the government, fitted them out, and believed he could go round the earth. That is what he thought. He said to himself: 'If we go from Europe over to the East, we find Asia there [pointing to the drawing], down there is peninsular India, and there's Indo-China.' He knew, therefore, that going that way by land one would come to India. He now wanted to go round the earth from Spain and reach India from the other side. That was his intention. He wanted to go round the world, for he was hoping to see the first practical use made of the earth's spherical nature. He wanted to go round and discover India from the other side. So he set out and came to America and absolutely believed it to be the other side of India. That is also why this area was called the West Indies, a name still used for part of it today.

So you see that the earth's spherical form gradually became knowledge through human thinking, and people only gradually discovered that they had reached the other side of America and that this was not India but a new continent. It was therefore in 1492, 431 years ago, that America was discovered.

But the discovery of America also meant something very, very different. To understand what it means, please consider the following. You see, as I told you, it was in 1493 that Christopher Columbus first set out and discovered America. In 1543, Copernicus[29] first presented the view that the sun stood still and the earth moved around the sun like the other planets. Something every child learns at school today has therefore only been known from that time. Just think — how many years would that be? It's only 380 years! So it is only since then that people have had the merest inkling of something which is taught in primary school today. Before that, people knew nothing of all this. But they gave all the more thought to the moon's influence on the human being. They knew that the moon drives the blood to the head, as I've just told you. They perceived the influence on the human being.

Now you have to consider what the discovery of America really meant. You see, people talk about things without giving it much thought and in history it is also presented like this: discovery of America; a stroke of genius! Yes, gentlemen, but you have to think of it also in a very different way. What kind of people do you think lived in America at the time when Columbus got there? Less than 500 years ago, copper-red native Americans lived there, and these American Indians did not think the way you do today in Europe, for example. They knew a great deal about the influence of the stars. So there was a population in America at that time who knew an extraordinary amount about the influence of the stars. They lived entirely according to the influence of the stars. And then the Europeans arrived, civilized humanity. Now you see, even in the nineteenth century the American Indians would still say that the Europeans always brought along such a strange thing, something white with tiny spirits on it. But those, they said, were very harmful spirits, terribly harmful spirits, and the Europeans would use them to cast spells on the Americans. That was what the American Indians thought. And do you know what it was that they were so afraid of and which made them think the Europeans were such dreadful people, causing such havoc with it? Those were books — pages of white paper with letters on them. The American Indians saw them, believed them to be magic, and said: 'These people use them to cast spells on us.'

That was how human beings encountered one another. And there followed the eradication of the American Indians. But where did the people come from who eradicated the American Indians? They came from Europe! And if the people who had lived in Europe would have got to America in 1323, their views would have been much more like those of the American Indians. For in 1323 people in Europe still knew about the influence of the stars. They would have had much more in common. But the people who actually went there later on no longer had anything at all in common with the American Indians, and all they could do was to eradicate them. And European people then lived and developed in the place where the American Indians had been. So you have to consider this. The Americans who developed there are really Europeans. You see, the ideas people often get from what they learn at school are sometimes really quite idiotically stupid.

I'd just like to draw your attention to one thing. Today people talk a lot about the French. But the people who live around Nuremberg today are still called Franconians. The French are simply ancient Germans who migrated there and adopted a variant of the Latin language. So all the things people keep saying when they do not know how things have come about, and the angry things they say because of the way things are taught in history lessons are sometimes extremely foolish, infinitely stupid. And in that case, too, we have infinite stupidity. People fail to consider that people from Europe, people who developed in Europe in the last three centuries, went over to America. The really major immigration only came much later, in the eighteenth, nineteenth centuries. That was when the settlers went to

America. And what kind of people went there? Well, illiterate people also went, but they did not have much of an influence. The people who went there and had a major influence were people who had been educated in Europe, above all in science, people who had learned the Copernican theories, and took a completely different view of the stars.

Just think how it all fits together in world history. On the one hand the earth was shown to be spherical, and people found that it was possible to go round the earth. And on the other hand it was shown that the sun did not rise there and then went down again, but that there was space everywhere and the earth moved around the sun; that the earth was not flat, that the sun did not go down into the water at night but that the earth moved around the sun.

You see, people do not give thought to the connection between the discovery of America in 1492 and Copernicus' new view of the stars in 1543. There is a close connection. Please do not think that what happened could have happened unless the stars had an influence on human beings. The stars played a role when Columbus thought: 'Now I'll go west.' You just have to consider how nebulous it all was. He did not know he was going to discover America. He merely wanted to go round the earth. It's just like a blind hen finding a grain. We can't say it was his rational mind that did it, for in such a situation people are driven by influences. And it is the influence of the stars that drives them. So we also have to say to ourselves when we ask ourselves why Copernicus thought about the stars: 'We must look for the reasons in the influence of the stars.'

There was a time during the Middle Ages—I told you it was still like this 600 years ago—when people's ideas still related to a very small world. And then they suddenly had ideas that went right round the earth and went right round in the heavens. All their ideas floated apart. Yes, gentlemen, there we have to think a bit more deeply about what is going on in the human being. We have to go into these things in a truly scientific way. I have by now told you many things about the human being. I'll now tell you something that has been thoroughly confirmed again, so that you may see how things are.

An Austrian poet, Robert Hamerling,[30] was appointed to teach at a secondary school in Trieste at a particular time, in 1855. He took a great interest in everything that went on. This Robert Hamerling was also very interested at the time in all kinds of swindlers who would always be passing through Trieste, people who produced abnormal things and were called mediums. He liked to go to such meetings, not being at all superstitious, but he really saw the swindling and cheating that went on with most of these things. But once, when he saw someone with a particularly remarkable medium, he thought he'd really check this out. Now before Hamerling went to Trieste he knew a young girl in Graz, where he then lived, and this girl died soon after. He had a lock of her hair. He'd made the lock of hair into a small circlet, tied it and fixed it to a small piece of paper which he put into a little box. He kept this as a memento. It had become quite precious to him when the person concerned had died. He had taken it with him to Trieste among other things. No one knew about it. He never told anyone about it — he remembered this very clearly — and had actually never shown the little box to anyone. Conditions were such, anyway, that he would not have liked to show it to anyone. It was something he felt rather embarrassed about. So he had a secret little box, as it were, with the memento inside it. He put this in his pocket when he went to the meeting with the medium. And what happened was that people would give the medium all kinds of things, putting them into envelopes or boxes. The medium would take this in her hand, touch it and tell what was in the box. Now there is often a lot of cheating going on with such things; one must have a very open mind in such cases.

I was at a meeting once, for example, when a medium was also brought in, and the person called the manager went around among the audience and asked them to write all kinds of things on bits of paper. He'd take these, but stay where he was. The medium wore a blindfold. And as he went on standing there he'd just say: 'What have I got in my hand?' and the medium would immediately say what it was. So if someone wrote down his own name and gave it to the manager, he'd read it and then crunch up the piece of paper. The medium could not see anything, but she'd say what it said on the piece of paper. Now you see the people around the table where I was sitting were terribly curious — for they were truly amazed — and they decided we should write something down that the fellow would not be clever enough to communicate; for they all thought he was communicating with the medium by some kind of signs. So I wrote the name Spinoza and the title of a work by Spinoza, the *Ethica*, for the people thought the manager would not know, of course, who Spinoza was. But he accepted Spinoza and his *Ethica* just as well, and the medium promptly gave the correct answer. People were really amazed by this. But, you see, the matter was quite simple. The manager was a ventriloquist, and the medium only pretended to answer as the manager spoke from his stomach in the medium's voice. Things really are like this and one simply must not allow oneself to be deceived. I have to stress this again and again. One must not allow oneself to be deceived. And that is exactly the difference between superstitious people who easily believe anything, and people who are able to form an opinion about these things.

But Hamerling took his little box and no one knew anything about it. He handed this little box, which no one knew about, up among all the other things. The medium was sitting at a table and he handed the box up. Now the other things were dealt with first. The medium did it quite briskly. And the moment she came to his little box, she picked it up and flung it away. Hamerling thought that they probably had some kind of arrangement with all the other things, whilst in his case there could be no arrangement, so the medium could not discover what was in it and therefore flung it away. He then went and said he would nevertheless like to know what was inside. The little box was picked up once more. The medium flung it away again. It was picked up again. And then the medium said, in something of a stammer: 'A lock of hair and a small piece of paper.' Now it was for him to be surprised, of course. There could be absolutely no question of cheating. So he asked why she'd flung it away again and again. And she said: 'Because it comes from a dead woman.' He was even more amazed then. So that was a case — I am only speaking of cases which you find in the literature, otherwise there'd be hundreds more I could mention — where there was no question of cheating.

What was behind this? At the time, the medium must not know what is there, but has to search for it from her unconscious. A quite specific influence was behind this.

I once told you that the influence of cooked buckwheat in the basement may sometimes still show itself on the third floor. You'll remember my telling you about this. Such an influence lies behind this, which only affects the head. And the medium will then say what's inside — why? Because the medium is someone whose blood is more subject to the influence of the moon than other people's are. The influence is not so strong that a haemorrhage will occur, but the blood is drawn towards the head, more so than in other people. This has a powerful influence; this is how such an influence can be there.

Considering this, you'll say to yourself: 'Yes, the mighty

influences from the stars do of course affect the human being all the time.' And everything Europe has experienced in relation to America and the whole earth has been under the influence of the stars. But what is the nature of this influence? Well, gentlemen, you have to consider the following. Imagine this to be the earth [*drawing on the board*]. There was that small part of the earth which was all people would know in earlier times. Above it were the stars—I'm of course only showing this schematically. People were under the influence of these stars. It was the time before the discovery of America. People had very definite ideas. If you look at the pictures and portraits of the aldermen of those times, you can see how definite their ideas were, how firmly they stood with both feet on the ground. That was because the relative positions of the stars were such at the time that the stars were close together. Since then the relative positions of the stars have changed. If this is the earth, the stars are much more at an angle, as it were, again drawn in a highly schematic way. If one were to draw it in detail, each would of course stand out, as it were. You'll say: 'But surely the fixed stars have not changed?' But they have, though not as much. So you see from this that the spaces in between have increased during the fifteenth, sixteenth, seventeenth, eighteenth and nineteenth centuries. The ideas have dissolved. And now a time is coming when the spaces in between are getting less again, with the stars coming more closely together. This is only a very little bit so with the fixed stars, but it is the case, nevertheless. If one draws the fixed stars one can see that they, too, must change their relative positions. And people are exposed to this, having acquired ideas under the influence of stars that were far apart. Now they have to get ideas under the influence of stars that are closer together again. The relative positions of the stars in the world are quite new now. You can see this if you have been wide awake in life from the last century into the present century. You see, I was born in 1861, and have therefore known the times of the 70s, 80s, 90s and now the twentieth century. Yes, it was very different when I was a boy than it is today. When I was a boy people simply did think differently from the way they do today. Everything has changed, and it has changed particularly in one area. When I was a young boy of 12, I did not have much money to buy books, but we were given a school programme every year as a present; it gave the most important ideas used in physics in those times. Now at first I really had to knuckle down to this. They were really hard to grasp. I had to study differential calculus in order to understand these things. But I do know the ideas which were then used in physics.

Today things are completely different. Someone studying physics at the university learns something completely different from what we would learn when we were boys. And it is possible to see from what has happened there that the ideas used in physics have dissolved. Today's physicists simply no longer know what ideas to work with. In those days we spoke of space and time as two different things. Today physicists speak of four dimensions, taking the first, second and third to be dimensions in space and the fourth dimension to be the equivalent of time. Most people have no idea of what is taught today. People outside the universities still live with the ideas I learned when I was a boy. But today's physicists are talking about something completely different. It shows that the ideas have been thrown into confusion. The modern physicist has not the least notion as to what he should do. Everything has become confused.

Well, gentlemen, the things going on in the human head show you that the relative positions of the stars are different now. For the situation is that modern people all have more blood in the head than people had in their heads for centuries, the moon now being supported by stars that once again are more close together. So if we study the evolution of man, we find that a wave of blood has gone up to the head because of the relative positions of the stars. But this wave exists not only in the human being but on the whole earth. And it is the same influence through which cold was once pushed up from south to north in the distant past, burying the mammoths in a kind of vast ice cellar, so that their meat is still fresh in Siberia today. And just as that cold was thrown up north in those times, just as the blood is driven up into the head by the moon, so today's volcanic eruptions are thrown up by the stars. We thus have the effect of the relative positions of stars today that comes from the other side of the earth. It passes across through North America, through Greenland, pushes the cold air across, so that vast masses of cold air are today thrown from west to east because of the relative positions of the stars.

And as I have told you,[31] going to Italy all one needs to do in some places is to light a piece of paper and vapours will rise from the ground. It is not the earth which throws up the vapours, but they come up because I heat the air above and so make it thinner. And now the relative positions of the stars are pushing air masses from west to east. We are exposed to this here, and this creates the climate we now have. It goes like this from west to east. And because of this the soil down below is made to throw up its masses, its fiery masses. They are first of all thrown up over there in America, where they have huge volcanoes, enormous earthquakes. Now it is moving further east. Etna, Vesuvius are all starting to be active, for the wave is going that way, and things become elastic down below. It is not pushed up from below, but brought to the surface by the relative positions of the stars. In human beings the blood is pushed up into the brain, and on earth air masses are pushed across and transported to other places. It is the same thing. It all comes from the stars.

If people understood why they are now thinking differ-ently, they would also understand why Etna is spewing fire and flames. But then people must first of all also know that this is not something one can consider on its own; it has to be seen in connection with the whole universe. That is indeed how it is. And people have completely forgotten how to consider things within the universe. It is really interesting that the animals are much more intelligent in this respect than people are, as I have told you before. Animals usually go away before there is a volcanic eruption or the like; people stay put. Why do the animals move away? Yes, when the different influence comes, the differ-ent influence from the stars, it is like this with the animals. An animal is essentially made in such a way that it has its legs there [Fig. 15], there its spine, the spinal vertebrae, and there its head. As the stars move along there, the whole spine is always exposed to the stars, vertebra by vertebra exposed to the stars, and they belong together; they belong together so much that we have 28 to 31 vertebrae in the spine and the moon takes 28 to 31 days to complete its orbit. The connection is as close as that.

Fig. 15

But humans walk upright. With them, only the head, this little bit of head, is exposed to the starry heavens. Their spine has been lifted out. So in humans only the blood is exposed to the star influence and not the nervous system. In animals, the nervous system is exposed to the star influence. This is why an animal will notice the star influence much sooner than a human being does and move away when earthquakes or volcanic eruptions are about to happen. The human being stays put. The very fact that the animal is able to move away, thus showing us that the influence of the stars affects it, is proof that we are not dealing with waves arising from the earth in some way, but that the stars are bringing their influence to bear from outside. Man is not just a creature of this earth, he is a creature relating to the whole world of the stars.

Now this will of course also make us understand that humanity, having lost its old knowledge of the stars, must gain it anew. So I'd say that it is truly the case that with anthroposophy we must give the human race something again in a new way which they need, otherwise they'll remain in a state of confusion. For the stars which are now closer together no longer fit the ideas held in earlier times; only the kind of ideas anthroposophy is able to give will fit.

I was actually given four questions today. We'll try and move on with these the next time we meet. I may have to be away on Wednesday and I'll then ask people to tell you when we'll have our next session.

Developing independent thinking and the ability to think backwards

We still have some questions that were asked the last time. I'm going to answer them in a slightly different order than the one in which they were put. The questions are the following.

How can one gain insight into the secrets of the world for one's view of the world and of life?

How far does a person have to go in modern science to find higher worlds?

Do the forces active in the universe have an effect on the whole of humanity?

How do plants relate to the human being, to the human body?

Now what I want to do—these are, of course, very complex questions—is to proceed in a way where the answer emerges gradually. One can't really do it any other way with such complex issues. For the question 'How does one gain insight into the secrets of the world?', for instance, really means: 'How does one get to the real science of the spirit?' This is something you certainly should not imagine is an easy thing to do today. For the truth is that when they hear that there is such a thing as anthroposophy or a science of the spirit, most people will think: 'I'll now also gain the ability to see things of the spirit. I reckon that'll take a week, and then I'll no doubt be able to know everything for myself.'

Well, the matter is not that easy, of course. We have to be quite clear in our minds that even ordinary science calls for quite a lot. To make even the simplest scientific observations one has to learn to use the necessary instruments. It is of course relatively easy to use a microscope, but to do proper scientific work with a microscope you can't just say: 'I'll now put a piece of muscle or something like that under the microscope and then I'll look down the microscope and know what is going on in there.' If you were to do that, you'd see nothing, of course. To see things under a microscope you must first of all make very thin sections. A piece of muscle will not do, therefore, but you have to cut thin sections with a fine razor, take off what may sometimes be a very small amount, make another thin section, and so produce a very thin layer. And in most cases even this will not get you anywhere. For if you put such a very thin layer of muscle or cells under the microscope and look at it, you'll see nothing at all as a rule. What you have to do is ask yourself: How can I make the material I am unable to see under the microscope visible? And one often has to impregnate the material with special stains, making it visible by staining. And one must then know that one has changed the material a little bit by doing so. One also needs to know what the material is like when one does not change it. All these are still quite simple things, however.

If you want to study the stars using a telescope, you first have to learn how to use the telescope. Mind you, that's still quite simple. You know there are itinerants who set up telescopes in the street for people to look through. But this, too, won't get you far. It will only get you somewhere if you know that you also have to have a small scope to go with it and a timepiece which you need to set, and so on. These are just examples to show you how complicated it is to investigate even the simplest things in the physical world we perceive through the senses.

When it comes to investigations made in the world of the spirit, things are truly very much more difficult. This calls for a great deal more preparation. People imagine you can learn it in a week. But that is definitely not the case. Above all you have to consider that we must first of all activate something that already exists within us. Something which really is not active in us all the time has to be made active.

To show you how things really are, let me first of all tell you this. You know that for investigations that penetrate into the world of the spirit, and also in ordinary science, one often has to start by gaining insight into something that is not normal. You only gain real knowledge of things if you have first considered something that is not normal. I have given you particular examples of this before. We have to consider this because people in the world outside often call someone who makes spiritual investigations mad, however normal he may in fact be. So we do indeed have to investigate things a little bit in such a way that we finally arrive at the truth. You should not think, of course, that your goal can be fully achieved by considering something that is not normal but pathological, but you will learn a lot from it.

There are people, for example, who are not normal because they have a mental disorder, as it is put. What does it really mean to say someone has a mental disorder? There can be no worse term in the world than this 'mental disorder'. For the mind can never be out of order. The mind simply cannot be in disorder. Take the following, for instance. If someone has a 'mental disorder' for 20 years — such things do happen — and then is normal again, what is really going on there? Now, of course, it can happen that for 20 years this person insists he is being persecuted by others; he is suffering from persecution mania, as it is called. Or the situation may be that he sees all kinds of spectres that do not exist, and so on. This may continue for 20 years. Now, gentlemen, someone who has such a 'mental disorder' for 20 years may certainly recover. But you'll always find one thing. If someone has been 'mentally deranged' for 3, 5 or 20 years and then recovers, he'll not be quite the same as he was before. You'll above all note the following. He'll tell you, once he has recovered: 'Yes, during my illness I was able to see into the world of the spirit all the time.' He'll tell you all kinds of things he perceived relating to the world of the spirit. And if you then check his story, having gained knowledge of the higher worlds whilst in sound mind, it will be true that he'll say much that is rubbish but on the other hand also much that is correct. So that is the strange thing. Someone may suffer from a 'mental disorder' for years, recover, and then tell you he was in the world of the spirit, where he experienced this and this and this. And if you know about this yourself, having been in sound mind, you have to agree that much of it is correct.

If you talk to someone during the time when his mind is deranged, he'll never be able to tell you anything that makes sense. He'll tell you the rubbish he experiences. For the truth is that people who have had a mental disorder for years did not in fact experience these things whilst they had their 'mental disorder', as it is called. They did not experience anything of the world of the spirit. But afterwards, when they have recovered and are, in a way, able to look back on the time when they were not of sound mind, things they did not in fact experience during their illness will seem to them to have been glimpses of the spiritual world. This awareness of having seen much of the world of the spirit thus really only comes at the moment when these people recover.

You see, we can learn a very great deal from this. We can learn that there is something in the human being that is not used at all when he is mentally ill. But it was there, it was alive in him. And where was it? He did not see anything of the outside world, for he'd tell you that the sky was red and the clouds were green—all kinds of things. He did not properly see anything that existed in the outside world. But this deeper human being who is inside him, whom he cannot use at all during his illness—that human being is then in the world of the spirit. And when he's able to use his brain again and to look back on the experiences this spiritual human being has had, the experiences gained in mind and spirit will come to him.

We see from this that when someone is in the condition we call 'mental illness' he is actually living in the world of the spirit with the part of him that is of the spirit. This part is in very good health. What is it, therefore, that is sick when someone is mentally ill? You see, it is the body which is sick when someone is mentally ill, and the body is then unable to use the soul and the mind and spirit. When someone is said to be mentally ill, it is always something in the body that is sick, and if the brain is sick you cannot think properly, of course. Nor can you feel things properly if your liver is sick.

Because of this, 'mentally ill' is really the worst term you can choose, for 'mentally ill' means that the body is so sick that it cannot use the mind and spirit, which in itself is always healthy. Above all else you need to understand that the mind and spirit is always sound. Only the body can get sick, and is then unable to use the mind properly. If someone's brain is sick, it is just the way it is when someone has a hammer that breaks every time it is used. If I say to someone who does not have a hammer, 'You are simply lazy, you can't use your hammer at all,' that's nonsense, of course. He can hammer perfectly well, but he does not have a hammer with which to do it. And so it is nonsense to say someone is 'mentally ill'. The mind is perfectly sound, but it does not have the body it needs to be effective.

We can get a particularly good idea of what can be learned from this if we consider the true nature of our thinking. You will have seen from what I have been saying that people have a mind but need a tool, the brain, to be able to think. It is not the least bit clever for a materialist to say that we need a brain. Of course we do. But saying this does not tell us anything about the mind. You also see from this that the mind itself may withdraw completely in the human being. And it is important to know this, for only then will one realize that at the present time—I am now going to say something that'll really surprise you—people cannot think at all. They think they can, but actually they cannot think at all. Let me show you why people are unable to think.

You'll say: 'But people go to school, and today you learn to think marvellously well even at primary school!' Well, that's certainly the way it seems. But the truth is that people are quite unable to think. It only seems that they are able to think. Now you know, at a primary school we have primary school teachers. They have also learned things, and it is said they have also learned to think. The people who taught them are 'brainy', as we say, meaning that from the modern point of view they are thought to be people of great wisdom. They have been to university. Before they went to university they went to grammar school or the like, and there they learned Latin. Now if you consider the matter a bit you'll of course be able to say: 'My teacher certainly did not know Latin!' But he studied under someone who did know Latin. And because of this the things you learned at school also depended on the Latin language, and everything people learn today is dependent on the Latin language. You can see this from the mere fact that when someone writes a prescription, he'll do so in Latin. This goes back to the times when everything was still written in Latin. It is not that long ago—30 or 40 years—that people were required to write their exam papers in Latin at the universities.

Everything we learn today therefore depends on the Latin language. And this has happened because in the Middle Ages—going back to the fourteenth or fifteenth century, which really is not that long ago—everything was taught in Latin. The first person to lecture in German in

Leipzig, for example, was a man called Thomasius.[32] That was not long ago, in the seventeenth century. People would always lecture in Latin. People who had some learning would also have Latin, and in the Middle Ages absolutely everything people were able to learn was in Latin. So if you wanted to learn anything else, you first had to do Latin. You'll say: 'But not at primary school.' But primary schools have only existed from the sixteenth century onwards. They only came into existence gradually, when people's everyday language also began to include terms for learned ideas. All our thinking is therefore influenced by the Latin language. All of you, gentlemen, think the way people have learned to think through the Latin language. And if you were to say, for instance, that the Americans, say, did not learn Latin so early, you have to remember that today's Americans are immigrants from Europe! Everything comes from the Latin language.

The Latin language has a particular characteristic, however. It evolved in ancient Rome and did so in such a way that the language itself is actually thinking. It is interesting to see how Latin is taught at grammar school. One learns Latin, and then learns to think—to think properly by studying the Latin sentence. All thinking then becomes dependent on something which is not done by the person himself but by the Latin language. You have to realize, gentlemen, that this is tremendously important. Anyone who has learned anything today, therefore, does not think for himself, and the Latin language does the thinking even in people who have never learned Latin. And so the strange thing is that independent thinking is today really only found in some people who have not got much education.

Now please note that I am not saying we should return to illiteracy. This is something we cannot do. I never want to see regression. But we have to see the situation as it is. Because of this it is so important that we can sometimes also go back to the things a simple person, who has not had much education, still knows. He finds it hard to tell people, because they'll always laugh at him, of course. But still, it is extraordinarily important to know that people do not think for themselves today; the Latin language is thinking in them.

You see, unless one is able to think for oneself one will be unable to enter into the world of the spirit. Here you have the reason why today's academic world is against all insight into the spirit. It is because Latin education makes them unable to think for themselves. The first thing one has to learn is to think for oneself. People are quite right when they say today that the brain is thinking. Why does the brain think? Because the Latin sentences come into it, and the brain then thinks quite automatically in modern people. They are Latin language automatons who walk about and do not think for themselves.

Something quite remarkable has happened in recent times. I mentioned it to you the other day we met, something you'll not have noticed, for it is not so easy to notice. But something quite special has happened in recent times. Now you know we have our physical body in us, and also our ether body and the others as well — I'll leave these aside for the moment. The brain is of course part of the physical body, but the ether body is also in the brain, and we are only able to think for ourselves with the ether body. We cannot think with the physical body as such. But it is possible to think with the physical body if the situation is as it is with the Latin language, when the brain is used like an automatic machine as we use it to think. But for as long as we only think with the brain we cannot think things of the spirit. We have to start to think with the ether body, with the ether body which often is not used for years when someone is mentally ill. This has to be made inwardly active.

The important thing, therefore, is that we learn to think

independently. It is not possible to get into the world of the spirit unless one is able to think independently. This does, of course, mean that one must first of all realize: 'Wow! You never learned to think for yourself in your young days. You only learned to think the things that have been thought for centuries by using the Latin language.' And when one rightly knows this, one also knows that the very first requirement for entering into the world of the spirit is to learn to think independently.

We now come to the thing I wanted to mention when I said that something remarkable had happened in recent times. It was the academics who were most of all thinking entirely along Latin lines. And academics developed the science of physics, for instance. They thought up physics, thinking it up entirely with their physical brains the way one does with the Latin language. When we were young, when I was the age of young Erbsmehl over there, for instance, we only learned the kind of physics that had been thought up with a Latin brain. That was all we learned then, the things thought up with the Latin brain. But much has happened since then, gentlemen. You see, when I was young the telephone was just being developed. It did not exist before that. Then came all the other great inventions which people today grow up with as if they'd always been there. They only came in the last few decades. Because of this, more and more people studied science who had not been drilled in Latin. This is a remarkable thing. For if you consider the scientific life of recent decades you'll find that growing numbers of engineers came into the world of science. They did not bother much with Latin and so their thinking did not become so automatic. This non-automated thinking was then also taken up by the others. And the result is that today many of the concepts, ideas, used in physics today are falling apart. They are most interesting. Professor Gruner[33] in Bern, for instance, spoke about a new orientation in physics two years ago. He said that all their concepts had changed in recent years.

You do not easily realize this because people will still tell you the things that were thought 20 years ago if you go to popular lectures today. They can't tell you the things that are being thought today because they are not able to think them themselves. If you take the concepts that were still valid 30 years ago, it is just as if you have a small piece of ice and it melts. The ideas are melting. They're no longer there if you want to think them through carefully. This is something we have to realize. The situation is that if someone who studied physics 30 years ago now looks at what has become of it, he feels like tearing out his hair, for he has to say to himself: 'I cannot manage this with the concepts I have learned.' That is the way it is. And why is it like this? It is so because in the course of evolution people have in recent years reached the point where the ether body should begin to think. And they don't want to do that. They want to go on thinking with their physical bodies. But the concepts simply fall apart in the physical body. And they don't want to learn to think with the ether body. They don't want to learn to think independently.

And you see, the situation is such that it became necessary for me to write this book on the philosophy of freedom in 1893. This book, *The Philosophy of Spiritual Activity*,[34] is not really important because of what it says. Of course, the things it says are something one wanted to tell the world at the time, but that is not the most important point of it. The important thing about the book is that for the first time all of it is completely independent thinking. No one who is only able to think in a dependent way will be able to understand it. From the very beginning he has to get used, page by page, to go back to his ether body so that he'll actually be able to have the thoughts which are in this book. The book is therefore an educational tool—it is a most important educational tool – and it should be taken as such.

When the book was published in the 1890s, people had no idea what to do with it. For them, it was as if someone in Europe was writing in Chinese which no one could understand. It was, of course, written in German, but in thoughts that were completely unfamiliar, for anything Latin had deliberately been stripped away. For the first time care had been taken, consciously and deliberately, to have no thoughts in the book that were still under the Latin influence, but only completely independent thoughts. The physical brain is truly a Latin scholar. The human ether body is no Latin scholar. And one therefore has to make an effort to express in words the thoughts one has in one's ether body.

Let me tell you something else. People did, of course, realize that all ideas had changed in recent decades. When I was young the teacher would write lots of things on the blackboard. We had to learn them to do well in our exams. Well and good. And now, in recent years, people have discovered exactly what Gruner said in his address, which is that all our concepts would be meaningless if there were no longer any solid but only fluid bodies. He imagined the whole world as a fluid body. And in that case our concepts would no longer have meaning, he said, and we'd have to think in a very different way.

Well, of course we'd have to think differently if there were no solid bodies any more! For then you'd no longer be able to do anything with all the ideas you learned at school. So if you were to grow really intelligent as a fish, let us say, and got the idea of going to a human university as a fish, you would learn something there which simply does not exist for fishes, seeing that they live in water. They only know solid bodies at the boundaries of their world, which they touch only to recoil immediately. If a fish were to start to think, therefore, its thoughts would have to be of a very different kind than those of a human being. But these are the kind of thoughts human beings, too, need today, for those other thoughts are slipping from their grasp, and they have to say to themselves: 'Wow, if everything were fluid, we'd have to have very different kinds of thoughts.'

However, gentlemen, did I not tell you of a stage in the development of the earth when no solids existed as yet, and everything was fluid, even the animals? I have told you about this. And surely you can understand that our present thinking cannot go back to such conditions. It simply cannot think them! Our present-day thinking therefore cannot tell us anything about the beginning of the world. And, we have to say that if the world were fluid, we'd have to have completely different ideas. There are no solid bodies in the world of the spirit! It is therefore quite impossible to enter into this world with the concepts in which people were drilled through the Latin language. We must first get out of the habit of using them.

You see, this is indeed a great secret. In the ancient Greek civilization, which preceded the Latin civilization — Roman civilization only developed five or six centuries before Christ, whilst Greek civilization was much earlier — in Greek civilization people still knew of the spirit. They were still able to see into the world of the spirit. When Roman civilization came, and with it the Latin language, the spirit was gradually eradicated. At this point I again have to say something you'll find rather strange, but you'll understand. Who used Latin through the centuries, nothing but Latin? The Church itself contributed most to this development. The fact is that the Church, which pretends to teach people about the spirit, has done most to drive the spirit out. And in the Middle Ages all universities were Church institutions. We do, of course, have to be grateful that the Church founded the universities in the thirteenth, fourteenth and fifteenth centuries, but it founded them on the basis of Latin scholarship, in which there is no possibility of getting to the spirit. And so it came about that people gradually only came to have concepts relating to solid bodies. Just consider how this was with the Romans. They introduced these dry, objective concepts that had no spirituality. Because of this, everything then came to be seen in material terms. Just think — if the Greeks had described a rite such as Holy Communion they would not have described it as if the physical matter used for this were blood and flesh! This has come about through materialism. Even Holy Communion is seen in a materialistic way, because it is all connected with the Latin language.

The Latin language is entirely logical all the way. You see, I have worked with many people whose culture was completely Latin, even though they spoke German. To be clear about anything, they would quickly translate it into Latin, because all thinking in Latin has become logical in more recent times. But this logical thinking only relates to solid bodies. To enter into the world of the spirit we need fluid ideas.

There's the Theosophical Society, for instance. They also wanted to enter into the world of the spirit. In this Society people also say that man has a physical body, an ether body, and so on. But it is a materialistic view, for they merely think: 'The physical body is dense; the ether body is a little less dense, and the astral body even less so.' But that's always bodies, it will never be spirit, for to enter into the spirit one has to develop ideas that are always changing. You see, when I make a drawing I even take account of this in the way I draw. I may draw the physical body, let us say, and in that case try to reflect the way the human being is as a physical body. But when I try to draw the ether body, I would not dream of drawing a figure for you in the same way as before. Instead I try to show that the human being

Fig. 16

has an ether body which spreads like this [Fig. 16]. You
have to know, however, that what I am drawing there is not
so much the ether body I am drawing, not so much a picture
of it, but only a momentary picture. It will be different the
next moment. To draw the ether body, therefore, I'd have to
draw it now, quickly erase it again, draw it differently
again, erase, draw again, erase. It is in continuous motion.
And with the kind of ideas people have today they cannot
keep up with this. The most important thing for you to
consider, therefore, is that your ideas have to grow mobile,
flexible. This is something people will first have to get used
to. And it is necessary for people today to become completely independent in their thinking.

But that is not all, gentlemen. Let me tell you something
else. Human beings develop, as you know. Not much
thought is usually given to their development in the course
of later life, but attention is paid to it when they are young.
People know perfectly well that a 4-year-old child cannot

yet write, do sums or read, whilst an 8-year-old may be able to do these things. There you see that development is taking place. In later life, however, once we are 'made men', we are so arrogant that we no longer admit to being in a process of development. But we actually continue to develop all our lives, and it is quite remarkable how we develop. You see, our development proceeds like this. Let us assume this is a human being—just a rough sketch [Fig. 17]. When the child is very young, all development comes from the head. Once the second teeth have developed, and one is therefore older, all development comes from the chest. This is why one has to be so careful about children's breathing between their 7th and 14th years, making sure they breathe enough, and so on. So that would be the age of an older child—today we'd really have to use another word, for today's children will no longer accept it; from their 14th year on one really has to call them 'young ladies' and 'young gentlemen'. Well, let's say

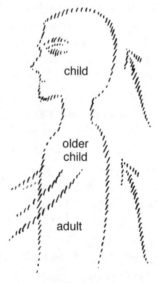

Fig. 17

'older children'. And it will only be when a person has reached sexual maturity that development comes from the whole human being, from the limbs. We are thus able to say that human beings are only in their full process of development when they have reached sexual maturity. This then continues. We develop further in our 20s and 30s. But you see, gentlemen — some of you can now see it in yourselves — when we get older, many things regress again. It is really true that many things will then deteriorate. It need not be like that if one has entered into a life in mind and spirit, but in normal human life there is deterioration when one gets older. It is actually the task of anthroposophy to see that in future people will no longer deteriorate in old age. But that, too, will of course have to happen slowly and gradually.

Now the situation is that there are people whose mental powers deteriorate quite dreadfully. But it is not the mind that deteriorates, but again only the body. It is interesting to note that it is often particularly intelligent people who show a terrible degree of deterioration in old age. You'll have heard, for example, that people consider Kant[35] to have been one of the greatest minds. Kant grew senile in his old age. His body deteriorated so much, therefore, that he was no longer able to use his wise mind. And that is how it is for many people. It is especially the intelligent people who have often grown really senile in old age. Again this is of course only a more powerful, intensive form of something that happens to everyone. As one gets older, one gradually is less able to use the physical body, apart from anything else because enormous amounts of calcium are deposited, mainly in the arteries. And the more calcium is deposited in the arteries, the less are we able to use the physical body. The degree to which development coming from the head went into the whole body up to one's 40th year, let us say, is also the degree of deterioration that happens. Coming from the 40s into the 50s, one needs to use the chest more again, and in old age one needs to use the head more again. But at that time, in old age, one should not use the physical head but the more subtle ether head. This, however, is something people do not learn to do with their Latin education. And it was above all the people who in recent decades had a materialistic Latin education who were most exposed to this senility.

We have to go back to childhood level in our old age, and this is something that gets quite powerful in some people. They grow mentally weaker and weaker, as it is put. The mind remains quite sound, however; it is only the body that grows weaker and weaker. In the end these people can no longer do the things they had been able to do first of all. Such things certainly happen. Let us say someone has grown old. He is now no longer able to do something he did previously. He can only do the things he did as an older child. Finally he'll also no longer be able to do these, but only play and understand the ideas he originally gained from play. There have actually been people who at a very advanced age were only able to understand the things their parents or nurse told them in their very earliest years. The saying that we grow childish in old age has its good reasons. We do truly return to our childhood again.

But so long as we have a life in the mind and spirit this is no misfortune, no misfortune at all. It is really a good thing. For as a child we are still able to use the ether body. When a child romps about, shouting and doing all kinds of things, it is not the physical body that does this—or at most only if the child has a tummy ache, but even then the tummy ache must first be transmitted to the ether body and astral body, so that the child moves because of the tummy ache. It definitely is not the physical body that is romping about there. Then you grow old and return to childhood level. You have gradually got out of the romping habit and now use the ether body which you used for romping about as a child for something better in your old age. It may be a good thing, therefore, that we go back again in this way.

This, then, would be the second thing. The first thing we have to learn in order to enter into the world of the spirit is the right way of thinking. We'll talk another time about the way one achieves this. Today let us first of all try and understand how these things go. The first thing is wholly independent thinking. It means abandoning much of what modern education offers, for modern education means the opposite of independent thinking, a thinking derived from Latin. Do not imagine that the thinking developed with socialist theories today is independent thinking! All of them have been learning from something that has come from Latin; they just did not know this. You know, a worker may decide to do one thing or another in the sphere of his will; but when he starts to think, he is using entirely middle-class concepts, and these have come from thinking in Latin. The first thing we need, therefore, is independent thinking.

The second thing is to learn to live not just in the present moment but always to be able to go back again into the life we lived whilst we were children. You see, someone wanting to enter into the world of the spirit will often have to say: 'Now discover how things were when you were a boy of 12. What did you do then?' And we need to do this not just superficially, in outer terms, but really imagine every detail. There's nothing more useful, for example, than to begin to say to yourself: 'Yes, I was 12 then—I can get quite a good picture of it. There was a pile of stones by the roadside and I climbed up on top. I fell off once. Then there was a hazel bush and I took out my knife and cut off branches, and I cut my finger.' To see again what one did many years ago, this will help us to enter into a condition where we do not just live in the present. Thinking the way people have learned to think today, you are thinking with your present physical body. But when you try to discover what you were at the age of 12, you cannot think with the physical body you then had, for it no longer exists. I told you that the physical body is a new one every seven years. You then have to think with your ether body. You therefore call up your ether body when you think back to something in the past, when you were 12 or 14 years old. This will get you into the inner activity that you need.

And we can above all get in the habit of thinking altogether differently from the way we usually think. You see, how do you think? Now you know we met at 9 o'clock today. I started by reading out the bit of paper with your questions. Then I considered a number of things, and we have now reached the point where we say: 'We have to think back to the life we knew when we were 12 or 14 years old.' Now when you get home you may, perhaps, if the matter is of special interest to you, think these thoughts through once more. Well, this is something one can do. Most people do this; they'll go through it again. But you might do something else. You might say: 'What did he say last?' The last thing he said was that one should think of one's earlier life, up to the age of 12 or 14. Before that he said one should be independent in one's thinking. And before that about the way Latin gradually came into people's lives. Even earlier he spoke of how someone who has not been of a sound mind will afterwards look back and say he had special experiences. He showed that people do not get mentally ill, but that only the body gets sick. You see, you'd now have gone through the whole lecture backwards.

Well, gentlemen, things do not go back to front in the outside world. I might perhaps have given the lecture backwards from the very beginning, but then you would not have been able to understand, for one starts from the beginning and develops the theme so that it is gradually understood. Once you've understood it, however, you can also think it through the other way round. But factual things don't go back to front, and so I come away from the facts. I then think like this: 'Just now I am not thinking the way things happen outside, but back to front.' This needs some effort. I have to grow inwardly mobile to think backwards. Just as someone must learn to use a telescope if he wants to look through it, so someone who wants to see into the world of the spirit must often think backwards, again and again think backwards. And one day he'll reach the point where he knows: 'Ah, this is where I enter into the world of the spirit.'

Once again you can see from this, gentlemen, that all your life you've got your physical body into the habit of thinking forwards. If you now start to think backwards, the physical body won't do it and something peculiar happens. When people ask again and again, 'How do I get into the world of the spirit?' the first piece of advice one gives—you'll also find it in *Knowledge of the Higher Worlds*—is to say: 'Learn at least to go back through the day's events; and then other things.' People have of course first of all learned to think with their physical body. They note this. They then make great efforts to think backwards, but they have only learned to think with their physical body, not with the ether body. And then the ether body goes on 'general strike'. Yes, it really is a general strike. And if people did not go to sleep so often when they think backwards, they would know: 'When I begin to think backwards I should get to the world of the spirit.' But they go to sleep the very moment they might begin to see, for the effort is too much for them. It therefore needs tremendous good will and all one's energy not to go to sleep. You need patience for this. It often takes years, actually. But you have to have patience.

You see, if someone were able to tell you the things you experience unconsciously when you've gone to sleep after thinking backwards, you'd see that it is something terribly intelligent. The stupidest people begin to have extraordinarily intelligent thoughts when they then go to sleep, but they don't know this.

So the first thing I told you was that one must first of all learn to think independently. It is something one can do. I won't say, for instance — not being conceited — that only my *Philosophy of Spiritual Activity* will serve the purpose, but it has been deliberately written in such a way that one will get in the habit of independent thinking.

Independent thinking, therefore.

Thinking back accurately to things that happened at the age of 10 or 12.

Or accurately thinking things one has learned over again, backwards.

With this, we have at least considered how we can tear ourselves away from the physical body; how we enter into the world of the spirit. And we'll continue with this on Saturday, taking the matter further, so that all four questions will gradually be resolved.

Creating boredom artificially. Opinions formed artificially. Opinions formed in the physical world are reversed in the other world

We'll continue to consider the questions that were put before. You need to understand, however, that the answer to these questions is one of the most difficult. I'll try and make it as simple as possible. As I told you before, to find a way of gaining insight into the spirit one must first of all be able to develop completely independent thinking. Secondly one must be able, as I told you, to think backwards. This means one must try to think things backwards which in ordinary life go like this: starting with the first, then the second, the third, and so on. If I give you a talk, therefore, you should try to do as I told you the last time and start from the end and think back to the beginning. Such things are the first elementary steps.

Today, very much in connection with the second question, I'd like to consider something else. You know that human beings can only live within a particular temperature range. If necessary they can tolerate a great deal of heat. If it gets quite hot in the summer, well, they'll sweat but they can bear it; but if the temperature were to go even higher, they would no longer be able to live. In the same way people can tolerate some degree of cold, but when it gets below their limit they'll freeze to death. And you see, the strange thing is that between these two temperatures — the low temperature where they begin to freeze to death and the heat they can only just tolerate — between these two temperatures, in the range in which human beings live, it is actually impossible to see spiritual entities. It is just like the situation I spoke of the last time where I said that the moment one begins to think backwards one would begin to see spiritual entities. But there one goes to sleep. Most people go to sleep unless they have first trained themselves so that they'll stay awake.

But now to something else. You see, if people were to live at higher temperatures than those they can just tolerate, they would perceive spiritual entities. But they cannot tolerate those temperatures. And they might also be able to perceive them if they were to make themselves a garment of snow, get themselves right into the snow; but they would freeze to death. Something that seems quite unbelievable to people is a fact, nevertheless. It is that the spirits withdraw from the temperature range which human beings are able to tolerate when they are in their physical bodies.

Human beings do not tolerate such temperatures in their bodies, but they can tolerate them in their souls. Only, as I said, the mind, the soul, then goes to sleep. For the mind, the soul, does not freeze to death, nor does it burn, but it goes to sleep.

There are however two ways we have of gaining a notion of how things would be if we were at a higher temperature than we are able to bear and also if we were at a lower temperature than we are able to bear. Let me give you an example. You see, when we develop a temperature ourselves we reach a higher temperature than we are able to bear, doing so inwardly. The temperature will not be so high that we'll immediately die of it, but with the temperature produced from the inside, we reach a higher temperature than we normally have. You know how people begin to talk like someone who's not on this earth when they get such a high temperature. The things people say in a fever do not relate to this earth. But a materialist would be. bound to say that these were thoughts cooked up at a high temperature, but they were not true, of course.

A situation therefore exists where people develop a

higher temperature, getting feverish and talking nonsense. Now you see, the soul cannot talk nonsense. However high the temperature, the soul cannot talk nonsense. It is talking nonsense because the body is out of order at a higher temperature. You'll have an idea of it if you think of the kind of glass spheres people sometimes put in their flower gardens to mirror the garden world that surrounds them. Looking into such a glass sphere you'll see a face you won't like! [*blackboard sketch*] It's the kind of face you'll not like. But you won't say either: 'Wow, just look what has happened to my face!' You'd not think for a moment that it actually was your face which looked so very different in the reflection. And if your mind begins to talk nonsense when you have a temperature, you won't say either that your mind, your soul, is beginning to talk nonsense. The things your mind and soul are saying are distorted because they are said out of a sick brain, just as your face looks squashed flat in such a faulty mirror.

You therefore have to say to yourself: 'When I have a temperature and talk nonsense, the situation is that the mind and soul is speaking out of a sick brain. My face has not changed when I stand before the reflective glass sphere, but it looks all distorted.' In the same way the things someone says in a fever sounds distorted because it comes from a sick body and a brain that is not functioning the way it should. But how come that the brain is not functioning properly? It is because the whole of the blood circulation is moving too fast. You only have to feel the pulse and you'll know it. The high temperature in the head is therefore due to the blood circulating too fast. The blood circulation produces heat which then rises to the head — you have a temperature. Your mind and soul then shows itself as if in a mirror that does not work properly.

The opposite may also happen, but in this case not by lying down in the snow and letting yourself freeze to death in the snow, for in that case you would really freeze to death. The opposite condition can only arise out of the mind and spirit. In this case one has to do something using the mind. And this, gentlemen, will produce something very strange. Just think: someone begins to think terribly hard about things, reflecting on the most insignificant details. It is better to reflect on the most insignificant details, things considered so insignificant that most people don't even want to think about them. Let me show you something. If you have a triangle [Fig. 18] and divide it into four equal parts, so that you have four triangles like this, you can say that the larger triangle is greater than each of the four small triangles. I can now put this in general terms and say there is a theorem which says: The whole is greater than its parts [*writing it on the board*]. Well, really, if you have a satisfied stockbroker and say to him, 'Just think about this: The whole is greater than its parts,' he'll say: 'Certainly not. I'd find that extremely boring.' And if you were actually to go to him and say: 'Look, the blackboard is a body with particular dimensions; the table is another body which has its own dimensions'—I now formulate the statement that all bodies have dimensions [*writing on the board*]. Now imagine you were at some kind of meeting and all the time you'd just hear things said about the statement that all bodies have dimensions. You'd go home saying it was a really insipid, boring meeting. And if I were now to come and say:

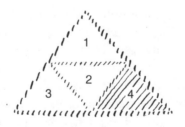

Fig. 18

'Look, the grass is green, the rose is red, and these things therefore have colour. Yesterday the judge in a court case passed judgment in some way or other, and that had no colour. And a court was also in session in another place where the judge passed judgment and again it was colourless. Judgments, or opinions, are colourless,' this gives us a third statement [*writing it on the board*]. Well, gentlemen, if someone were to talk for an hour on the subject that opinions are colourless, you'd say to yourself: 'I've been hearing that opinions are colourless for an hour, but this is terribly boring; it is utterly and completely boring!'

But why do you find such opinions boring? I should not write these things on the board for you, nor should I say them in a fairly humorous way, but I should enter the room walking stiffly and briskly, like a professor, and then say: 'Gentlemen, today we shall talk about the statement that opinions are colourless.' And I'd then have to spend a whole hour proving to you that the statement is correct. The way I am presenting it to you here is still quite amusing. But I'd have to come in like that and talk a whole hour on the statement 'Opinions are colourless' or on 'All bodies have dimensions'.

You might also draw a line like this to get from one point to another [*drawing on the board*]. One line is straight, the others are curved. But looking at it you'll immediately say: 'The straight line is the shortest route, all others are longer.' Now I can write this on the board as well: 'A straight line is the shortest route connecting two points.' If I wanted to talk a whole hour on this subject as well, you'd find it equally boring.

The whole is greater than its parts
All bodies have dimensions
Opinions are colourless
A straight line is the shortest route connecting two points

There's a German professor, however, who says that we can indeed perceive something of the world of the spirit, but we can only perceive the kind of thing of that world which can be put in the form of such statements. He presents the statements that allow us to perceive something of the world of the spirit to his students: 'The whole is greater than its parts. All bodies have dimensions. Opinions are colourless. A straight line is the shortest route connecting two points,' and so on. He says this is the only thing we can know of that other world. His students get terribly bored in his lectures. But the situation is such today that people have come to think that science has to be boring. And the students will generally be particularly enthusiastic about a professor who says such things. This merely by the way, of course.

The situation is really this. When you take in such opinions, form opinions or statements such as 'The whole is greater than its parts; a straight line is the shortest route connecting two points,' the back of your head grows cold. And because coldness develops in the back of the head, and a person is beginning to feel cold, he immediately wants to get away from such statements. They bore him. For that is the strange thing. When we are bored, the back of the head gets cold. It is not that the whole person gets cold, only the back of the head. It begins to want to die of cold. And this is not because of snow or because of ice now; the person is feeling cold because of the soul principle, because he is thinking things that are of no interest to him.

You see, we may make fun of such statements. But the fact is that to be patient and think them through again and again, that is, enter into boredom again and again with great patience, is one real way of gaining insight into the spirit. It is a strange thing, for people have to do exactly what they do not really want to do. I can tell you that mathematics are boring for some people, but because they are so difficult and one has to make an effort, and because it is so cold and one has to make a real effort with mathematics, it is the easiest way of entering into the world of the spirit. People who are able to overcome their reluctance and take up those statements again and again in a living way, artificially creating boredom for themselves, will find it easiest to enter into the world of the spirit.

I told you that when you get a temperature your pulse goes faster. You get hot, and you then get heat into the head, into the brain. So you then get into a hot condition and you talk nonsense. But if you struggle with statements like these here, where you really want to stop thinking altogether, the blood will not get more mobile but it will come to a stop in the back of the head. And when the blood comes to a stop back there, salts collect. Salts collect back there. They have two effects, these salts. Most people get a belly-ache from them. And because they notice this belly-ache quite quickly — things get uncomfortable in the belly when they are supposed to think such statements — they'll soon stop. But when someone thinks such things all the time, as Nietzsche[36] did, a great man who lived towards the end of the nineteenth century and was always battling with such statements in his youth, many salts are deposited in the head, and Nietzsche was always suffering from migraine. And one must now find a way, you see, of thinking such statements without getting migraine, without salts being deposited, and also without getting a belly-ache. You have to stay perfectly healthy and be able to create boredom for yourself artificially. Someone who is honest about telling you how to enter into the world of the spirit will therefore have to say: 'You must first of all be able to create artificial boredom for yourself; otherwise you'll not get into the world of the spirit at all.'

Consider the times we live in. What is the general desire? The general desire is to avoid boredom at all costs. Just think of the way people rush from one place to another, just so that they won't be bored! They always look for entertainment. That is to run away from the spirit. It is true — if there might perhaps be something somewhere that is of the spirit, people of our time will immediately run away. They do not know this; it happens unconsciously. But seeking entertainment is a matter of running away from the spirit. That's the way it is. And the only people who will be able to enter into the spirit are those who are not afraid to do without entertainment for once and live artificially in statements like these [see above]. And having got so far that one is able to live in such statements artificially, without getting a migraine or a belly-ache, but really being able to manage to live in such statements for many hours, it will gradually be possible to see things in the spirit.

But then something else will have to change as well. A time will come when you realize that having lived in such statements you then find they begin to go the other way round! So I've been thinking for a long time that the large triangle is greater than its parts. If I do this for a long time, the statement reverses itself and I develop the following idea: 'If this is a triangle here, and I take a quarter of it and want to take it out, it begins to grow [*drawing on the board*], and it is no longer true that the whole is greater than its parts. The quarter is suddenly bigger.' I see that the quarter is bigger, and I then have to say: 'The whole is smaller than its parts' [*writing on the board*].

The work I have done has now brought me to the point where I perceive the way things look in the world of the spirit. For they look the other way round from the way they are in the physical world. In the physical world, the whole is always greater than its parts, whilst in the world of the spirit the part is greater than the whole. You'll be unable, for example, to perceive the true nature of the human being unless you know that the part is greater than the whole. In modern science, people always want to look into the smallest things. But if you want to know the human liver here in the physical world, it is smaller than the human being. If you want to see it in the spirit, it grows and grows to gigantic proportions; the liver becomes a whole universe. And if you fail to take note of this, you'll not be able to understand the liver in the spirit.

You must first of all have arrived at the statement in an honest way which says that the whole is smaller than its part, and the part is greater than the whole. In the same way, if you have thought the statement 'All bodies have dimensions' long enough, so that you are facing the terrible danger of your brain freezing to death back there, all bodies will shrink, cease having dimensions, and you finally have the statement 'No body has dimensions' [*writing on the board*].

And now something really funny. It is funny in the physical world, but a most serious matter in the world of the spirit. You see, you may think there's nothing more silly than my saying that the court was in session in Wigglesham and a judgment, an opinion, was given that was colourless. And another was given in Tripshill and it was equally colourless. But if you think the statement long enough, the opinions will gain colour. And just as you are able to say that a rose is red so you'll be able to say the judgment in Wigglesham was a dirty yellow, and the one in Tripshill was red. Well, you may get some that are a beautiful red, but it does not happen often. So you see you reach the point where you say: 'All opinions given by people are in colour.' And it is only now that one actually is able to think about the world of the spirit, for there everything is the opposite: opinions are in colour [*writing on the board*].

A straight line is the shortest route connecting two points—this is so true that it is served up to you as one of the first theorems in geometry. In the physical world it is as true as it can possibly be. But if you think about it for a long time: if someone who is not a physical but a spiritual entity wants to get from village A to village B, the route will seem terribly short to him if he goes in a semicircle [*drawing*]. And you form the opinion that a straight line is the longest route connecting two points [*writing on the board*].

The whole is smaller than its parts
No body has dimensions
Opinions are in colour
A straight line is the longest route connecting two points

This is certainly something to make your jaw drop! The world will not consider such things, however. People will say that someone who starts to say that judgements or opinions are coloured has a temperature or that he is mad. But the situation is that one can come to these things without one's body, whilst of sound mind, for in the spiritual world properties are the opposite of what they are in the physical world. And you have to get to this by means of the simplest statements, for the simplest statements are the most incredible. You know, if someone starts to talk about the world of the spirit in an interesting way people will, of course listen, the way they also do if someone tells ghost stories. But they won't listen if someone says: 'You just first of all get in the habit of creating artificial boredom for yourself.' This has to be done artificially. Nothing will come of it if one gets bored with conventional science. But to develop boredom artificially, making an inner effort, and not get migraine or a belly-ache, that is, without involving the body. If the body is involved, you'll immediately get migraine or a belly-ache.

Just listen to what people say when they hear that they should not let the professor bore them, for that would not help them, and that to be seers they must gradually over-come the migraine and the belly-ache. You see, your student sits there, and the professor bores him most dreadfully. He should really get a migraine or a belly-ache, but he doesn't. The matter then moves to other organs that don't hurt so much. And people really get sick then, because the physical body is involved. If you produce boredom in this way today, which is what happens in modern science, you'll just make people ill. If you tell people to produce boredom for themselves by their own inner efforts, and if they go through this boredom, they will bit by bit enter into the world of the spirit, but this needs to be grasped in the right way, for the very first opinions you gain in that world will be the other way round. So there is an extraordinarily good way of working effectively on oneself. It is this. If you have come across something in the world that is really, really boring, and then afterwards, seeing it was so boring that you ran away, that you did not like it at all any more, or were glad when it was over, you start to think about it, doing so very, very slowly.

You see I myself—this is something I know from experience—learned an enormous amount from this. I used to hear terribly boring lectures in my young days. Indeed, I used to look forward to this, knowing that the lecture was going to be boring, because this would get you out of yourself, just as going to sleep normally does. So I used to be really pleased to know that I was about to hear boring lectures for some hours. But once the lecture had started and the professor would be speaking, I would always feel that he was disrupting my boredom by talking and talking all the time. Afterwards, however, I'd give deep thought to every detail he had said. It was not the least bit interesting to me, but I went through every session again from the beginning, really going through it, and sometimes would go through a one-hour lecture in such a way that it would take two hours, and so I created boredom artificially.

Gentlemen, this is where you make a strange discovery. It

was particularly at the end of the nineteenth century that you were able to make a very strange discovery. Just imagine you have been listening to a lecture given by a real clot — they do exist — and were then able to meditate on this boring lecture. You therefore bring back to mind all the things that bored you so terribly. And gradually something will show itself behind the person who produced the most boring things, this real clot; something like a higher human being, a wholly spiritual human being will show itself. And the lecture theatres are transformed in your mind in a way that can be grasped when you are entirely of a sound mind. And I knew many professors at the end of the nineteenth century where that was the case. But please don't talk a lot about it, otherwise people will think it was something quite dreadful, for the most intelligent spiritual human beings appeared behind those men.

Now what was going on there? It is not at all true that inwardly, unconsciously people are as stupid as they appear to be. They are actually much cleverer, and it is the most stupid who are sometimes really clever. The reverse happens again. But they cannot grasp their own cleverness. This is a dreadful secret. For the element which is people's true mind and soul is often there behind them and they cannot grasp it themselves.

Yes, this is indeed how you get into the worlds of spirit. As you know, we had materialistic science at the end of the nineteenth century. People are still blindly following that science today. I myself must say that it has been tremendously useful to get to know this materialistic science, for from beginning to end it always produced the most boring statements. Now if you just think yourself the cat's whiskers, having grown so clever, finally knowing that man is descended from the apes, as we are told in science — well, in that case, nothing will come of it. But if you think this statement through again and again, using all your inner energy, it will finally change into one that is correct in the spirit and you realize that man has not descended from the apes at all but from a spiritual entity.

There are, however, various differences. A boy was sent to school once. There he heard for the first time — from his teacher — that man is descended from the apes. It emerged that it was too early for him. At home he told his father: 'Dad, I heard something new today. Just think, man is descended from the apes.' 'Rubbish,' said his father, all upset, 'you're just stupid! It may be true for you, but not for me!' You see, he, too, found the story unbelievable. He related it only to the mind, however.

But you see from all the things I am telling you that it is also possible to find one's way into modern science in two ways. And I can certainly tell you that if someone has not learned that science the way very many people did in the nineteenth century and still do today, but if instead of repeating everything you are told you think meditatively, thinking things through again and again, for hours and hours, they will turn around, and what you get is the truth in the spirit.

When you have thought for a long time about plants and minerals and for a long time about the things people tell you today in such a dreadfully materialistic way, simply thinking it through, you will finally reach the point where the significance of the zodiac, the significance of the stars, all the secrets of the stars are apparent to you.

But the safest way is to start with statements like 'The part is greater than the whole. No body has dimensions. Opinions are coloured. The straight line is the longest route connecting two points.' You will then have torn yourself away from your physical body. If you go through all this, you will be able to use your ether body instead of your physical body. You can then begin to think with the ether body, and the ether body must think everything the opposite way round from the way it is in the physical world. For with the ether body you gradually enter into the world of the spirit. But there things will come to a halt after all, and you'll have to develop yet another habit.

You know, when we read something today, something rather odd may happen. I was in a town in southern Austria once, for instance, and someone gave me the evening paper. This had a leading article, as it is called. A terribly interesting story was told in every detail, a major political story. You read the first column, the second column, the third column—terribly interesting. And right at the bottom, still on the same page, was a brief note saying: 'We are sorry to say that everything written in today's leading article is based on the wrong information and not a word of it is true.'

You see, such things can happen today. It is an extreme case, but anyone reading the papers today may find that every now and then, on every page, he sees something that is simply not true. He only finds out afterwards that it is not true. You see, I think most people have grown so unthinking today that truth and lies are all one to them. Well, this will not get one into the world of the spirit.

I told you the last time we met: when someone goes mad only his body is sick. The mind, the soul does not get sick, it remains sound. Today I told you that when someone talks wildly in a fever, his thoughts become mere caricature, but the mind and soul is still all right. But one has to get into the habit, if one wants to enter into the world of the spirit, of feeling inner pain when something is not true, and that one's soul rejoices when something is true, that one will be as happy about the truth as if someone had given one a million—I mean a million Swiss francs, not Deutschmark! (*Laughter*) That is how happy we should be on hearing the truth, and that is how we should suffer in our souls—it is not the body but the soul that must be able to suffer if one finds that something somewhere is a lie—just as the body suffers if it has a terrible illness. It is not that the soul should be sick, but the soul must be capable of feeling pain and pleasure, just as the body does when it is sick or wholly at ease, or when one knows pain or pleasure in the ordinary way in this world.

It means we must come to feel truth the way we feel joy and happiness and pleasure in physical life; and we must come to feel untruth to be pain, grow as sick inwardly in our soul when we meet untruthfulness, as we otherwise only get sick if there are disorders in the body. So when someone has been lying his head off, you have to be able to say, but in such a way that it is truly the case: 'He's given me deadly nightshade berries to eat!' But it must be an inner truth.

Now, of course, if you consider our modern times, the newspapers, for instance, you are made to swallow deadly nightshade berries all the time. And if your mind and soul is to stay healthy, you need to vomit all the time at the soul level. And seeing that we cannot do without the papers, you need to get into the habit, if you wish to enter into the world of the spirit, of getting a bad taste in your mouth from the papers and getting pleasure when you read something decent, where someone writes in a truly inward way. Your pleasure should be like the pleasure you have from eating something, if you like, that tastes really good. The truth and the striving for truth must taste good to you, and lies, if you become aware of them, must taste bitter, poisonous.

You therefore have to learn not only that opinions are in colour, but also to say: printers' ink is usually like the juice of deadly nightshade berries today. You must, however, be able to feel this in all honesty and with great probity. Then, gentlemen, then you have come to something which is known as transformation in the spirit.

People talk about alchemy and think it can be used to change copper into gold. Mountebanks will, of course, tell you this in all kinds of ways even today; superstitious people have believed it for a long time. But such things are possible in the spirit. Only you have to believe in the truth of the spirit. There you have to be able to say to yourself: 'The ink the printer used is the same substance everywhere, whether he's printed a book that is true or a lying newspaper. But on the one occasion the printers' ink is genuinely the juice of the deadly nightshade berry, and on the other occasion it is as if liquid gold is flowing. Things that are one and the same in the physical world are very, very different in the spirit.'

But if today's clever people come and you say to them, 'Printers' ink can be like liquid gold or it can be the juice of deadly nightshade berries,' they'll say, 'You are speaking metaphorically; it's just an analogy.' Well, gentlemen, the analogy, the picture, must become truly spiritual, and one has to understand what things become in the spirit.

Let me give you an example that actually comes from the history of the Social Democratic Party. You may not have been so much aware of it, but there was a time when the Social Democratic Party split in two. One group were people who followed Bernstein[37] and similar people. They entered into all kinds of compromises with the middle classes. And the other group were the radicals, with Bebel[38] the leader of the radicals until he died. You'll know about Bebel from the literature if nothing else. There was a party conference once in Dresden, and Bebel got pretty wild about the others. He said he'd create order in social democracy. He gave a tremendously weighty speech, in the course of which he said: 'Yes, if that and that happens because of the other group, a louse will run over my liver!' [German saying when something rubs one up the wrong way. Translator] Now everyone will of course say that this is just an analogy, for no real louse would be running across Bebel's liver. But why do people use such phrases? Bebel did not use it, of course, because a louse actually ran over his liver; it was something he'd heard and he used it to say that the thing would really annoy him. But why do people have such a phrase? Why can one say that a 'louse' runs over the liver?

Not everyone is like the man who would always collect lice off his head, and when someone once asked him, 'Tell me, dear chap, how come you are so clever and always catch a louse?' he said, 'No problem. If I miss one, I get the one next to it.' It's not like that for everyone, that he misses the louse he wants to catch but still picks one up. It is usually highly unpleasant when people have lice; they feel terrible about it. You should have seen it. When I was a family tutor, one of the boys in my care came home one day. He had been out, sitting on all kinds of benches in the city, and he gradually developed a pain in his eyes, a terrible pain in his eyes. Now there was some uncertainty as to which specialist to call in, because the boy had such a terrible pain in his eyes. I said: 'Let's first of all try an ointment for lice and put it on his eyebrows.' Quite right. When they took a look he had lots of lice, and when the ointment had worked, his eyes also stopped watering. Now you should have seen his mother's and his aunt's faces when the boy was suddenly found to have lice! They felt this right down to their livers. Things felt very strange in their bellies: 'Oh dear, the boy has lice! How terrible!' And then it does very much seem to one as if the louse runs across the liver. The phrase comes from a very real sensation people did have once when someone had lice.

Now people don't catch lice at a meeting or party conference. But they do something that gives them such a horror, as if in earlier times or among people of a particular class lice had run across the liver. So you see the phrase reflected a real situation when it was coined. Later on such phrases are only used for things affecting the mind or soul.

But one has to bring this about artificially, gentlemen. One must be able to do it, so that one feels it really and honestly and not just as the sound of a phrase. I have a newspaper and most of what it says will probably be the kind of thing where the printers' ink is deadly nightshade juice. I'd like to know what people would really do if they had such a feeling today! Just think how much deadly nightshade has been used to consider whose fault the War was and who was not at fault, and how people feel good simply because they belong to the one nation or the other; not because the things that are said are true but because the papers say they were not at fault, writing all kinds of untruths to say they were not at fault. But how are people to get into the world of the spirit in the present day and age? One must simply resolve, strongly resolve to be very different from the people of today, and yet one must of course also live with these people. For it will do no good to get up on a speaker's platform and start to shout at them. But one has to find an alley-way for the truth. And that is hard, as hard as I have shown you today.

I've had to speak of difficult things today, so that you may indeed see that it is far from easy to enter into the world of the spirit. We'll get to other things again that will not be such an effort for you. But you'll find that it is a good thing that we have been considering difficult things. The next time we continue I'll show you how the whole way into the world of the spirit goes.

Developing inner honesty

Gentlemen, in the last talk I gave you I said that human beings cannot gain insight today, for the thinking we use is not really suitable for this. In earlier times, even just 1,500 years ago, let us say, someone who wanted to learn something first had to develop his thinking. They did not believe that one could in any way grasp the world of the spirit with one's ordinary thinking, and they had a way of training one's thinking. Today all the education we have does not encourage people to develop their thinking at all. Because of this they also are not really able to think in any real way.

Let me explain this by giving you an example, something you'll have been reading about in the papers these days.[39]

> A frequently recurrent dream is the dream of flying. We dream that we are flying, floating or falling, and this often happens immediately after going to bed.

Well now, you all know this thing about flying in your dreams. A man who is used to thinking only in the modern scientific way now wants to explain this. You'll see in a minute that this kind of thinking does not get one anywhere when one is dealing with things like these.

> This dream, Dr Richard Traugott writes in *Natur*, is caused by a sudden start we give, something that really happens.

So what does this man think? He thinks that the body gives a start when we are on the point of going to sleep. Now I ask you, gentlemen, you've no doubt given a start sometimes, even when awake? When do you do this? I think you give a start when you have a shock, when you experience something that gives you a fright and perhaps causes fear, coming as a sudden surprise at that moment. Then you give a start. You may also give a start, for instance, if you walk around out there, let us say, and suddenly see someone who you thought was in America; seeing him startles you, because you are taken by surprise. But you'll never imagine, as you begin to give a start, that you think you're flying. Never in your dreams, I'm sure, would you think you are flying when you give a start. So you see the confused notions people have when they deduce that one might have the idea one is flying when the body gives a start. You can see from this that people give some thought to things, but the moment they want to use those thoughts to explain something in the human being, they do not work. Such thoughts will work for as long as one experiments with lifeless matter in a laboratory, but the moment you are intending to explain something, it no longer works.

Now it goes on.

> The reason for such a start lies in the fact that muscle tensions are different when waking and asleep. When we are awake, energy currents are continually going to the muscles in the body from the central nervous system,

(he assumes, therefore, that electrical currents, energy currents, are passing from our nerves to our muscles all the time we are awake)

> which gives our muscles the tension needed to keep the body in balance and keep the musculature functioning in a regular way; in sleep, this muscle tension has largely gone and since the reflex excitability of the spinal marrow is enhanced during the first sleep period,

(meaning as soon as one's gone to sleep)

> the process of muscle relaxation, or the stimulus this means for the spinal marrow, will easily trigger that startle reflex,

(he is saying, therefore, that a stimulus is applied to the nervous system in the spinal marrow; this, he says goes further and tenses the muscles more than before)

> meaning the start given by the body. Other sensations one actually has of organs may have an even more direct effect in creating the sensation of flying, floating in the air, swimming — especially the rhythmical movements of the respiratory muscles and of the chest as it goes up and down,

Now just think. When you start to huff and puff and your chest tightens — did you ever have a feeling that you were flying? You would feel even heavier in that case —

> and above all also loss of the sensations of pressure and resistance from anything we rest on, which we have in any part of the body that rests on anything whilst we are awake.

Well, gentlemen, you see, if one is walking, when awake, the physical base one rests on is very small; you have the feeling that you are walking on the soles of your feet. And when you are sitting down whilst you're awake you have a slightly larger base to rest on than just the soles of your feet. Yet even if you add this to the size of the area on which the soles of your feet are resting, it is still very small compared to the area you rest on when you are sleeping. The gentleman is saying the pressure of lying on something has gone. But the area you lie on and the pressure is greater when you have gone to bed than when you walk or sit in your waking hours! You can see, therefore, that with this kind of thinking one gets to say things that are simply nonsense. And that is the knowledge one gets of the human being with modern science!

He says, therefore, that electric currents go into the nerves. They are stronger when we are asleep, the muscles twitch and you get the notion of flying, that is, you think you are flying, or the area you lie on is not there when you sleep! One simply cannot believe the things that are said.

Also loss of the sensations of pressure and resistance from anything we rest on, which we have in any part of the body that rests on anything whilst we are awake.

One cannot think why the man does not consider the objection that we lie on a much larger supporting area when we sleep. But he does not do this, for modern thinking either makes people talk nonsense or does not provide any explanations whatsoever.

Now let us look at some of this—for then you'll see, gentlemen, how insight is gained into a higher, spiritual world—seeing what really happens when someone goes to sleep.

Let me first of all draw you some pictures. You know that it is just something to show you. But let us assume this is someone's physical body [Fig. 19, left]. In this human

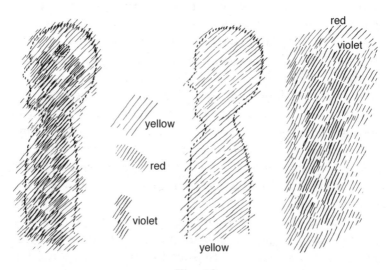

Fig. 19

physical body we have an extra body, the ether body, which is not perceptible to the senses; I'll make it yellow. This is inside, it fills the other one. And this one is invisible.

These two bodies, the physical body and the ether body, remain in the bed when we sleep. Now that we are awake, the astral body is inside these two bodies – I'll show this by going over it in red – and then there is also the I in there, the fourth body. I'll make it less distinct [violet]. That is the human being when he is awake – physical body, ether body, astral body and I; these are one inside the other.

Let us now look at a sleeping person. He only has the physical body and ether body lying in bed [Fig. 19, middle]. This, here, lies in the bed. Outside the bed are the astral body – it has gone outside – and the I, the I-body [Fig. 19, right]. The part which remains in bed is like a plant, for a plant also has a physical body and an ether body. If the plant did not have an ether body it would be a stone. It would not be alive then, would not grow. So the part that remains in bed is like a plant. The plant does not think. The part that lies in the bed – you know this very well – also does not think in such a way that the thinking comes to conscious awareness. The thoughts are in there, as I explained to you the other day, and are even brighter than the thoughts we use when we are conscious; but there are no conscious thoughts. It is just as it is with a plant.

But when he is outside, the human being is in a state where he feels that he no longer has any boundaries. You can even see why it is that consciousness ceases when we go out of the body like that. For if you are in your body, you must make your astral body the size of your physical body. When you go outside, the astral body suddenly begins to grow to giant size, to go out in all directions, for the physical body no longer draws it to itself, no longer makes it small. The moment you go to sleep, therefore, you move out of your physical body; you then grow bigger and bigger.

Now just imagine you are having a glass of something—lest people start saying I am speaking in favour of alcohol; you know this is an unpleasant subject just now in Switzerland—so I'll say you are drinking a glass of water with a bit of raspberry juice in it. If you put a little bit of raspberry juice in a glass of water you get the taste of the raspberry juice. But imagine you are taking not this glass but a large container large enough to hold five bottles of water and you only put as much raspberry juice in it as you put into your glass before. You stir well, and the raspberry juice then has to spread through a lot more water; so the taste of raspberry juice is less. Now you see, as a young boy I grew up near a wine merchants where they had a barrel with a capacity for 400 buckets of wine in the cellars. If one had filled that with water—a barrel holding 400 buckets filled with water rather than wine—and added those few drops of raspberry juice, stirring the whole, you could have drunk the water and would not have tasted the raspberry juice at all. That is clear. Now, gentlemen, for as long as your astral body is as small as your physical body, it is like the raspberry juice in a glass of water. Your astral body then only goes as far as your physical body does. When you go outside in your sleep, the physical body no longer holds it together. The astral body then spreads, just as the raspberry juice spreads in the 400 buckets of water. And you then no longer have conscious awareness in this astral body, for conscious awareness develops when the astral body contracts.

Now you'll also get a proper explanation for what is supposed to happen when we go to sleep. While we are awake, the astral body is in our fingers, in our toes; the astral body is everywhere in our muscles. Now when we feel the astral body in our muscles, we have the feeling we are dependent on our physical body. The physical body is heavy. We feel the weight of the physical body. The moment we go outside, we leave the physical body and its weight behind. At this moment, before conscious awareness has gone in our sleep, we no longer feel heavy. We do not feel as if we are falling, for we are rising up; but we do feel that we are floating upwards. This increase in size, being no longer bound to the physical body — this is what we experience as flying or swimming. We are able to move freely until consciousness goes and we are completely asleep.

So what does a modern scientist say? He says: 'We give a start in our muscles.' Well, if we give a start in our muscles we feel them more than we usually do. We do not imagine we're flying in that case, but when we give a start we feel more bound to the physical body than ever. Just think — someone standing there who is amazed will open his mouth wide. Why does he open his mouth wide? Because he is so much in his muscles that he cannot control himself. So this startled reaction, this living in one's muscles, is the opposite of what we have when we go to sleep. When we go to sleep we actually go out of our muscles. So it is not a question of muscles contracting but of muscles relaxing. When we lie down, so that our body is supported by a larger area, we do not need to hold our muscles together with our astral body; they relax. And it is not because they tense up but because they relax, seeing that we no longer have to exert an influence on them, that we feel ourselves to be free of our muscles, and we float away with our lighter astral body.

Now remember how I told you the last time that we need to learn to think the other way round. Here you see it. Someone who thinks the way people are generally in the habit of thinking today will arrive at the opposite of the truth when he wants to explain something in the human being. So we must first of all get used to thinking the right way, so that we are also able to think the opposite of what exists in the physical world. People have got out of the habit of thinking in the right way, thinking in such a way that one's thinking takes one into the realm of the spirit.

Now there are really very many people today who may speak our language, and our language also has the word 'spirit' in it, but people cannot get any real meaning of this word. They can only think of things that are physical. And, as you have seen, if one wants to think of things in the spirit, one has to come to something that has no physical properties at all, something one does not see in the physical world. People's thinking has gone so far awry today that they want to see things of the spirit as something physical. They then become spiritualists. You see, the physical body can move a table. People say: 'If I can move a table I exist. If a spirit is supposed to exist, it must also be able to move a table.' Well, so they then start table tipping, and they take the table tipping as proof for the spiritual world. This is because their thinking is crooked, bent. Their thinking is materialistic, wanting the spirit, too, to be physical. Spiritualism is the most materialistic thing there is. You just have to see it first.

Now maybe one or the other of you will say: 'But I have been there when people sat down around a table, linking their hands in a chain, and tables moved, jumped, and all kinds of things.' Superficially that is right. You can sit around a table, make a chain around it, and the business may on occasion set the table in motion. But you see, that is just as it is when I make some other small movement and cause a big movement. Just imagine you have a railway train. The train has an engine in front, with an engine driver on it. Now the engine driver does not get down from the machine and go to the back of it and push. I doubt if he'd manage to get a fast train really moving that way. You know, the engine driver makes just a very small movement, and the train goes very fast, with the machine pulling many carriages. Why? Well, because the gears function the way they should. In that way a small movement results in a big one and does so by physical means.

In the same way it is a purely physical process when people link hands around a table and then begin to twitch just the tiniest bit and so on. And lo and behold, those tiny twitches are converted into big movements through matter, for this is most cleverly put together. So to begin with it is a perfectly ordinary physical process.

Now if there is someone in the group who has particular ideas in his subconscious mind, these thoughts pass through his twitching fingers. And you will then also get answers in this way, answers that can be read off, using the alphabet. But the answers you get are always in the subconscious mind of someone who is there, ingenious though they may be. I did explain to you that when human beings go down even just a little into the subconscious, they are more ingenious than they are in their conscious minds. This also shows itself in table tipping. The fact that people have become spiritualists thus actually proves that materialism is powerful in our age.

Our ordinary thinking cannot provide explanations of any kind when it comes to the human being. So you see we have a situation where someone tries to explain a dream, the dream of flying, in this newspaper article I quoted today. He explains it exactly the opposite way from the way it should be explained. But people really are no longer able to study such things, things that are extremely interesting. I have told you things about dreams on several occasions before; today I'll concentrate once again on some of the major facts.

Just think of someone dreaming, gentlemen. In his dream he is crossing some square in Basel. But suddenly — such a thing is possible in dreams — he finds a fence in his way, with a picket here, a picket there, then a picket missing; he's got a picket here, another one there, then one's missing again [*drawing on the board*]. He then dreams that he wants to jump over the fence and gets impaled on a picket. It hurts. Now he wakes up. And he realizes: 'Wow, you did not get impaled on that picket at all, but you have a terrible toothache!' He has the toothache and wakes up with an aching tooth. He has a gap up there in his teeth, and another one up here. So that is what he saw as a fence with missing pickets. It is just like his upper teeth with the gaps where teeth are missing. He then touches the one tooth and that is exactly the one that is hurting. It has got a hole in it and it hurts. That is a dream one can certainly have.

But what actually happened there? Now you see, the whole process actually took place in his waking life. You can say to yourself: 'I was happy when I was asleep, for then I didn't have this dreadful toothache.' But why did you not have the toothache when asleep? Because you were out there with your astral body. The physical body and the ether body do not feel the toothache. You can hammer a stone as much as you like, knocking a piece off it; the stone in itself will not feel it. You can also tear a plant apart; it will not feel it because it does not yet have an astral body, only an ether body. I'm sure some people would stop pulling off roses and picking flowers in the meadows if the plants were always hissing like snakes because it hurts. But the plant does not hurt. And human beings are like plants in their sleep. While they are asleep the tooth does not hurt. Slipping in with one's astral body, however, one will come to the teeth with one's astral body. You see, you have to be completely inside the body before you'll feel any hurt there is in the body. When you're not yet quite inside, something that hurts will seem to be an outside object.

Imagine, gentlemen, I am striking a match here; I watch it burn. If I had been inside it, I would not only have seen it through my astral body but also felt it as pain. When I am not yet wholly in my body but just in the process of slipping in, the row of teeth is like an outside body. I feel it to be an outside body and create an image which is similar to it. Just

as I create images of objects in the outside world, so I create
an image of my teeth when I am still half outside. And since
I am not yet able to create the right image—this is something I can only do if I have the science of the spirit—I create
an image of a fence rather than a row of teeth. And there are
pickets missing from the fence just as I have gaps in the row
of teeth. You see, the confusion due to my not being completely in my body makes an error arise. You take the inner
for the outer, simply because you are outside when you are
asleep. Then the inner is something outer.

You see, I have actually seen this happening with young
children. When you teach them, they do not yet have a
feeling for speaking quite correctly. And I have really
known an occasion when a boy who had just started to
write put '*Zaun, Zäune*' for '*Zahn*' [*Zaun* = fence, *Zäune* =
fences, *Zahn* = tooth. Translator]. And then he was told:
'That's wrong!' And he grew anxious in his slipping in—not
slipping out, but slipping in. Then you'll not dream of flying but have a bad dream. The child is afraid, as in a
nightmare, and makes this of it, and so the tooth has become
a fence. The child made the error. And you'll see again and
again that such connections between words actually create
dream images. There will always be some kind of connection between words. And so we can now see what is really
going on there.

You see when someone talks like that—this Richard
Traugott has actually written a lot about dreams,[40] all of it
just as nonsensical as what he is writing here about the
dream of flying—and if he only has the completely ordinary
thinking of our time, he'll say the opposite of what is really
true. For he does not understand that he feels like a flyer on
leaving the body because the astral body gets big then, and
that he feels like someone who has to force his way through
when he comes in again because the astral body is then
squeezed in. To tense his muscles is equated with a bad

dream. The bad dream comes exactly when the man who has written the article says one dreams of flying. Going to sleep, too, you'll have only bad dreams if the going-to-sleep process is not quite going the way it should. Imagine you are lying down somewhere and you get a feeling that someone is throttling you. This happens because you are on the point of going to sleep, but there is a restlessness somewhere, and so you can't get to sleep properly. So then you keep trying—now going out, now coming in. When you want to come in, which, however, you can't do because you're still tired, you get a throttling sensation because the astral body wants to come in, pushing in hard, but yet cannot get in properly. Once you know it you can explain all these things much better.

And this will also make you realize that something else is needed if we want to get to know the world of the spirit. You have to be perfectly clear in your mind that the physical body cannot have any part in this. One must be able to live exactly in the part which is the astral body. To get to know the world of the spirit you thus need to achieve something over which you normally go to sleep. If you slip out of the physical body with your astral body in ordinary life, you'll go to sleep. You see this is the business of the wine barrel again, of which I spoke before. The astral body grows to giant size. If you want to get to know the astral body you must have the inner strength to hold it together. Just imagine what happens. For the moment I'll just go back to the drop of raspberry juice again instead of the human astral body and I. Let us get a really good picture of this [drawing on the board]. There we have the glass of water, and in it a drop of raspberry juice. The drop of raspberry juice spreads [colouring it in]. You'll still know it is there if you have a glass of water. But now think of something a hundred thousand times bigger—I can't draw this, of course. You'd no longer see any of it if I were to try and make the colour light enough to match the distribution. Nor would one sense any of it. But now imagine that drop is a devil of a fellow and I put it into this wine barrel which holds 400 buckets of water — sorry, not wine, just water. Now this drop of raspberry juice, a real devil of a fellow, says to itself: 'I won't allow myself to be mixed in! I'll stay a drop of raspberry juice!' So there you have your wine barrel, or water barrel, and the drop of raspberry juice stays quite small. Now if you were to get in there with your tongue, licking your way through the water until you came to the place where the drop of raspberry juice has stayed small, you would taste the sweetness of that drop of raspberry juice. It has to resist events, therefore.

I said it's a devil of a fellow, just to have a way of putting it. The people who oppose anthroposophy are sometimes very funny indeed. In a Hamburg paper it was said, first having vilified anthroposophy in every possible way, who I was. It said I was really the devil! They were perfectly serious about it, saying that the devil had come into the world. I am only saying the drop of raspberry juice would be a devil of a fellow if it kept small when one put it into the water. Now it is something different for the astral body to keep as small as it was in the physical body when it comes out of it. You have to develop the strength that makes it possible to keep the astral body small. You can do this by developing the ability to think very clearly. I have told you that one has to develop independent thinking. Independent thinking is more powerful than the weak thinking of these people. The first requirement is a powerful ability to think. The second requirement is the ability to think backwards. In the outer physical world things go forwards. If you learn to think backwards, you gain more power in your thinking. And if you also learn the thing I told you last time, 'the part is always greater than the whole' — which contradicts the physical reality — you learn to put yourself into a world which is certainly not like the physical world but the opposite. You then learn to put yourself into the world of the spirit.

All these things make it possible for the astral body to stay smaller, even though it leaves the physical body, and not to stream out into the general astral ocean.

This, then, all goes together. But you also have to be very clear in your minds that these things have to be considered in the same sober, scientific way as are the objects in outer physical life. As soon as you start to fantasize, you'll no longer have the science of the spirit. You certainly must not indulge in fantasies.

Let us assume, for example — well, I want to show this very clearly — you have a pain in your big toe. You only feel this pain in your big toe because of your astral body. If you only had your physical body you'd not feel any pain. If you had only your ether body, you'd feel no pain, otherwise a plant would squeak when you took hold of it, a flower would squeak when you took hold of it. Now you will squeak if you have a pain in your big toe — well, not you personally, perhaps, but you know what I mean. We squeak, therefore, if we have a pain in the big toe. The question is, why do we squeak? You see, we have the astral body spread throughout the whole physical body. When we come to the place with our astral body where something or other is not right in the big toe, we take this up to the brain with our astral body. There we form an idea of the pain.

But now imagine someone has a sick brain. When someone has a perfectly sound brain, he'll also have a place in that brain where he can perceive the pain in his big toe. One needs a healthy spot in the brain to be able to perceive the pain in the big toe. Let us assume, however, this spot in the brain is sick. I have told you, the soul cannot be sick, the astral body cannot be sick, but the physical brain can be sick. Now if this spot in the brain is sick, the pain in the big toe cannot be perceived. So what does the person do? Well, gentlemen, a small part of the physical brain is sick; but you see, the brain's ether body is still there in that spot. The ether part of the brain in that place is no longer supported by the physical part. So what does the ether part do? The ether part makes your big toe into a mountain. It does not just take note of the big toe, but makes it into a mountain. And it makes the pain in it into a lot of small spirits, mountain sprites sitting in there. So you see [Fig. 20]: here's your big toe; you've put it out into space because you have a sick brain. And now you swear there's a huge mountain in front of you. But all of it is really just your big toe. It is a delusion.

Gentlemen, you have to be careful not to have such delusions when you want to enter into the world of the spirit, for then you get involved in fantasies. How can we achieve this? Again we must first of all do it by training. You

Fig. 20

have to know all the things that may come from the physical body if there is sickness in it anywhere. Then you'll no longer confuse the genuine spirit that appears to you with something that merely comes from your physical body.

So in addition to active thinking, to thinking backwards, to the kind of thinking I described to you the last time we met, where one thinks in a very different way compared to the way one does in the physical world, there must also be the proper knowledge: this and this comes from your physical body. All these are necessary preparations.

You see a particular art would be practised in the preparation people had in earlier times, so that they might enter a little into the world of the spirit in the old way. It was called the art of dialectics. It meant one had to learn to think. Today, if you were to ask someone to learn to think first—well, he'd tear out every hair from your head, for everyone believes he's already able to think. The truth is, however, that when we go back to earlier times we find that people first had to learn to think in a particular way. And that was called the art of dialectics. You had to think forward and back, and had to learn to establish concepts in the right way.

Now why was it like this? It was like this because people learned to think by learning to talk. I have told you on a previous occasion that a child also learns to talk first and then to think, but this would of course be in a childlike way at first. Today people remain childlike like this all their lives, but this does not serve in later life. Learning to think all the time from talking, one gets the air to come in and go out again every time one breathes in or out. Much depends on being prepared to speak properly, for this will also make one breathe properly. Someone who is able to breathe properly will be able to talk for a long time; someone who is not able to breathe properly will soon get tired when talking for a long time without interruption.

The art of dialectics taught people to speak properly and therefore also to think properly. Today people cannot think properly, for their breath is all the time colliding with their breathing organ. Just listen to an academic speaking today. Well, in the first place, only few of them speak; they usually read things off. They use quite different things to help them then, their eyes, and so on, and this gives them support. But just listen to them talking. They usually appear to be short of breath and always colliding with their own physical body.

In this way everything becomes an image of the physical body. You may have a sick spot here in the brain and so your big toe becomes a mountain with all kinds of sprites, or you may keep running into things with your breath all the time you are thinking, unable to let it go out. In either case, the whole world seems physical to you because you are all the time colliding with it in your breath. Where does this materialism really come from? Materialism develops because people are not able to think properly, to breathe out properly, bumping into the physical. They then believe the whole world to be all pressure and push. Pressure and push is what they have inside them because they did not prepare themselves beforehand by thinking in the right way. And so we might say that when someone is a materialist today this is because he cannot get out of himself, keeps bumping into himself everywhere inside.

Let us take another look at Mr Traugott. He really ought to say: 'The dream that one is flying develops because we go out of ourselves and the astral body is beginning to get bigger.' But he does not realize this, for he keeps thinking and thinking, he does a terrible lot of thinking! Well, gentlemen, just think, if someone starts to think who is not really able to think, what does he do? He first of all wrinkles his forehead, and then, because this still will not get him to think, he'll strike his forehead with his fist. What is he really trying to do? He wants to tense his muscles; he tenses his muscles. And if they are not tense enough he wants to hit them, so that they'll really tense up. So what does Mr Traugott do when he thinks about a dream? Instead of looking at things the way they are, he tenses his own muscles, and he then finds exactly the thing he is doing: 'Muscle tension,' he'll say, 'that's it!' Dream thus equals muscle tension. But he is merely confusing his thoughts about the dream with the reality.

You'll only learn something about Mr Traugott — about what happens to him when he thinks about things — if you read this thing. That is how it usually is today. If you read what gets printed, you find out what they imagine things to be. If you read the paper today you have to say to yourself: 'You'll learn little about what is happening in the world from the paper, but you will find out what the gentlemen who sit in the editorial office would like to happen in the world.'

And that is also how it is with materialistic science. You'll not learn from it what the world really is, but what materialistic professors think about the world today. Once you've found that out, you'll see that in anthroposophy the aim is not to deceive the world but to offer honesty instead of craftiness and illusion and things that are often quite deliberately untrue.

So you see that honesty, inner honesty, is the fourth quality we need to enter into the world of the spirit. Looking at the world, you'll see that there is not much honesty there. No wonder that there is also not much honesty in science.

We have been considering four qualities needed in our thinking — clear, independent thinking; thinking in a way that is independent of the outside world; thinking in a way that is completely different from the physical world, and also to be honest in our thinking. We'll consider other qualities the next time we meet.

Getting to be at home in the outside world.
Questions relating to nutrition. Effects of potatoes,
beetroots and radishes

There still remain some of the questions that were asked the other day. Just as the other day I started from an academic person's comment on dreams, so I want to take my starting-point today from something that seems to have proved quite a headache to the present-day scholar — we'll also get to our discussion this way — and that is the lizard's tail. You know if you have a fairly large lizard and want to grab it by the tail, the tail will break off. People say the lizard is brittle. And it is really very difficult to get hold of larger lizards by the tail; it'll break off and the creature runs off quite nimbly, without its tail. Scientists are doing experiments to establish if the animal's tail is actually torn out or if it is left behind by the creature. Modern science bases itself on materialism, and so people think that the animal has very weak muscles to hold this part of the tail together and is unable to hold these muscles together when it is caught.

There is a strange fact, however, and this is something people do not consider a great deal. This is the fact that lizards that have been caught and have been living in captivity for quite a long time lose this ability to drop their tail so easily. The tail grows stronger, and it cannot be torn out so easily; it'll stand up to more. This is a strange thing, that lizards easily lose their tail when they are out there and it proves stronger when they are in captivity. What can be the reason for this?

You see, people reflect for a long time how this might be brought about by the small muscles there in the tail. Yet the fact I have just described easily shows why it happens that the creature's tail is less easily torn off in captivity. It happens because the creature will be a little bit afraid when you want to catch it out there. It is not the usual thing for it to be caught out there. Something is happening to it for the first time. It will be the first time that a human being comes near it, and it feels afraid, and being afraid it grows so brittle that it loses its tail. When it gets used to people, being in captivity, where people come near it all the time, it will no longer be afraid and lose its tail.

Quite a superficial look will therefore tell us that the lizard's fear and terror plays an important role. Now we have to take things further and say: 'Yes, the fear the lizard has when a human being comes near it and wants to catch it only comes out in the creature when the human being catches it, but it is always there inside the creature, and it is this fear which holds the creature's matter, its physical substance, together and makes it strong.'

I am going to tell you of a very strange thing that happens in human beings. You'll have heard of people who are very dependent on their soul life and get diarrhoea when they feel fear. Anxiety causes diarrhoea. And what does this mean? It means that the material in the bowels is no longer held together. The question is, what did hold the stuff in the bowels together? You see, when fear goes up into the soul, it no longer holds the things together in the bowels. But when the fear is down in the bowels it holds the stuff together.

And that is how it is with the lizard. If we look at a lizard [*drawing on the board*], it is all the time full of fear, the whole of it, just like our own belly. It is filled with something that has soul quality. And the tail in particular is filled with fear. When the animal expresses its fear, the tail breaks, but the fear remains in the creature. When it is in captivity it does not feel the fear because it has got used to people, and the result is that the fear can then hold the tail together. So we see a quite specific soul quality having particular significance for the consistency of the body.

We humans also have fear in us. In our big toe, in the legs, in the belly — there's fear everywhere. It does not dare go above the diaphragm, however, except when we have nightmares. But the fear is there in us. The fear has its purpose, however. It holds our organism together. And we have more fear in our bones than anywhere else. The bones are so solid because there is a terrible fear in them. It is fear which keeps the bones together. The moment you feel your bones too much, you get softening of the bones. You'll see this confirmed in anxious individuals, people who were anxious even in their young days, when the bones had not yet hardened but the people were anxious. And it is also possible to cure children with rickets by influencing the soul, by finding a way of driving out their fear. But it would be quite wrong to say we thus have fear in us as a soul quality. We only need to take the fear up a bit higher and we'll gain higher insights. That would not be a good thing, for in that case we would make ourselves sick in soul and body.

You see, to gain insight into the world of the spirit — I have told you the other things that are needed — we must find our way properly into the outside world, really live in it. How do people find their way to the outside world today? This is something you could see most beautifully again these last few weeks. You'll remember, we were all of us ever so cold, and then we really sweated. This is the way most people live with the outside world, knowing no more but that on one occasion they get into a real sweat, and on the other they were ever so cold. But that is not the only way of living with the outside world. Instead one develops a particular ability, so that one does not just feel cold when it gets cold but points to the cold and gets a kind of fear, knowing that the fear will go when it gets warm. If one develops this inner faculty, that one has a kind of fear of the snow, and a certain feeling of well-being in the warmth of the sun, this is simply something that leads to higher insight; it is another quality in addition to those I have described to you. And the situation simply is that someone who wants to gain higher insight must feel something when he comes up to a piece of red-hot iron, and he must feel something when he comes up to a pebble. Coming up to some red-hot iron he must inwardly have the feeling: This is related to your own warmth; it does you good. But when he picks up a pebble this should give him an uncanny feeling; he should feel anxious.

Well, gentlemen, you can immediately see from this that it is no good fighting shy of things, as we put it today, if you want to gain higher insights, for then you'd drop the pebble as soon as you pick it up, because it frightens you. You have to have courage and bear the anxiety. On the other hand you should not be like the moth which takes such sensual pleasure in the light that it actually rushes into the flame and dies. Looking at the insect rushing to die in the flame you can see that the flame is related to the element of spirit and soul.

We are thus able to say that we need to acquire an inner feeling, an inner response to the natural world outside. What purpose will this serve? Well you see, gentlemen, in the first place the earth is solid rock [Fig. 21]. Materialists believe in this solid rock which is part of the earth, for they are able to walk on it. It is hard to the touch. Materialists put their faith in solid rock. But someone who is hoping to gain higher insight develops some degree of anxiety on coming face to face with this very rock.

This anxiety does not appear at all when we are in heated air. I'll draw this heated air above the solid rock. When we consider the heated air this anxiety does not arise at all, for the heated air — I'll show that it has heated up by making it a

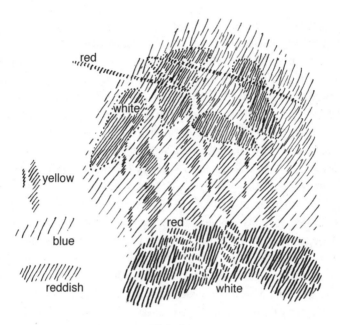

Fig. 21

bit red—does not make us anxious. But one can also reach the point where the heated air makes one anxious. This will actually be the case when one tries more and more to cope with the feelings one has towards the heated air by liking it. Just think, you've got someone there who feels more and more at ease in the heated air. But now the heated air also begins to make him anxious! The more you feel at ease in it, the more does the heated air make you anxious.

So if one gets into the habit of feeling really at ease in the heated air, getting more and more used to the warmth, as it were—such things are necessary; you have to enter into the whole of nature to gain higher insight—the business begins to get really peculiar. Let me show it to you even more clearly. Most people want to cool down again when they feel hot. All they know in that case is that they'd like to be less hot. But if you put up with the heat, if you stay with it, and actually feel comfortable in it, the parts I have drawn rather schematically in the air here [Fig. 21, yellow] oddly enough begin to fill up with all kinds of images [white, at the top] and the world of the spirit literally begins to show itself, the world of the spirit which is always present in the air though people do not feel it in the air, perceive it in the air, because they do not want to bear the heat.

Once one has got used to seeing all these spirits that are present in the air, spirits people do not perceive because they do not want to put up with the heat in the air — once you have got used to seeing these spirits you will gradually also begin to perceive something peculiar where the solid rock is concerned. You'll find that if you say to yourself: 'Yes, a stone is hard if I put my clumsy paw on it. But if I begin more and more to perceive the things of the spirit, if I enter more and more into the realm of the spirit, if not only the things we perceive with the senses are all around me, but more and more also the things of the spirit, I'll not, of course, be able to slip into the soil with my physical flesh-and-blood body, but I can begin to slip into the soil with my astral body.' I've told you about this. This is most interesting. The moment one begins to perceive things of the spirit in the air, using all the means I have told you about, at that moment you yourself slip out of your body far enough so that you'll no longer feel the stones to be an obstacle but enter into the solid ground the way a swimmer does into water. You yourself enter in there [Fig. 21, red, down below]. This is extraordinarily interesting. You can't enter into the air in the spirit, because other spirits show themselves there. But it is easy to creep into the soil (this is actually empty as far as the spirit is concerned), you can immerse yourself in it like a swimmer.

And you see the middle state is that of water [blue]. The water goes up as it evaporates and then comes down again as rain. Lightning will often develop up there—this is something you've seen for yourselves [red, up top]. The water is between the solid ground and the air. It is less dense than the solid ground; it is denser than air. Now what does this mean? It means something you can best see by looking up at lightning. The academic view is that lightning is a spark of electricity. Why do academics see it as a spark of electricity? Well, you probably know it already—if not, I'll tell you now. If you take a stick of sealing wax and rub it with a piece of leather it becomes electrified, and if you have little snippets of paper they'll be attracted to the stick of sealing wax. And one can make all kinds of different bodies electrical by rubbing them or in other ways. This is something children are shown at school.

But there is something quite specific that is needed. For if your schoolroom is fusty, no stick of sealing wax will ever be electrified—nor any of the other things you then use in your experiments—for everything must first of all be thoroughly wiped with a completely dry cloth, since the watery element does not produce electricity. And then you can produce electricity. Now the academic people say: 'Up there you have the clouds, they form ranks and create the electrical spark, the lightning.' Yes, but gentlemen, any child might come along and say: 'But you actually have to keep the watery element away, for if you have even just a little bit of damp on your apparatus you don't get any electricity!' Any child might raise that objection. So that is the kind of nonsense people talk. It is, of course, absolutely out of the question that the clouds rub against one another up there.

But just think, when water evaporates and goes up there, it comes more and more into a region of spirituality, going further away from the matter which is lacking in spirit down below and entering into spiritual nature up there. And it is indeed the spirit which produces the electrical spark, the lightning. For as we go higher and higher we come into the region of the spirit. The earth only has matter near to it. Higher up it is surrounded by the spiritual element. So there we truly enter into the realm of the spirit. And the situation is that the moment the water vapour goes up and comes into the region of the spirit, lightning can arise out of the spirit. The water grows spiritual up there and comes down again condensed. In pursuing the study of nature one must therefore also come to the spirit. And it is only if one absolutely refuses to take account of the spiritual element that one arrives at all kinds of absurdities like those I've told you about — the dream of flying, or the lizard's tail, or the lightning. One simply always finds that it is not possible to explain the natural world unless one first enters into the realm of the spirit.

Now you can also understand the following. When we stand on the soil we are really always made in such a way from below upwards that we are related to the spiritual from below; we can enter into it, as a swimmer enters into water. So when we go out of the physical body and out of the ether body at night with our astral body and our I, we are really entering everywhere into our solid surroundings. We unite with the things that are solid, for we cannot enter into the airy element, and we literally move about in the solid element.

This wandering about in the solid element is very important, however. If we relate in the right way to heat, the way I have told you before, we come to see the spirits that are in the air. But when we go out of the body at night and as spirit connect with the earthly element, the situation may be that when we wake up again we still have something of what we experienced in the solid element of the earth. We still have something inside us there; we have something in our soul element.

Now this is something that is extraordinarily interesting.

You will have noticed that one easily hears things as one wakes up. And if you pay careful attention on waking up you will have the strange experience where you'll say to yourself: 'Someone has just been knocking on my door!' This is a very strange thing. When you enter livingly into the air with your soul, you will see something; images will arise. But when you enter livingly into the solid element, into matter, with your soul, like a swimmer immersing himself in water, you will experience sounds. The extraordinarily important thing is that all solids are continually sounding, but we do not hear the sounds because we are not inside the solids. Every solid always has sounds in it, and you will still hear these as you wake up, because you are then still half inside.

But these sounds may certainly mean something, and it is absolutely true that if someone living a long way off has died, for instance, and someone else wakes up and hears something like a knocking on the door, this has to do with the person who has died. Human beings are, of course, unable to interpret these things correctly. For just imagine all of you were unable to read, that is, interpret the black marks on paper, not having learned to read. And in the same way you are quite unable to interpret the marvellous thing that is afoot when you hear sounds as you wake up. You don't have to think that the person who has died is actually standing there and knocking at your door as if he used fingers. But the person who died, and who after all is still on earth during the first days after death, lives in the solid bodies. And this is something that need not seem at all strange and wonderful to you, that the very fact of uniting with the solid element creates sounds, which is what people have always been saying in the days when they still paid attention to such things. The fact that people have an inkling that someone has died far away has real significance. Someone has died. At first he is still connected with the solid earth in his soul. And the sounds then arise that come from him. The human being is resounding as he leaves the earthly realm. You can of course hear this just as well if you are a long way off, as you can read a long way off what someone has taken to the post office in America. A telegram can be read in America. Such long-distance effects based on earthly matter exist; they do exist on earth, they always exist. And in the days when people paid heed to such things, they certainly knew of the connection between the spiritual element and the earthly world. That is not just a tale, it is truly something people perceived in earlier times. As you can see we come to quite specific things here that are considered superstition today, and which can be scientifically proved just as other things can be scientifically proved.

However, you also have to know these things exactly. For you see, if one were to get to the point of perceiving the world of the spirit in the air, that is, if people were not quite such wimps as they are today—you know, the more civilized people get the more do they tend to be wimpish in some respect, and people who because of their work, let us say, have to live in a terrible rush do not have the time while they are working to perceive the world of the spirit—they would not fail to see the world of the spirit that exists in the air. But this seeing of spirits in the air would really be something fairly free from danger. Anyone could easily do it without getting into any danger.

But this hearing can be dangerous if it takes hold too much of people, and if they get too much into a state where they hear all kinds of things. The thing is this. There are people who gradually reach a condition where they hear all kinds of words. All kinds of things are said to them. These people are in the process of going mad. Now if one sees spirits by looking for them in the air, one is never really threatened by any danger. Why? Well, I have to tell you this

by using an analogy. If you go in a boat and fall into the
water you may drown. If someone pulls you out of the
water, you may also experience all kinds of things, but you
won't drown. It is just like that when the human soul goes
out in an upward direction and sees all kinds of things.
Nothing can happen to it. If it goes downwards, into solid
matter, it may drown spiritually, I'd say. And this drown-
ing in the spirit happens when people lose consciousness in
such a way that all kinds of things are then told to them
inwardly. And that is what is so bad. You see, when
someone sees the spiritual element outside, it is just as it is
when he walks about in the world, and just as he's not
afraid of the chair he sees, so he'll gradually also not be
afraid of the spiritual outside, but actually come to like it.
But something people hear inwardly—we sink down into
the solid ground with the whole of our spirit and the whole
of our soul—anything we then hear inwardly will completely absorb us. You can drown in it most miserably. We
must therefore always be a bit cautious when people say
they are told all kinds of things inside. This is always a
dangerous situation. Someone who has gained a really firm
foothold in the world of the spirit and knows his way about
will know what is actually being said there. He'll know that
in that case it is not particularly sublime spirits who speak
to one but really always spirits that are more of a lower
kind. You see, gentlemen, I have told you these things quite
openly so that you may see that as a human being one really
needs to consider the outside world in a very different way
if one wants to enter into the world of the spirit.

There are of course people who'll say: 'But why have the
spirits made it so difficult for us to get to know them?' Yes,
but just think what kind of human beings we'd be if we did
not have to make any effort to enter into the world of the
spirit, if we were always in it. We'd be absolute spiritual
automatons. We only gain the right relationship to the

spirits because we have to make an effort. And it does take the greatest inner effort to be able to do research in the world of the spirit.

It is of course easy to be the great scientist at the laboratory bench and make all kinds of experiments; it is easy to cut up dead bodies and discover all kinds of things. But it really calls for a great deal of inner work to enter into the world of the spirit in a real way. The educated people of today are too lazy for this. And it is really always out of this laziness that people say: 'I did the exercises given in *Knowledge of the Higher Worlds*, but I did not see anything.' They think it should be given to them from outside and that they should not have to do inner work for it. Gentlemen, that is the problem! People want to have everything presented to them today. I told you before that they want to film everything today; they want to have films made of everything, so that it may come to them from the outside.

To make real progress in the spirit one must always see to it that anything one takes in from the world is worked through. People will therefore be more likely to get to the spiritual element if in future they avoid as much as possible having everything shown to them in films and instead try to think things through as much as possible when they learn anything about the world. And you see, I haven't shown you a film. There isn't the time for it, of course, but even if we had the time I would not attempt to show the matter to you in a film. Instead I made drawings that developed as we went on, and you were able to see what I intended with every line I drew and were able to think along with me. And this is also what we need in teaching children today—as few finished drawings as possible, and as much as possible to arise out of the moment, with the child seeing every line as it is drawn. The child then joins in the effort inwardly, and this encourages inner activity. The result will be that people find their way into the spiritual element more easily and develop an understanding for spiritual things again. You also should not present children with whole, complete theories, for this'll make them dogmatic. What matters is to get them to be active in themselves. This'll also make the whole body much more free.

I'd now like to go on to something else that is another part of one of the questions. You will no doubt have heard that the potato only came to Europe at a particular time. The people of Europe have not always been potato eaters.

A rather peculiar thing happened on one occasion. You see, there's an encyclopaedia[41] which I actually also helped to write, though not the article I am now talking about. It says something very funny in that article, and that is that everyone believes a man called Drake brought the potato to Europe, which was a great merit for him. There's a Drake monument in Offenburg, which is now occupied by the French. Now it really felt very odd to me to look it up in the encyclopaedia one day and it really said: 'They put up a monument to Drake in Offenburg because he was reputed, wrongly so, to have brought the potato to Europe.' So when someone is reputed to have done something, he gets a monument in Europe! However, that is not what I want to talk about. I want to talk about the fact that the potato was brought to Europe at a particular time.

Let us look at the potato. We do not really eat the roots of it [*drawing on the board*]. If that is the potato plant, the rootlets are like this. The potato itself is a stem tuber. So with an ordinary plant you have the root, and then the stem grows. But if the stem thickens the way it does in the potato, you get a tuber. It is really a thickened shoot, so that the potato is not a root but a thickened shoot or stem. This is something you should remember well. If you eat a potato you are eating a thickened shoot. You are essentially taking your nourishment from a thickened stem. We now have to ask ourselves what significance it had for people that they learned to eat what essentially is a thickened stem when the potato came to Europe.

Looking at a whole plant you have the root, the stem, the leaves and the flower [Fig. 22]. It is a strange thing with a plant. The root down there grows very similar to the soil, especially in containing a lot of salts, and the flower up top grows very similar to the warm air. Up there it is like a continuous cooking process in the heat of the sun. The flower therefore contains oils and fats, especially oils. Looking at a plant we thus have salts being deposited below. The root is rich in salts, the flower in oils.

The consequence is that when we eat the root we get many salts into our gut. These salts find their way up to the brain and stimulate the brain. Salts thus stimulate the brain. And so it is quite good, for instance, for someone suffering from headaches—not migraine-like headaches but head-

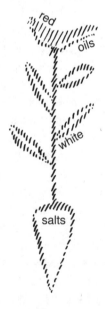

Fig. 22

aches that fill the head — to eat roots. You can see that many roots have a certain salty harshness. You can tell from the taste. But if you eat flowers, that is where the plant is really half-cooked already. Up there you already have the oils; that is something which above all greases the stomach and the gut; it has an effect on the abdomen. A physician has to take account of this when he prescribes a medicinal tea. If someone makes a tea from flowers he'll never get much of an effect on the head. But if he has the roots boiled and gets the patient to drink that, he'll get a powerful effect on the head. So you see, whilst we have to go from the belly to the head in human beings, from below upwards, we have to go the opposite way in the plant, from flower to roots. The root of the plant is related to the head. The flower of the plant is related to the gut and so on. If we consider this, we'll begin to realize something about the significance of the potato. For the potato has tubers, something that has not quite become a root. So when we eat many potatoes we are largely feeding on plants that have not quite become root. If one limits oneself to eating potatoes, and eats too many potatoes, one does not get enough food into the head. It stays down in the digestive tract. The situation is therefore that with their potato eating the people of Europe neglected their head, their brain. This connection is only seen when one works with the science of the spirit. Then one says to oneself that people's heads have grown less capable since the potato has come to be eaten more and more in Europe.

The potato will mainly stimulate the tongue and the gullet. Going down in the potato plant we do not go quite as far as the root. And it is the same with the human being. When we do not go quite as far as the head and stay with the tongue and gullet, these are specially stimulated by the potato, and people find the potato makes such a good part of a meal, a good side dish, because it stimulates the parts that are below the head and leave the head unmolested.

When we eat beetroot, gentlemen, we get a terrible longing to think a lot. We do this quite unconsciously. When we eat potatoes, we really get a longing to eat something again quite soon. The potato will soon make us hungry again because it does not go all the way to the head. Beetroot will soon fill you up, for it does actually go up into the head, which is the most important thing, and the head is the most important part, and it completely fills the head with activity when it goes right up into it. For people do of course find it most unpleasant to have to be able to think, and so they'll sometimes have potato rather than beetroot, because potato does not encourage thinking. It does not encourage thinking, you get lazy in your thinking. Beetroot on the other hand is a powerful stimulus to think, but it does it in such a way that you actually want to think, and someone who does not want to think does not like beetroot. If you need something to stimulate your thinking, you should particularly use the salty stimulus of radishes, for instance. This will be good for someone who is not very lively in the head, for it'll get his thoughts moving a bit if he adds radish to his food.

So you see we have this strange thing. We can say that radishes stimulate our thinking. And you need not be all that active in your thinking; eat radish and the thoughts will come, such powerful thoughts that they'll even create mighty dreams. Someone who eats a lot of potatoes does not get powerful thoughts; but he'll get dreams that make him heavy. And someone who has to eat potatoes all the time will really be tired all the time and always want to sleep and dream. It therefore plays an important role in the history of civilization what kinds of foods are actually available to people.

Now you might say, gentlemen: 'Yes, but the thing is that we really live altogether on matter.' That's not true, however. I have often told you that as human beings we have a new body about every seven years. It's renewed all the time. The matter we had in our bodies eight or ten years ago is no longer in there. It's gone. We cut it away when we cut our nails, cut our hair; it's gone away in our sweat. It all goes away. Some of it goes quite quickly, some goes slowly, but go it does.

Now how do people think this goes? You see, they imagine it is something like this. I'll draw it in schematic form now [Fig. 23]. So that would be the human being [white]. He is all the time giving off matter and is all the time taking in new matter [blue arrows]. People therefore think that matter comes in through the mouth and goes out again through the anus and in the urine, and the human being is a kind of tube. He takes in matter with his food,

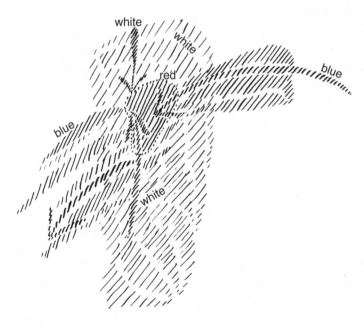

Fig. 23

keeps it for a time and then throws it out again. That is more or less how people think man is made.

But the truth is that nothing of the earthly matter enters into the real human being, none at all. That is just an illusion. The matter is like this. If we eat potatoes, say, this is not in order to take in something from the potato. The potato is merely something which stimulates us, stimulates us in the jaw, the gullet and so on. It is active just there. And then the power develops in us to throw the potato out again and, as we drive it out, the principle which builds up our body in the course of seven years comes towards us from the ether [white arrows], not from the solid matter. We actually do not at all build our bodies with earthly matter. We only eat the things we eat to get a stimulus. The whole idea people have of food coming in there and going out there, remaining inside for a while in between times, is quite wrong, therefore. We just get a stimulus. And there a power comes from the ether, and we build up our whole body from the ether. Everything we have as our bodies has not been created out of earthly matter. You see if you push and there comes an opposite push, you must not confuse that second push with your original push. You should not confuse the fact that we need food to stop us from getting lazy in restoring our body with the fact that we take this food into us.

Now the situation is that irregularities may of course occur. For if we take too much food the food stays inside us for too long. We then collect unjustifiable food in us, grow corpulent, fat, and so on. If we take in too little we do not get enough stimulus and do not take enough of what we need from the world of the spirit, from the etheric world.

But this is something most important, gentlemen, this fact that we do not build ourselves up out of the earth and its matter but that we build ourselves up out of something that is beyond the earth. If it is the case that the whole body is renewed in seven years, the heart will also be renewed [red]. So you no longer have the heart inside you now that you had eight years ago. It has been renewed, renewed not from the material substance of the earth but renewed out of the element that surrounds the earth in the light. Your heart is compressed light! You really and truly have a heart that is condensed sunlight. And the food you have eaten has only given the stimulus for you to compress the sunlight so far. You build up all your organs from the light-filled sur-roundings, and the fact that we eat, that we take in food, only means that a stimulus is given.

You see, the only thing our food gives us is to let us have something like a couch inside us. We sense ourselves and have a feeling of self in ordinary life because we have physical matter in us, physical substance. We get a feeling for ourselves just as if you were to sit down on a couch. Then you also feel the pressure of the couch. And that is how you sense your body as something that is all the time exerting pressure on something you have created out of the universe. You don't feel it when you're asleep because then you're out of yourself. You sense your body; it is a kind of couch made for you, harder for a bony person, softer for someone else. It is a kind of couch on which the real human being lies down, and we do of course also feel the difference between a soft feather bed and a wooden bench! And so the human being gets a feeling for anything that is hard in him and anything that is soft. But what he feels there is not the actual human being, for the actual human being is the something that sits there inside him.

The next time I'll explain to you what this has to do with gaining higher insight. The people who want to gain insight today do not in the least consider the human activity but only what the couch presents to them.

Human and cosmic breathing. The earth breathes light. Fertilization in plants and humans; fertilization of water through lightning

If we take the things we considered the last time a bit further, we come to the following. In the days when I was young, very young still, there would be a lot of excitement when a travelling hypnotist would give performances with people. Now we need not give special praise to people who make a public show of extremely serious things, and I certainly would not want to sing great praises of Hansen,[42] a man who in the 1870s and 1880s, especially in the 1880s, gave public performances on a subject which scientists had not at all been considering in those days and about which nothing was known in science at that time. But scientists have since taken up the subject, particularly as a result of Hansen's public performances.

Let me first of all tell you of an experiment that had long been forgotten when Hansen started to do it over and over again, to the amazement of his audiences. He would take two chairs, place them at some distance from each other [*drawing on the board*], and then hypnotize someone simply by the power of his own personality, as people put it, that is, get him to enter into a sleeplike state to begin with. It was a sleeplike state, however, that was much deeper than ordinary sleep. He would then take this person and position him in such a way that his head would be on one chair and his feet on the other. Now you know that if this happens to someone when they are in their ordinary state of consciousness, they'll simply fall between the chairs. This person did not fall between the two chairs to begin with. He lay where he was put, as stiff as a broomstick. But that was not enough. Hansen, quite a hefty fellow, then went and boldly stood upright on the person's stomach. So there he would stand, this man Hansen. The person did not stir, but lay there like a plank of wood, in spite of the fact that Hansen stood on him.

So this is certainly something that can be done, has been frequently done since then, and scientists cannot doubt it, having known nothing about it earlier on and having to be shown it by Hansen, who was not a particularly pleasant person. You see, someone in this state is said to be cataleptic.

When something like this happens, that someone may lie there like a plank of wood, and someone else may even stand on him, and it is a temporary state, brought about under the influence of that other person, it is just an experiment and not a very serious matter. But we can certainly say that this condition also exists in everyday life, though on a much smaller scale. You'll sometimes come across it. It will then, of course, only be apparent to someone able to observe it as a physician. It occurs when people develop a particular condition which is called a mental illness.

There are people, for example, who have been resolute and effective in their work and then suddenly begin to think in a way that is as if all their thoughts were frozen. It may happen that someone went to work regularly at 8 o'clock in the morning, let us say. Suddenly he finds it is very nice to stay in bed. He wants to get up but cannot find the will to do so. And if fear finally takes over — he's got his watch lying there, it shows a particular time — and he has got up at last, he cannot find the will to eat his breakfast, and then again to leave the house. He finally comes to say to himself all the time: 'I can't do it; I can't do it,' finally behaving like a stick, unable to decide on anything. And it will go so far that he gets into a state where one can also see it in his body; he's rigid. Before he'd have moved his arms quickly, now he moves them slowly; he'd walk at a lively pace before, now he finds it difficult to take one step and then the next. The whole person grows rigid and heavy. This is a condition which sometimes develops in people when they are still quite young.

It is the selfsame condition, only not so marked and now not occurring all at once but very gradually. When someone begins to be cataleptic, you won't be able to put him across two chairs in the same way and stand on him, or to sit on him. But the condition is such that he can no longer manage his body in the right way.

This is the one state. But Hansen also showed people other experiments. These would be copied a great deal in those days, and scientists have now also taken note of them. They did not take them up until Hansen, amateur and showman, drew their attention to the matter. These other states were like this. Hansen would ask a member of the audience to come up. Some fools would say he'd arranged this before-hand, but that's nonsense, of course. He would spot the people who'd be suitable for this among the members of the audience. It can't be done equally well with everyone; but he'd developed an eye for those who would be right. He'd let a member of the audience come up and again bring his personal influence to bear. He would stand there, his own thick legs firmly placed on the floor. His eyes were such that people would think they'd enter into and go right through you, a penetrating gaze as one says. And he'd always have the eye like this, you see [*drawing on the board*]. When he looked at someone, the eye would be such that the white of the eye was visible both above and below; the eye would be open in that way. Now usually the lid covers the white, so that one does not see the white above and below the pupil. But he had developed a fixed look, as one says.

This would of course make a tremendous impression on the individual he had picked to be his victim, who'd immediately start to be a little bit unconscious, as one says. He lost consciousness, but something very strange would happen. Hansen would then say: 'You can't move from the spot. Your feet are fixed to the floor.' The man would try — he couldn't move, could not take a single step. He simply could not do it and stood where he was. Hansen would also say to suitable victims: 'Now kneel down!' The person would kneel down. 'Look, an angel is appearing up there.' The person would put his hands together in prayer, and be transported as he looked up to the angel. Hansen would do all these things with people he picked for his victims. He would of course pick people whose conscious minds were not very strong, and with them he could do all these things right before the audience's eyes. There would be no deception — many people said he cheated — but these things have since then been done at scientific institutes and so they are valid.

Then he'd also do the following, for instance. He'd take a chair and put it there for someone who no longer had no thoughts of his own but only the thoughts Hansen gave him. Hansen would stand there and say: 'Here's an apple.' You know apples are good, they taste good. But he'd take a potato and give it to the man who'd bite into it with the greatest pleasure, eating the potato as if it were an apple. Hansen therefore was not only able to persuade people that they were seeing an angel, but also that a potato was an apple and could be eaten as an apple. Then he'd take some water, for instance, and say: 'I am now giving you some very special sweet wine.' And one could see the man delighting in the sweetness. Those were the kinds of experiments Hansen made. It was the other kind of experiment he did.

What did he do when he stood on someone? He had

killed the person's will, so that he no longer had any will at all. With the people he treated the way I have told you just now he only influenced their thoughts. They just had to think the way Hansen said; if he said, 'That's an apple,' and so on, they had to accept his taste, and if he said, 'That's an angel,' they would follow his thoughts and see the angel.

And you see, Hansen was able to do many other things as well. He'd do the following, for example. He'd ask someone from the audience to come up who he thought would make a good victim, and he'd first of all hypnotize him, that is, make him such that he had no conscious mind of his own, that he'd take up any ideas Hansen would present to him. He'd then say: 'There'll be an interval of ten minutes. After those ten minutes I'll wake you up. You'll then go to the man who is sitting in that corner over there and take his watch from his pocket like a pickpocket.' He'd wake the man first — in the meantime Hansen had done all kinds of other things with other people — and the man would grow restless, get up, go to the man sitting over yonder in the corner and take his watch from his pocket.

People will use Latin names, of course. As I told you, Latin can always be used if one wants to use logic. And the first kind of experiments I described are called hypnotic experiments, whilst those where the man has been woken up and then does the thing afterwards are called post — post meaning 'after' — they are called post-hypnotic experiments. People now speak of hypnosis and post-hypnosis and it is known that people can be in such states.

These things give deep insight into human nature, however, for at a later stage the post-hypnotic element in particular was taken much further. If you put someone into a deep hypnotic state and tell him to do something or other three days later he will do it — if he has the right kind of personal make-up. These experiments have been done.

Now you know that these things are never as acute as that

in ordinary life. But they do occur in a milder form, as I have shown you in the case of someone unable to move. The other state also occurs in ordinary life. You'll have known not only people who are completely paralysed and no longer know what to do with themselves, so that in a sense they are cataleptic, but also people who suddenly begin — before that they were really perfectly sensible people — to be extremely talkative. You can't keep up with them; their thoughts pour forth, they talk, talk, talk, like a running wheel. With them, the situation is just as it is with someone who'd eat a potato thinking it to be an apple, except that in this case Hansen was in control, whilst the people who keep pouring forth their thoughts depend on their own bellies. For this is what is so interesting, that the belly — I have told you a great deal about the way the liver and so on goes on thinking in the belly — thinks much faster than the head. And when someone gets so weak in the head that he can no longer put up the necessary resistance to the thoughts that come from the belly, cannot slow them down sufficiently, the thoughts will just pour forth. These people are therefore hypnotized by their own bellies.

This is altogether a remarkable thing in life. Man has these two opposite organs, his head and his belly. Both of them think. But it is certainly true that the head thinks slowly and the belly thinks fast. The head thinks much too slowly, and the belly much too fast, but as you know very well, if you pour together a thick liquid and a thin one you get a medium thick liquid. And that is how it is with the human being. The conditions in the head slow down those in the belly, and conditions in the belly make those in the head go faster, and a balance is created.

You see, the things that go on in the world all depend on the interaction of opposite states or conditions. Much still has to be learned about this in modern science today. Let me tell you something about this. Imagine you have someone who is reasonably normal. If he lives to an age of about 72 years he will have lived 25,920 days—you can work this out, I have spoken of it before. That's 72 years. People normally live that many days. And if you count the number of breaths people take, you'll find that they take exactly that number of breaths in a day. Someone who lives a normal life and whose organism is not destroyed too early—in which case he can't reach the age of 72; someone who does not live to 72 has been destroyed in some way—has as many days in his life as the number of breaths he takes in a day. That is how human beings live. Every day, from one sunrise to the next, they take 25,920 breaths, and all things being equal, they reach patriarchal age, living for 25,920 days.

Now what does it mean that we live for 25,920 days normally, reaching patriarchal age? It means that we go 25,920 times through day and night here on earth. We go through days and nights, an experience we may have 25,920 times. What does the earth do when it goes through day and night? Now you see, gentlemen, the important thing— Goethe already had some idea of it, and today we can be definite about it—is that when dawn comes, the earth draws the powers of light, powers of the cosmos, to itself in the place where we happen to be. It is different in the other hemisphere; there it is the other way round, but it is the same process. The earth and everything that is in the earth thus breathes in light. It breathes out again when it is night. The earth does within a day what we do with the air in the short time needed for breathing in and breathing out.

You can see therefore that the earth is very much slower than we are, terribly much so. We take as many breaths in a day as the earth does in the whole of our life. This is what you can see. Now if we consider this more fully we discover something special in relation to man. Human beings breathe in such a way that the blood needs the breath. The blood is produced in the intestines, that is, in the belly, and the abdomen therefore wants to breathe that quickly. We are therefore able to say that human breathing has to do with the abdomen, the belly.

You see, if we consider the head in a truly scientific way, as scientifically as only the belly is studied in modern science today, the situation in the head is that the head is really always trying to hold the breathing back a little. The breathing also goes up into the head. The head wants to breathe in such a way that it only takes one breath each day, breathing in and out only once in a day, though we actually breathe in and out every four seconds. The head really wants to slow the breath down, make it much slower. We are therefore able to say that the head is really doing cosmic breathing; only the breathing from the body is all the time rushing up to the head, fast, and the breathing then goes slowly from the head to the body.

Now if you have someone whose will is inhibited, someone who grows rigid, what happens in his case? The breathing in his belly is not functioning properly, and the slow head breathing wants to spread to the whole body. So the fellow lies there and Hansen stands on him. The head breathing wants to control the whole body and he grows rigid. But when someone is talking and talking and talking, the head breathing no longer tends to function properly, and the fast body breathing comes up, and he talks. In that case we have not hypnosis but flight of ideas, as it is called.

Now you may say — yes, you may truly say this: 'But the world is really not at all well organized, for with our head-breathing not in tune with our body-breathing we are all the time in danger of becoming imbeciles, with either the body-breathing or the head-breathing not getting its due.' So that's a serious problem. We are always in danger of becoming imbeciles because of this. You may say: 'Well, really, the world is not at all well organized!' But let me tell you something else, gentlemen.

Consider women, for instance. Since a woman is a human being, her body-breathing is faster and her head-breathing is slower. The slower breathing is the cosmic way of breathing. But the woman only does this in the head. In the rest of her body she has the fast body-breathing. The two merely influence one another. But let us assume the woman conceives. What happens then? You see, head-breathing is brought into a small area in the body-breathing area, in the womb, by the matter with which she is inseminated. During her pregnancy the woman therefore has the slow breathing in the head, but she also has slow breathing in her pelvic region. Slow head-breathing is brought into the body-breathing, and she then has head-breathing twice over. And what develops? First of all the head. So what has come into the body when she conceived? You see, the cosmic breathing which we otherwise have only in the head has come in there. The human being takes in the whole world in the breathing process. What happens when a woman conceives is really that where the human body normally only has the human body-breathing, cosmic breathing is implanted in the body for a period of nine months, the kind of breathing human beings only have in the head otherwise.

There you see the relationship between the human being and the whole universe. At the place where the human being develops in the womb the mother wants to breathe in such a way that a single breath takes a whole day. In this way she slows down the processes in that area and so is able not only to live but also to produce a new human being. With those slow processes in the head we have a life span of 72 years. When we say that human beings normally live for 72 years, and when we see that it takes nine months for a new human being to develop, it is not at all surprising that a new human being develops in nine months, for human beings live for 72 years and we merely compress the 72 years in the breathing process, and then a new human being develops. This is something that lets you gain deep insight into the whole of nature and may also give you a foundation for the other kind of thinking.

Consider the earth and the plants in the earth. Let us say this is the root of the plant, this the stem with the leaves, and up above the flower [Fig. 24]. When you look at the root, it has salts everywhere around it in the soil. You have salts everywhere down there. These salts are heavy. The root is therefore wholly within gravity. But it is a strange thing with gravity. For it is overcome. If you were to take human heads that had been cut off, they would have quite a weight. The human head is heavy. Or take a pig's head — it is heavy. You don't feel the weight of the head as it sits on your shoulders, because gravity is overcome. In plants, too, gravity is overcome. For if the plant were to feel heaviness in its leaves it would not grow upwards but more and more downwards. But a plant grows upwards, overcoming gravity. In overcoming gravity the plant opens up to the

Fig. 24

light. The light becomes active in it, and the light comes down from above, which is the opposite direction to gravity. The light is active in it, and the light comes down from above, in the opposite direction to gravity. The plant thus goes more and more up into the light, grows more and more. As a root it was implanted into the salts of the earth; now it is exposed to the sun and its light. As it is exposed to the sun and its light, fertilization occurs here. The ovary develops and the seed, and a new plant develops under the influence of the light. The cosmic breathing of which I spoke in human beings, implanted at conception, is brought to the plant year by year through the light. The plant thus grows from gravity to light and thus also fertilization.

We shall say, therefore, that something which we can only discover in human beings by using our mind, so that we know that cosmic breathing comes in there, and a little bit of head develops then in a particular place inside the human body, we can also see with our eyes when we look at plants. This is extraordinarily interesting. Looking at a flower, one is able to say: 'There the universe—the cosmos is also the universe—fertilizes the flower.' The rest of it, with the pollen grain coming in and so on, is merely by the way; it has to be there because in the physical world everything has to happen physically. But in reality it is the light which comes from the universe and fertilizes the flower, and this creates the seed for the new plant.

But, gentlemen, surely you can see what is really happening? We cannot really see what happens because it is so small. But we can see it after all! Let us consider what is happening with the plant in a completely different way. Let us assume this is the earth [Fig. 25]. Don't look at a plant now, but at the earth, how mists rise at a distance—maybe looking at it from a mountain, there it is easiest to see. There the mists are rising. They consist of water. If you were to look at a plant, the situation would not be all that dissimilar,

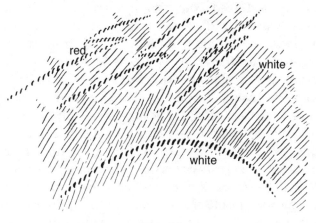

Fig. 25

it would be similar. Looking at such a plant—you'd have to sit there for a long time, however, observing all the time—you'd see that to begin with it is low, then it rises, opening out into leaves. But the mists also open out as they rise. So look at the earth here. It is only water which rises, not the solid parts you get when a plant is growing. But the water is rising. When the plant reaches a certain point up there it is fertilized out of the cosmos. When the water, here rising as mist, reaches a certain point, it is also fertilized out of the cosmos. And what happens then? Lightning develops, gentlemen! It does not happen all the time, of course, but when fertilization occurs and things are as clearly apparent as they are in summer—the lightning also comes at other times, but then it is invisible—the water is fertilized with light and heat by the universe. The same process which occurs in the plant also happens up there, and lightning makes it visible. And when the mist has been fertilized up above it comes down again as fruitful rain. So when you see a cloud of mist rising it is really a gigantic but extremely thinly spread plant. This opens up its flower up there in the cosmos, it is fertilized, contracts, and the fertilized droplets come down again in the form of rain.

This explains lightning for you. People imagine huge Leiden flasks up there or giant electricity generators; but that is not so. In reality the waters of the earth are fertilized out there, so that they can fulfil their function on earth again. And the process which happens in the plant only happens much lower down because the plant is more solid. You always get these tiny flashes of lightning up here in the region of the flower when it is the right time of the year; it is just that we do not see them. But these tiny flashes of lightning cause fertilization to occur. The rain and mists show you the same phenomenon which also occurs when a plant is fertilized. And this then also goes as far as the human being, where cosmic breathing, the breathing of the universe, which normally is only in the head, occurs in the human abdomen.

Now take a cataleptic person. What has happened in his case? Well, gentlemen, if one were to examine the cataleptic body one would find that it has grown particularly rich in salts. It has grown similar to a plant root, particularly in the head. If our head gets as rich in salts as a plant root, we grow imbecile, with the rigidity of the head spreading to everything else. So if you see people who cannot decide to go, or even to lift a hand, or get out of bed in the morning — they've got too much salt in their heads, have grown too much like the root of a plant. If you see people who are always talking and talking, they have grown too much like a flower. For when we talk we really only say part of what we know. But the people who keep talking all the time really always want to tell us everything they can. They would really always want to create a complete human being, because it is really their belly which is talking. And in drawing the world to itself, taking it into itself, the belly then becomes a head. But it is going too fast then, the way it does in the belly and in human breathing.

We are therefore able to say that Hansen made the people he placed across two chairs before he stood on them too much like a plant root in their heads. There you see the relationship between the human head and the plant root. One can actually make the whole head similar to a plant root. And he made the people whom he persuaded to eat a potato as if it were an apple similar to a flower. There you see the similarity between the belly human being, that is, the abdominal human being, and the flower. The things Hansen showed to the scientists are still being done today, but people have not yet found the explanation, an explanation which bit by bit takes one into the whole universe.

So, now we can also answer the question if nature is really so badly organized that we may grow imbecile by breathing wrongly either in the head or the belly, on the one hand cataleptic with head-breathing, on the other hand talkative because we suffer from flight of ideas and cannot use the will. Now if someone considers this extremely stupid and says that if he had had the task of creating the world he'd have made it a bit differently, so we would not face the danger of growing imbecile in one of two possible directions, we can say to him: 'If this were not the case, if we were not able to have head-breathing also in the human abdomen, the head-breathing that develops when we grow rigid, the human being could never develop and there could be no fertilization. So then there would be no human beings on earth.'

You see therefore that the risk of growing imbecile is connected with the fact that we are actually able to come into existence. So if there had been the intention anywhere in the natural world that there should be no human beings, then, you see, there would also be no problem about people growing imbecile. But as there had to be human beings there also has to be the risk of growing imbecile. We have no reason to rail at nature because we can see how things are connected. After all, someone might also come and say: 'Really, how silly it is that 2 times 2 makes 4. I wish it would make 6, for then I'd have more.' But this cannot be. And in the same way it cannot be that the human being exists on earth without there being a risk of growing imbecile. We simply have to understand these things properly. We shall then also be able to see things in the right way everywhere.

Looking at lightning, one would then say: 'Is the lightning only up there?' Oh no, the lesser lightning is there all summer as the plants are fertilized — passing over the pastures, over the woodlands. And finally there is a lightning that always happens in us. Everywhere within us we have the same phenomena which we see occasionally when there's lightning, for our thoughts flash up like lightning in us. But compared to the tremendous flash of lightning outside, the process in our thinking is only a faint one. But now you'll also be able to say to yourselves: 'It does mean something to say, as I look at the lightning, that I am seeing cosmic thoughts. For this is the same process which is also inside me.' You need to look at things scientifically and not in a superstitious way.

You see, it is certainly interesting that by the end of the nineteenth century scientists had reached a point where such important things were not taken note of, and it needed a charlatan, a mountebank like Hansen to come along and show them. It was only after this that attention was paid to these things. You can see, therefore, that science was not as good in the last third of the nineteenth century as people like to say it was. Yes, major discoveries were made in outer ways, X-rays and so on were discovered, but people actually had no desire to know anything decent about the inner life of human beings, and still do not have the desire to this day. Because of this our modern science does not apply to human beings and does not help at all when it comes to humanity. You may build as many universities as you like, the processes that are active in the human being will not be explained to you if you go to them. At the same time they also won't tell you what really happens when plants are fertilized. And when mists rise and rain falls the explanation is that it is not much different from when you cook something on a stove—the vapours rise and then come down again. But that's not how it is, for when the vapours rise they reach a sphere up above where they are fertilized by the universe. And lightning is proof that they are fertilized. And there we actually see fertilization take place, a process that also happens elsewhere.

The situation is that this has great significance. Take a year. You have winter and summer in a year, just as you have day and night within 24 hours. And a human life has 25,920 days. If you take 25,920 years you get the time when the earth did not yet exist and when it will no longer be. We are now more or less a little bit beyond the mid-point, with the earth in existence for something above 13,000 years. After another 11,000 years or so it will perish again. Just as man lives 25,920 days, so does the earth live 25,920 years, the way it is now. It changes. It was young once, is now getting old. And it is extremely important for us to know that the waters need to be exposed to the universe year after year. At some point, in some place on this earth, the water must be exposed to the universe every year, otherwise the earth would not be able to live. The earth lives with the universe as we live with the air. If someone were to take away the air that is around us on earth, we would not be able to take our 25,920 breaths each day. If someone were to take away the sun, that is the light, the earth would not be able to live. Thus the earth lives with the help of the whole universe, just as we live with the help of the air that surrounds us. It would thus be right to say that we go for walks on the earth, and the earth goes for walks in the universe. We breathe on earth; the earth breathes in the universe.

You see, we could develop a peculiar science. The human head is round, as you know [*drawing on the board*] and has hairs on it here, unless a person is very old. Now there are creatures in these woods—this may not be desirable, but it happens. Let us assume they take the dandruff here and create a place where the cleverest of them always get together to teach the ignorant ones. That would be a louse university on the human head itself. Well, we can imagine such a thing. What would the clever lice teach the ignorant ones? They would teach: 'The head is lifeless, for we walk about on it. Lifeless dandruff develops. Digging down a bit we come to lifeless bone.' The clever lice would explain all this to the ignorant lice at their louse university up there. They would explain the human head more or less the way we explain the earth at our human universities. The louse professors—forgive me, I do of course mean the ones up there on the head—would therefore have no idea that the head is alive. They would develop a geology of the head and declare the head to be dead. But gentlemen, this is what people do in our universities! The earth is declared to be dead. They know nothing about its breathing. For one would never discover anything about human breathing at the louse university and therefore nothing about it would be explained. They would say: 'Man is dead; the human head is a dead sphere.' And unless the head lice were to make contact in some way with the body lice, the head lice would never know that there is a body.

And that is how it is. Unless human beings on earth make contact with other entities of a higher kind they'll never discover that the earth sends its waters out into the universe and is fertilized, that it breathes and is fertilized. Yes, taking the idea of the kind of science taught at the university on our head, we can really get an idea of what science on our earth is like. For that is truly how it is. And you can see from this that it will indeed be necessary for us to go beyond the things we can easily understand. We have to go beyond.

And a true science of the spirit that proceeds in an equally scientific way will be able to take us beyond and therefore also explain the things which Hansen first presented in his day.

Well, gentlemen, we've not yet finished with this question of hypnosis and with the rest of it. I'll say a few things about them the next time we meet, for they need to be compared with the situation in natural sleep. At 9 o'clock next Wednesday I want to talk to you about what happens when people sleep, what happens when someone develops catalepsy—for in ordinary sleep you can't lie on two chairs and be trodden on—the difference between sleep and hypnosis, the difference between catalepsy and flight of ideas.

How conscience developed in the course of human evolution. Unbornness and immortality. Teachings of Aristotle and the Roman Catholic Church

Well, gentlemen, if you have something you want to discuss or ask today, please do.

Question: Conscience is a marvellous thing people have. If you've done something, you'll think of it. And even if you are no longer thinking of the things that lie in the past, you do know you have a conscience. It would be interesting to know if the conscience can also be killed, so that it may be forgotten. The way people are today one would assume that conscience is dead for a large part of the human race.

Rudolf Steiner: You see, gentlemen, that is really a big question, but it does relate to the things we have been considering in the previous talks. I have tried to explain to you, step by step, that the human being, consisting of physical matter, also contains an ether body—which is a body of a very different kind that cannot be perceived or seen with our ordinary senses—an astral body and I organization, or one might also say I body. The human being has these four parts.

We now have to think about what happens when a person dies. As I have told you on a number of occasions, when a person sleeps, the physical body and the ether body remain lying in his bed. The astral body and the I go outside, so they are then no longer in the physical body and ether body. But when a person dies, the part that is laid aside is the physical body. It is then a real physical body; the other three parts—the ether body, the astral body and the

I—go out of it. As I told you, the ether body remains connected with the I and the astral body for a few days. Then it separates from them in the way I have told you, and the human being then lives in his I and his astral body. He lives on and on in the world of the spirit which is the one we really seek to discover in our life on earth through the science of the spirit. We are therefore able to say that now, whilst we are on earth, we know something of a world of the spirit; then we shall be in that world.

We come down to earth again after a time, however. Just as we go from birth to death in life on earth, so we then go through a world of the spirit and finally come down again. We assume the physical body which is the gift of our parents and so on. So we come down from the world of the spirit. This means that we were spirits, let us say, before we came into this world. We have come down from the world of the spirit. You see, gentlemen, it is extraordinarily important for people to know that they come down from the world of the spirit with their I and their astral body. Otherwise there can be no reason at all for people to talk about spirit in any way as they grow up. If they'd never been in the realm of the spirit they simply would not talk of the spirit.

You know there was a time on earth when people did not talk about life after death as much as some people do today. But they would talk a lot about their life before they came down to earth. In earlier times people did altogether talk more about the way things were for human beings before they assumed flesh and blood than about the way things were afterwards. In earlier times people felt it was much more important to remember that they were souls before they became human beings on earth. Now, the evolution of the human race on earth is something of which I have not said so much until now, but because of the question that has been asked, let us talk a bit about this today.

Going back in time by 8,000 or 10,000 years, let us say, we would find conditions here in Europe to be pretty wild still. But at that time, about 8,000 years before our time, life was extremely highly developed over in Asia. There's a country here in Asia [*drawing on the board*] that is called India. This would be the island Ceylon, up there would be the Ganges, a mighty river, and up there a mountain range, the Himalayas. The people who lived in this India — as I said it is over there in Asia — had a highly developed cultural life. I'll call them Indians today. At the time the name did not yet exist. But today we call the country India and so I'll use the term. Now of course, if we were to go back and ask those people, 'What do you call yourselves?' they would say: 'We are the sons of gods,' for they would be speaking of the land in which they were before they were on earth. There they themselves had still been gods, for in those times people would have called themselves gods when they were spirits. And if you had asked them: 'What are you when you are asleep?' they would have said, 'When we are awake we are human beings, when we go to sleep we are gods.' To them, to be gods merely meant to be different from the way you were when awake, to be more in the spirit.

These people therefore had a highly developed civilization and it was not so important to them to talk of life after death but rather of life before one is born, of this life with the gods, as they put it.

You see, no written records have come down from these people. But they did, of course, continue — you know there are also Indian people today — and at a much later time they wrote great literary works called the Vedas. The singular is 'Veda'. It really means 'the word'. People said to themselves: the word is a gift of the spirit, and in the Vedas they wrote down what they still knew of the other world. They did know much more in earlier times, but today we have only the Vedas as physical records that can be studied. They were written much later. But from them, from these things written down much later, we can see that those people still knew quite definitely that the human being was in a world of the spirit before he came down to earth.

If we now go back to about 6,000 years before our time we find civilization to be much less highly developed in this area. Civilization in India was then going down. The ancient Indian civilization of which scholars still speak today will by then have gone down from its original high level. But there, to the north of it [*drawing on the board*] — this would then be Arabia — there to the north, up there, a civilization was developing in an area that would later be Persia. I have therefore called it the Persian civilization. A completely different civilization developed there. It is quite remarkable. You see, if we go back to the ancient Indians who lived 2,000 years before these people here, we always find that they really thought very little of the earth world. They would always be mindful of having come to this earth world from the world of the spirit. They knew this very well. They did not think much of the earth world; they only had regard for the world of the spirit, and they would say they felt as if they had been cast out. Anything that existed on earth was not particularly important to them. But here in this place, that is, 6,000 years before our time, in the area known as Persia today, esteem for the earth arose for the first time. They had regard for life on earth in such a way that they would say to themselves: 'Yes, light is indeed most valuable, but the earth, too, is valuable in its darkness.' And the view gradually developed that the earth is equal in value and that it fights against heaven. And this struggle between heaven and earth was what people considered particularly important for 2,000 or 3,000 years.

Then, going back just 3,000 or 4,000 years, we come to a country over there, going from Arabia across to Africa, where the Nile is — Egypt. The Egyptians were the people who were more towards the west over there in Asia, more towards Europe, and they liked the earth even more. Going back 3,000 or 4,000 years we thus find these Egyptians, we might say a third kind of people—Indians, Persians, Egyptians—building those enormous pyramids. But the main thing they did was to manage the Nile. The river would flood the land with its rich soil year after year, and they channelled it in such a way that those floods would prove a benefit in every direction. They developed geometry, as it is called. They needed this. Geometry and the art of the surveyor were developed. People came to like the earth more and more. And you see, to the degree in which people came to like the earth when on earth, they were less able to see that they had come from a world of the spirit. I'd say they forgot this more and more as time went on, for they came to like the earth more and more, and in the same way it also became more important to them to say that one lives on after death.

Now, as we have seen, life after death is a certainty for human beings, but in earlier times, before the Egyptians came along, people did not give so much thought to immortality. Why? Because they took it as a matter of course. Knowing they had come from a world of the spirit, and had merely assumed a physical body, they never had any doubt but that they would be in a world of the spirit again after death. But here, in Egypt, where people were not giving so much thought to being in the realm of the spirit before life on earth, the Egyptians got terribly afraid of dying. This enormous fear of death is something which has not really existed for more than 3,000 or 4,000 years. The Indians and Persians had no fear of death. We can actually prove that the Egyptians had this terrible fear of death. For you see, if they had not had this appalling fear of dying, it would not be possible for English people and others today to go to Egypt and then exhibit mummies in their museums!

People were embalmed in those times, using all kinds of ointments and substances. They put people in their coffins looking the way they had looked in life, carefully preserved. People were embalmed and made into mummies because it was thought that if one kept the body together the soul principle, too, would remain for as long as the body still existed on earth. They preserved the body so that the soul principle would not suffer any kind of harm. So there you have the fear of dying. The Egyptians would use all the powers in earthly matter to bring about immortality. They also knew a great many other things that later came to be lost.

The next people to attract our attention were a bit to the north of Egypt, in Greece, in what is Greece today. Ancient Greece was very different, however. You see, the Greeks had almost completely forgotten about life before birth. Only a few individuals in particularly advanced schools called the 'mysteries' would still know of it. But generally speaking, people in Greek civilization had forgotten about their life in the spirit before birth, and they loved life on earth more than anyone. A philosopher who lived in ancient Greece in the fourth century before the Christian calendar began was Aristotle.[43] You see, we are now close to the Christian era. Aristotle presented a view that had not existed before. The view he presented was that when a child is born it is not only a body which is born but also a soul. So it was in ancient Greece that the view first developed that the human soul is born with the body, but that it is then immortal, that is, goes through death to live in the world of the spirit. Aristotle then developed a peculiar view. He had really forgotten all the wisdom of earlier times and his view was that the soul is born together with the body. But when someone dies, the soul remains, having only one life on earth behind it. And it then has to look back on that one life on earth for all eternity.

Just think what a terrible prospect that must have been! If someone had done something bad here on earth, he would be unable to make this good for all eternity, but would always have to look back, always see the scene where he did something bad. That was the prospect Aristotle offered.

There followed Christianity. During the very early centuries people understood Christianity a little bit. But when the Roman Empire absorbed Christianity, which then had its firm seat in Rome, people no longer understood it. People did not understand Christianity.

Now the Christians always held Councils. High Church dignitaries would meet and decide what the large herd of the faithful were to believe. You know, the view was then that there are shepherds and sheep, and the shepherds decided at those Councils what the sheep should believe. At the eighth of these Councils the shepherds decided for their sheep that it would be heretical to believe that human beings lived in the world of the spirit before they were born. And so Aristotle's earlier views became the dogma of the Christian Church. Humanity was literally forced to know nothing in this way, never even to think that the human being has come down from the world of the spirit with a soul. This was forbidden.

When materialists say today that the soul is born with the body and is nothing but a bodily element, this is exactly what people have learned from the Church. The thing is, people think they go beyond the Church in becoming materialists. But no, people would never have become materialists if the Church had not got rid of perception of the spirit. At that eighth ecumenical Council in Constantinople the Church got rid of the spirit, and this continued all through the Middle Ages. It is only now that we have to discover again, through the science of the spirit, that the human being existed as soul before he was on earth.

This is the important thing, the most tremendously important thing.

Anyone who looks at human evolution on earth can see very clearly that people originally knew that human beings exist in the spirit before they come down to earth. It was merely forgotten as time went on, and later was actually forbidden, following the decision made at the Council.

Now we have to understand what this means. Just think, people who lived until Egyptian times, that is in early millennia, knew: 'Before you walked about on this earth you were in the world of the spirit.' Yes, they did not just bring down some kind of vague, general knowledge from the world of the spirit, but an awareness of having lived there with other spirits. And their ethical impulses also came from this. 'I can see what I am meant to do here on earth from the way things are here on earth,' those ancients would say; 'and as to anything else I am meant to do, I merely need to remember what was before birth.' They brought their ethical impulses down with them from the world of the spirit. You see, if you had asked people in those ancient times, 'What is good? What is evil?' they would say: 'Good is what the spirits want with whom I was before I was on earth; evil is anything they do not want.' But every single one of them would say this to himself. Today, gentlemen, it has been forgotten.

In Greece, the situation was a strange one. People had so much forgotten that there is life before birth that Aristotle was moved to say: 'The soul is born with the physical body.' The ancient Greeks therefore no longer had any idea that they had had a life before birth. But they felt something of that life in them. You know, whether one knows something or not really does not influence the real situation. I can say for as long as I like, 'There's no table behind me, I don't see any table' [*stepping back and bumping into the table*], but the table is definitely there, even though I do not see it. Life before birth continued to be there, and people felt something of this inwardly. And in about the fifth century before the Christian calendar started they began to call this their conscience. In about the fifth century before the Christian calendar started, the word 'conscience' first came up in Greece. It did not exist before that. The word 'conscience' thus came into being because people had forgotten life before birth and gave a name to something of it which they still felt inwardly. And it has been like this ever since. People sense life before birth in themselves but they'll say, 'Well, that's how it is. It comes into existence somewhere down there and then it comes popping up,' but they don't take any real note of it.

You see, that was a good thing for the Church. For what was it then able to do? Well, gentlemen, in early times, when people knew they had lived as souls before they came to earth, they would say: 'Ethical principles lie in the things we know of our earlier life, of life before earth.' Now the Greeks only had a sense of conscience. And then the Church came in and controlled people's consciences. You know, the Church took hold of the situation and people were told: 'You do not know what you are meant to do. The sheep do not know this; the shepherds do.' And rules were established to control their consciences.

You see, there was need to do this, to get rid of the spirit by decision of a Council, for it was then possible to control the conscience which was what remained of the spirit for people. And the Church then said: 'No, nothing existed of the human being before he existed on earth. The soul is born with the body. Any who do not believe this serve the devil. But we, the Church, know what goes on in the world of the spirit and what human beings are meant to do on earth.' This is the way in which the Church took control of human conscience.

It is possible to give chapter and verse for this. For you

see, this continued to play a role even in the nineteenth century, sometimes in a most terrible way. There was someone in Prague, for instance, in the 1830s and 1840s whose name was Smetana.[44] He was the son of a Roman Catholic verger who, of course, was a good Catholic. The father felt that one must believe what the Church says. He had a son. People were rather ambitious in those days and sent their children to grammar school. But they did not really learn very much at the kind of grammar schools they had in Prague in those days. Basically they learned very little. Young Smetana was thus educated at a grammar school. And the way things were in those days was that anyone who really wanted to learn anything would become a priest. Young Smetana therefore also became a priest. The situation in Prague and also in the rest of the Austrian Empire in those days was that grammar schools, too, would be staffed by priests. And when he had to teach others himself, Smetana would read somewhat different books from those that were prescribed reading for priests. The result was that he gradually came to doubt things, above all one particular dogma. He said to himself: 'Surely it is a terrible thing that a person is said to be born, live his life on earth and then go through death, and if he was an evildoer he must then look only at the bad things he has done on earth for all eternity — the Church would illustrate the matter as required — and never be given the opportunity to change for the better!'

Now you see, this man Smetana lived in an establishment of his order. But when he became a teacher, he felt too confined there and moved into a temporal home where he gradually read more and more — anthroposophical books weren't available then — of Hegel, Schelling and so on, people who wrote at least some sense, the beginnings of sense. Smetana then began to feel more and more in doubt about the eternal nature of punishment in hell, for according to Aristotle an evildoer goes through death and must then live on as an evildoer for ever and ever. The dogma of eternal punishment in hell which was then adopted by the Church at its Council came from this idea. It is not a Christian dogma but came from Aristotle. It is not at all true to say that it is a Christian dogma, this dogma of punishment in hell; it came from Aristotle. But people did not know this.

Smetana did come to see it, however. He then started to teach something that was not entirely in accord with the teaching of the Church. It was in 1848 that he taught something that was not quite in accord. He was first of all given a serious warning, a long letter written in Latin in which he was told to repent and return to the bosom of the Church, for it had made the shepherds extremely angry that he was teaching the sheep something that had not been laid down by the shepherds. He replied to that first letter, written in Latin, that he felt it was hypocritical to say something that went against one's convictions. A second letter in Latin brought an even more severe warning. And when he did not reply to this, for that would have been pointless, it was proclaimed in all the churches in Prague one day that a most important ceremony was to be performed at which one of the lost sheep, who had actually become a shepherd, would be excluded from the Church.

Old father Smetana, the verger, was one of the people who had to distribute the notices. He was still a faithful Catholic. You can imagine what it meant that the whole of Prague was called on to come and condemn Smetana's son, who was to be excluded from the Church for all eternity, and so on, and the father had to take the notices around himself! The church had never been as full in Prague as it was on that day. All the churches in Prague were full. And it was proclaimed from every pulpit that the apostate Smetana was cast out by the Church.

The consequence was — the Smetana family did of course have a disposition for tuberculosis — that first of all Smetana's sister died of grief, then the old father died of grief, and soon after Smetana himself died of grief, of the pain. But this is not the point for us, is it, but the fact that Smetana no longer proclaimed eternal punishment in hell, the way he saw it.

All this has to do with the idea of conscience evolving in human beings. Something human beings have retained in them from their life before earth lives in them and speaks as the voice of conscience. And when it comes to conscience, we can say to ourselves that conscience cannot have originated in the physical matter of the earth. For just imagine someone has a tremendous yearning for something, let us say. Such a thing has been known to happen. It is the material substances in his body, the physical matter of the earth, which urge him on and keep pricking so that he develops this yearning. His conscience will tell him: 'You must fight such desires.' Well, gentlemen, if the conscience had also come from the body this would be just as if someone were supposed to walk forward and back at the same time! It's nonsense to say our conscience comes from the body. Our conscience is connected with something we bring with us to earth from the life we have in the spirit before we are born. But, as I said, the awareness that our conscience comes from the world of the spirit has been lost to human beings, and in the case of someone like Smetana it began to dawn again in the nineteenth century because of this terrible business of punishment in hell. Conscience belongs to the human being himself. He has it in him. What good would be all the conscience one has in one if one were to go through death and then had to see for ever and ever how bad one has been? One would not be able to help oneself in that situation, and in that case, having a conscience would be quite pointless!

We can say, therefore, that if this is the human being [*drawing on the board*], his conscience lives in him. His conscience is something he has brought with him from the world of the spirit into life on earth. The voice of conscience in him says: 'You should not have done that, and you should not have done that!' A human being on earth says: 'That is what I want to do; it is my wish.' His conscience says something different, for it comes from the eternal human being. And it will only be when the human being has laid aside his physical body that he will realize: 'It is you yourself that always spoke with the voice of your conscience. It is just that you did not notice this during the time you lived on earth. Now you have gone through death. Now you have become your own conscience. Your conscience is now your body. Earlier, you did not have a conscience. Now you have your conscience and you live on with it after death.'

But the conscience must also be said to have a will. You see, all the things I have told you about have happened. The Greeks had forgotten about life before earth. The Church had made it a dogma that people must not believe in a life before earth. The conscience was completely misunderstood. All this had come to pass. And then there have of course always been great scholars. But the great scholars of medieval times did, of course, think there could be no life before earth, for the Church had forbidden people to believe this.

One man who had to face this dilemma, for example, was Thomas Aquinas who lived from 1225 to 1274. Being a Roman Catholic priest, he had to adopt the dogma of the Church. But he was a great thinker. And he had to say, with regard to the things I have told you about today: 'When someone dies, he will see only his past life on earth, in all eternity, never anything else. He will see just this.' So what did Thomas Aquinas do? He said people had only their thinking mind for all eternity, but no will. They had to look at their life when they had died but could no longer change anything. Thomas Aquinas was one of the great Aristotelians of the Middle Ages exactly because he said: 'When someone has done something bad on earth, he will have to look at it for ever; when someone has done something good, he'll for ever see the good.' The soul was said to have a mind, therefore, but no will.

This is not in accord with the truth. The truth is that after death we do look at what we have been, be it good or bad, but we still have the will, the whole power of soul, to change this. And so it happens that when we look at our past life we shall, of course, see it as it has been, but we then go on to live in the world of the spirit and see what should have been different. And it will then be quite natural for us to want to come down again and make amends. We'll get things wrong again, of course, but there will be further lives still, and we shall reach the goal of developing into a complete human being.

In the Middle Ages, Thomas Aquinas was only able to believe in the mind and its insights and not the will. And nineteenth-century people like Smetana still suffered from this. The result was that other people then came in the nineteenth century who got really angry about this idea of the mind and its insights. For it still went back to the dogma of punishment in hell, though these people did not realize this. Schopenhauer,[45] for example, got really angry about it all, and he then said it was all a matter for the will. Yes, but if you say it all has to do with the will, then this will is too stupid and foolish. Schopenhauer therefore said the whole of creation and everything was due to the will. People who thought about things would get caught up in a terrible inner dilemma, as Smetana did in Prague. There were many such people. That was just an excellent example, where the difficulties have been put down on paper. But there were many such people.

And so we have to understand that human conscience is an inheritance from life before earth. The spirit speaks in our conscience. Something we were before we came to be on earth has entered into the flesh and speaks as our conscience. And when we shall have laid our bodies aside, the soul will continue to speak as our conscience after death, but it will not be powerless; it will have a will and need to make amends, to continue doing things.

You see, that is the difference between anthroposophy and all the things that have become Christian dogma today, for example. There nothing is known about the power possessed by the human soul to be active. There the human being dies and can then only look for ever on the things he has done in one life on earth, for it is said that the soul is born with the body in that one life on earth. To show it in diagrammatic form one would therefore have to say: 'If this is one human life on earth [Fig. 26, upper part, circle], it also has soul from its beginning, and when the individual dies — this is his birth, this his death — the life of his soul goes on for all eternity. I won't continue the drawing across a second board, for that comes too expensive, though I'd actually need a third as well! It goes on for all eternity. And the mind is said to look at the badness of that one life on earth for all eternity, for the mind was born together with the physical in life on earth. The man who established this was really the first materialist, and that would in fact be Aristotle.

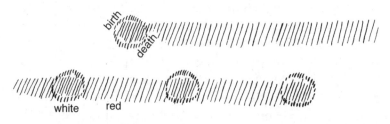

Fig. 26

Well, in anthroposophy we find that there is not just the one life on earth but that there are the lives that went before and those that follow as well. The individual has always something that is left over from the previous life; he does not know it exactly, but it is there inside him. That is his conscience. He then lays his body aside and lives on in his conscience. There [Fig. 26, lower part, red, left] he is basically all conscience until he is born again. Here [circle in the middle] conscience is again inside as a voice that speaks; and then [red, to the right] it lives in the outside world; it is there again.

It is actually the human being who creates new lives on earth for himself again and again on earth. This does, of course, go completely against the grain for a teaching where man is said to be nothing at all, and man is in all respects seen only as a creature. He is no mere creature, however, for he has creative powers himself. And that is the difference between anthroposophy and those other views. In anthroposophy, investigations show that those creative powers are also in man; man is creative. And the most creative part of him is indeed his conscience, which is a sacred inheritance from life before earth and which we take out into the other world again when we go through death.

Modern science here still takes its views from the Church. And it is an area where we should see things very clearly. For the matter went like this. Only things that were logical on the one hand and materialistic on the other went over to Rome. Modern nations then adopted it. But in the German language we sometimes still have something that has come down from the past, even if people do not realize this. This is truly strange. We can see from this how the human being is connected with events that happen on a large scale.

If we look at these countries up there in Asia today [pointing to the board], we have Siberia there. Those are regions with small populations now, but there was a time when they had large populations. The rivers would have been much, much bigger then. Siberia is a country that has gradually dried out, rising up higher, and people then went to the west, over to Europe. This was because the ground rose in Siberia. As a result many ideas people had in Asia came across to Europe, and these ideas live on in the European languages. And we have to say that the further west we go the less do we find of this idea of conscience. Yet the very word does show that among the people who created it there was a feeling that there was something there in the human being.

What does the word 'conscience' really mean? We have just said what the matter itself means: it is our inheritance from life before earth, something that remains part of our humanity. But the word 'conscience', what does it mean? You know, if we look at life on earth we say to ourselves there is no certainty about events that will come in two or three years' time; but one thing that is certain is that the human being has a spirit in him which existed before he came to exist on earth and which will continue after his existence on earth. And the word 'conscience' also relates to this 'knowing with certainty',[46] it is the most certain thing there can be. So the word actually points to something in the human being that is eternal. It is highly significant that the German word has a different content than the English 'conscience', for example, or other words used in the West. 'Conscience' is what comes together as knowledge on earth, knowledge massed together on earth.[47] But the principle in us that is called 'conscience' in German is the most certain thing there can be; it is not indefinite but absolutely certain. And it is absolutely certain that human beings on earth do not only believe in a life after death — which is the view held by Aristotle and the Church's believers — but also develop the will to shape it better and better, to shape the earth in an ever better way out of the spirit, meaning that the will lives on after death just as the mind does. Thomas Aquinas knew only of the mind living on. Now we must understand that the will lives on.

You see, gentlemen, it really is like this. We truly do not have to belittle a great scholar such as Thomas Aquinas was in the thirteenth century because he taught these things at that time. But it is a different thing for Thomas Aquinas to teach the only thing that could be taught in the thirteenth century than for people founding a Thomasian Society in Paris today to teach the same thing as was taught in the past — and indeed for Pope Leo XIII to instruct all priests and scholars in the Roman Catholic Church in the nineteenth century to speak only of the things which Thomas Aquinas taught in the thirteenth century.[48] Thomas himself would no longer say the same today!

These two things are now in opposition in the world, something like the Thomasians in Paris, who want to take people back to the past, and anthroposophy, where things are taught the way they are at the present time. When we consider something like human conscience, the most important thing about it is that it makes us see the eternal in the human being. But you cannot understand the eternal rightly if you do not also consider life before earth but think only of the idea of life after earth, called 'immortality', which has really only come into existence in Egyptian times.

You see, gentlemen, it was only 3,000 or 4,000 years ago that people started to talk about being immortal, meaning that their souls do not die when their bodies do. Before that people would say they were not born as souls when the body was born. They had a term we have to call 'unbornness'. That was the one side of it. And immortality is the other. Modern languages only have the word 'immortality'. The word 'unbornness' needs to come into existence again. Then people will say: 'Conscience is something in the human being that is not born and does not die.' And it is only then that people will really be able to value their conscience. For it only has meaning when we are able to appreciate its true value.

We'll continue at nine o'clock on Saturday, gentlemen.

Lung knowledge and kidney knowledge

Good morning, gentlemen! Have you thought of anything else you want to ask? — If not, I'd like to say something that relates to our previous subject, so that you may see how proof that the soul principle is present everywhere in the human physical organism, that is, in the human physical body, can be now found whichever way we approach the matter. Let us look at the human blood circulation from a particular point of view. As you know, blood flows in the blood vessels in our bodies. It goes from the lung, which has its arteries and in which oxygen is taken up as we breathe, to the heart, from the heart to the rest of the body. It is red during all this time but becomes more bluish as it passes through the body. This blue blood goes back to the heart and the lung where the oxygen makes it red again, and so the blood circulates, we might say, through the whole body.

Let us hold on to the thought that the blood flows through the body. A very simple flow cycle can serve to illustrate it. Just think we have a circular tube [Fig. 27]. Into it we put some red fluid so that it will show clearly. Now if we have such a tube in the outside world we need to have some kind of pump somewhere to set the fluid in motion. Let us imagine, therefore, we have some pump or other here [arrow] and that sets the fluid in motion. If I leave a hole at the top, the fluid will, of course, spray out there. But I don't want that, and so I add a tube up there. And now I set the fluid in motion so that it keeps going round and round. Can you imagine this? The fluid is made to go round. Now consider this. If the fluid is driven round

Fig. 27

by a pump here, then a small amount will rise in the tube here [at the top]. But it will only be a small amount as we keep the fluid moving. If I make the pump powerful, the fluid will rise a bit higher here; if I apply only little pressure it will rise less high. I am therefore able to measure the pressure in the circulating fluid by the height of the fluid up here.

Now you see, I can do something similar to this with human blood. If I insert such a little tube somewhere in a blood vessel the blood will rise some distance in that tube. I can thus insert a tube into some blood vessel — but not all of them. Imagine I have an artery somewhere — in the arm, let us say — and put in a tube here that is rather like an ampoule [*drawing on the board*]. The blood from the artery will flow up the tube a little bit; it goes through here and into the tube here. This small tube will be such that, depending on the person concerned, the level of blood in it will be higher or lower. With some people the blood will rise to a very high level, with others it will be less high. This shows that people have different blood pressures, for it is the pressure which is applied that shows itself in the tube. So you see, if the blood exerts a bit more pressure on the blood vessels, it will rise higher in the tube, if it exerts less pressure it will rise less high.

The materialistic view is that human beings also need a pump to drive the blood around. But this is an external instrument I have been drawing for you. In reality human beings do not have such a pump anywhere in their bodies, nor is the heart a pump. Human beings do not have a pump, but the blood moves because of something else. This is what we want to consider today.

But let us first of all consider the difference in height in this column of blood by which we measure the blood pressure. In a healthy person it is always at a particular level, between 120 and 140 mm, let us say, when someone is between 30 and 50 years of age. If the column is only 110 mm high, for example, when we apply such an instrument — we may call it a manometer — the person would be sick. He'd also be sick if it were 160 mm. If it is 160 mm, his blood pressure is too high; the blood is pressing too hard in his body. If it is only 110 mm, his blood pressure is too low, the blood is not pressing hard enough. You can see from this that we always have to have a specific blood pressure in our bodies. The blood must always exert a specific pressure. We have this blood pressure everywhere inside us. If we climb a really high mountain, the air around us will get thinner, of course, and because the outside air gets thinner the pressure from inside gets much greater. The blood will then come out through the pores. That is mountain sickness. You see, therefore, that we have to go around the world with a quite specific blood pressure.

Let us first look at people whose blood pressure is too low. People with low blood pressure grow extremely weak, tired, pale, and their digestion suffers severely. They grow feeble inside and do not properly manage to perform their bodily functions, and so they will go into a gradual decline.

If the blood pressure is too low, therefore, people grow tired and weak and sick.

Now let us look at people whose blood pressure is too high. There you sometimes see quite strange things. You see, if you push something like this instrument — it has to have a sharp point in front — into the skin, if you measure a blood pressure that is too high with it, you can be sure that such a person's kidneys will gradually grow useless. The kidneys start to develop their blood vessels, everything there is inside them, in a way they should not be. They calcify and grow enlarged; they degenerate, as people say. They no longer are the shape they should be. If you cut out the kidneys of such people with very high blood pressure after they have died, they look quite dilapidated.

The question is, where does all this come from? This connection with blood pressure and kidney disease is not really understood at all by those who think in materialistic terms. We have to realize that our astral body — I have told you about this; it is an invisible body in us — lives in this pressure we have in us, in the blood pressure. It is not true at all that the astral body lives in some substance, some form of matter; it lives in a force, in our blood pressure, and the astral body is healthy when our blood pressure is right, that is, between 120 and 140 mm in mid-life. If we have the right blood pressure, our astral body enters into the physical body as we wake up and feels well in there. It can spread in all directions. So if the blood pressure is right, about 120 mm, the astral body really spreads out in our blood pressure, and it can enter into every part of the physical body when we wake up. And whilst we are awake the whole astral body spreads everywhere in us if we have this 'normal' blood pressure, as it is called.

You see, it is the astral body which makes sure that our organs always are the right shape, the right configuration. Gentlemen, if we were to sleep all the time, so that the astral body would always be outside, the way it is when we sleep, our organs would soon grow fatty. We would not have proper organs. We need the astral body to stimulate the ether body so that we'll always have organs that are sound, having the right configuration. The astral body therefore always has to have the right blood pressure so that it may spread out.

Let us imagine someone goes into a room that is filled with carbon dioxide rather than air. He'd collapse; he'd be unable to breathe. The astral body and the I cannot live in such a body where the blood pressure is not right. They have to go out every time we go to sleep. Let us assume the blood pressure is too low. If the blood pressure is too low, the astral body does not enter properly into the physical body when we wake up. There is little astral activity in there then and the individual feels something rather like a continuous slight state of unconsciousness inside him. He will be weak as a result and his organs cannot be developed in the right way, for they have to be newly developed all the time. You remember I told you the organs have to be made new every seven years. The astral body must always be able to function in there.

Let us assume the blood pressure is too high. Now if the blood pressure is too high, what will happen? You see, I once told you that if the mixture of oxygen and nitrogen in the air were different we would find it hard to live. The air contains 79 per cent of nitrogen, the rest is mainly oxygen. The amount of oxygen is small, therefore. If the air contained more oxygen we'd be old people at the age of 20. We would age rapidly. It therefore also depends on the astral body if the body ages early or late. If the blood pressure is too high, the astral body likes being in the physical body. It is really in its element in our blood pressure and will then go in really deep. And what is the consequence? The consequence is that we have the kind of kidneys at 30 that we should only have when we are 70. We live too fast when the blood pressure is high. The kidneys are sensitive organs, and so they will degenerate early. Growing old has to do with the organs growing more and more calcified. And if the blood pressure is too high, the sensitive organs will calcify too soon. The kind of kidney disease one gets with high blood pressure is really a sign that the person has aged too soon, that is, whilst still young he has made these sensitive kidneys be the way they should only be in old age.

Now you see, gentlemen, the whole of this explanation which I have given you allows you to see that the human being does have something like a soul principle in his physical body, something I call the astral body, which goes out during the night. And so we may also say: Man lives in the forces that develop in his body. He lives in those forces, not in the physical matter.

Wherever you look, therefore, you find materialistic science has nothing to offer when it comes to the kind of thing I have just been explaining to you. It does not help people to discover what this is about. You'll always find it says in the books: if the blood pressure is high one must always fear the individual has kidney disease. But, it says in these books that they cannot show the connection. In reality they are therefore saying that they do not want human beings to have something that is supersensible in them, something spiritual, something with soul quality. They are saying they do not want this.

But we cannot explain these things without it. And this is really why people do not know where to turn today and have to admit this to all the world. It truly is the case, gentlemen, that the things that happen today, the overwhelming misery in the world which will get much, much worse in the immediate future because people simply do not want to accept anything that is of the spirit—for you must first of all know about something—this misery has come because people are not prepared to know anything about reality. And you cannot know anything about reality unless you consider the spiritual aspects. The way things have gone in the nineteenth century is that people were really only taught about superficial things. No one took care to see that they understood something about the soul element, about the spirit. And so people go about today and really have no idea at all that the elements of spirit and of soul do after all exist in this world.

You see, gentlemen, something extraordinarily important has happened as a result. One day, when much time will have passed and they are prompted by circumstance, people will overcome their reluctance and come to look at things again in the light of the spirit. Those people will say, at that future time: 'Yes, something tremendously important happened in human history at the beginning of the twentieth century.' Everything one is able to tell about the wars of earlier times is nothing compared to what has actually happened here in our day. Sometimes it is really quite unbelievable how people fail to realize that compared to what has been happening from 1914 right until now all those wars we read about in our history books are mere trifles. Those historical events are not at all great compared to what has been happening between human beings in the times we live in. And you see, to see what this is really about we have to look deeply into the reality of it all. But people don't do this today.

Now one thing to which I drew your attention is that the potato only came to Europe at a particular time. Now if you ask what do people eat most of today, the answer is: potatoes! And if you see the threat of starvation somewhere, the first thing people think of is how to get hold of potatoes. Today it is really so that people think of potatoes as something that has always been there. Well, gentlemen, if you'd lived five centuries ago you would not have eaten potatoes at all in Europe, for there weren't any! You would have been eating something else. But when one knows that everything depends on the spiritual realm one also knows that eating potatoes or not eating potatoes depends on the spiritual realm. And that is also how it is with many other things. There have been tremendous changes in human history in recent centuries, and all that talking in theories is of no value to us. You can have the best possible theories — Rousseau's theories, Marxist theories, Lenin's theories, anything you like, but these are all thought up, and you can't do anything with them if you lack the right knowledge. Thoughts only have value if you know what to do with them. All these people who have developed such excellent thoughts were utterly ignorant, if the truth be known. And it is a characteristic of our present time that people are really utterly ignorant. They want to present theories to people as to how to make the earth into paradise, yet they don't even know what happens to the human body when people eat potatoes. This is what causes one such heartfelt concern today, that people have not the least desire to know something. Now the masses are, of course, unable to do this, for they are persuaded that the knowledge possessed by those gentlemen at the university is absolutely right. And so schools are created for the people and they want to know what the others know today. But the truth is that exactly the people who ought to know things, who have made the business of knowing their profession, actually know nothing at all. And because of this people talk about all kinds of things today, but basically no one knows anything at all.

Now the potato is not, of course, the only thing, there are many other situations, but I am mentioning the potato because it is a particularly extreme example. An awful lot has really happened in these last centuries, and now, I'd say, it has led to a major discharge at the beginning of our twentieth century, so that enormously many things have happened. Today let us consider one of the things that happened, something that is extraordinarily important.

You see, gentlemen, I am going to mention something that may well make you laugh at first, but it is a serious matter nevertheless. You see, when a young fellow goes to university today or some other kind of college, he will be taken to a laboratory. He has to study there—he'll loaf around quite a bit as well—but you know, he has to study because he'll have to sit his exams later. You can more or less imagine how it all goes. But if we now go back to the people of whom I also told you also the last time we met, let us say to the ancient Indians—you'll remember the drawing I made for you, Asia—there the young fellows who were to be taught were not taken to a laboratory or a hospital but they would be told that above all else they must with great patience examine their inner parts. They had to sit down, their legs crossed, and always look at the tip of their nose, not look out into the world but always look at the tip of their nose. Well, gentlemen, what did this achieve? This was of course already at a time when the matter was falling into decadence. But there are still people who do this today, even in Europe; they want to get particularly clever inwardly and so they copy this. But it will achieve nothing today. But the people who did this in earlier times shut themselves off from the whole of the outside world in this way, for as you can imagine, you don't see much in the tip of your nose. All you practise is getting a squint in your eyes, if you always look at the tip of your nose. And if you don't walk but take all the weight off your legs, you also do not have gravity inside you. These people therefore eliminated gravity, eliminated all sensory impressions, they firmly plugged their ears and gave themselves up completely to their own bodies. That was what it was all about—not a matter of looking at the tip of your nose, which after all is not all that interesting, but of closing oneself off from the outside world.

This completely changed their breathing, however. It was the breathing, the lung, which became different in these people. When they used such a procedure to make their lungs function in a different way, images would arise in their mind's eye. They did indeed gain specific knowledge by this means, and were then able to tell people how things really are. Those people did know, for example, what happens with a plant, the way I have told you, because they had gone through this procedure. Today our young fellow at the university would say 'thank you very much' if they were made to sit in a row along the wall and asked to look all the time at the tips of their noses. People would consider that nonsense today. But you see, the only difference I get when I make experiments with things outside or on human beings is that when I do laboratory experiments I get to know about physical matter; when I do experiments on the human being I get to know the human being. Those people of old know the human being better than modern people do. And what was it they insisted on particularly, those people? That their lungs would function in a different way. And the lung would in turn stimulate the brain. In those earlier times it was thus truly the lung from which all the great knowledge and early wisdom came.

So it would be reasonable to say that if we have the lungs here in the human being [Fig. 28], and between them the heart, knowledge went from the lungs up into the head in those early times. This is in fact the secret about knowledge, that the human head is really quite unable to do anything. The head does not really know much of the world, it only knows what is inside. Gentlemen, if we had only the head and neither eyes nor ears, but just a head that was closed off all round, we would know a great deal about ourselves, but nothing about the outside world. And the most important

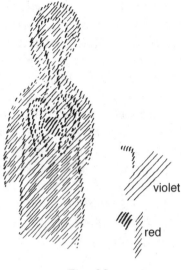

violet

red

Fig. 28

thing that comes into us from the outside world is the air. The air also stimulates the head, through the nose if nothing else, but very thin air also comes in everywhere through our eyes, through our ears everywhere. It is the air which sets the head in motion. We are thus able to say that if we go a long way back to those early millennia of which I have told you the last time, 6,000, 8,000 years back, we find people practised their breathing a lot in order to gain knowledge. They knew they had to press the air into the head in a different way and then they'd gain knowledge.

All people know today is that if they get air into their lungs it will vitalize them. But those ancients knew that if they drew in the air in a special way, as they looked at the tip of their nose, the muscles of the nose would be compressed, the air would be drawn in in a special way, and then knowledge would come in the head.

But you see, it went on like that until the Middle Ages, and even most recent times. Four hundred years after the birth of Christ, people then ceased to know anything. The knowledge vanished. But they still had things to remind them in their books. For that is the difference between earlier times and the times that began in about the eighth or ninth century before the birth of Christ. In those earlier times people had heads with which to know things, and in later times they had books by which to know things. That is indeed the difference. You know, in those ancient schools called mysteries it was not considered important to write down everything they knew. They would train people so that they were able to read in their heads. Someone who had been truly educated would be able to read in his head to know what was out there in the vast air space. His head would be a real book, we might say, but of course not in the sense in which we speak of bookish people today. Through breathing, the head had become something where wisdom could be found.

Then came the times when human heads were no longer worth anything. People did still have them, of course, but they were empty, and everything was written down. For some centuries before and also at the time of the birth of Christ, much, very much still existed in writing of the ancient wisdom. These things were burned by the Church, for they did not want this ancient wisdom, which people gained from their heads, to be passed on in any way to their descendants. You see, the people of the Church really had a terrible hatred of that ancient wisdom, and they eradicated it. With anthroposophy, the aim is to give people a head again that is not just an empty vessel. But it is something the Church really hates. Well, you can see that it does not exactly like it! Gentlemen, human beings are to be in a position again where they know things that you cannot find in books at all today, for the ancient wisdom has vanished, it has been burned, and the new things people have written in books is only about superficial things.

Well, everything people were thinking until the nine-teenth century was really only inherited from earlier times. It was, if I may put it like this, stimulated by the lung. Lung knowledge, we might say. The head stimulated by the lung, by the breathing — lung knowledge.

You see, the nineteenth century brought great scientific discoveries, but no thoughts. The thoughts were all taken from earlier times. It is really true that thoughts only existed in earlier times of human evolution. On the surface, great discoveries were made in the nineteenth century, but peo-ple were only thinking the old thoughts. That was still the old lung knowledge. And it seems rather amusing that we are able to say to a modern scientist: 'You despise the ancient Indian who would sit down, cross his legs, and look at the tip of his nose in order to have thoughts about the inner life. You don't do this any more. But you do use the thoughts he had, for they were written down, and you used them to discover X-rays, and so on.' It really is like that. All this was discovered with the old thoughts.

In the course of the nineteenth century, the human lung became completely unable, however, to give anything to the head. The human lung altogether went through a major change in the nineteenth century, and something else, the organs called the kidneys, actually became much more important than the lung in the course of the nineteenth century. These are in the first place strongly connected with the functions of the heart. The stimulant effect has moved from the lung to organs that lie lower down in the human being, and this has caused the great confusion in which humanity finds itself.

You see, the world of the spirit is, in a sense, still keeping an eye on the lung. When human beings had lung knowl-edge, they would be breathing in air and in doing so receive the stimulus for knowledge. Today people have to depend on getting the stimulus for knowledge from the kidneys.

But the kidneys will not give anything to the head of their own accord. You have to make an effort first, as I have described it in *Knowledge of the Higher Worlds*.[49] So in the first place we have to say that when the lungs still provided a stimulus for the human head, people were able to gain knowledge because a spiritual principle was still flowing into their lungs. Anything of the spirit that flows to the kidneys is at an unconscious level, so that people cannot know about it unless they go through the things in mind and spirit which I have described in *Knowledge of the Higher Worlds*, doing so in a fully conscious state.

What happens if people are not prepared to make such an effort? Well, gentlemen, the lung will remain in a condition where it provides no stimulus, and people will be completely dependent for anything they are able to know on their bellies, their kidneys. The change from lung to kidney knowledge has happened now, in the twentieth century, the time we live in. Lung knowledge still had a spiritual quality. Kidney knowledge has no spiritual quality for the human being unless we give it a spiritual quality.

Man has thus gone through a major change. This happened in the two decades we have lived through. Such an important thing has not been before in human nature, that the whole apparatus for gaining knowledge has slid down from the lung into the kidney. The astral body then did not find anything in the kidneys, and that is why there is such confusion, such a materialistic chaos, in all human heads.

So what would one say if one wanted to describe the real reason why there have been so many people in the twentieth century who did not know their way about in the world, who did not know what to do, and finally, when this was admitted, we got ourselves into this giant war? What was really going on there? If we want to find out what was going on, we must first take a bit of a look at the time that went before. You see, gentlemen, in the Middle Ages and later, terribly many people went to a particular place of pilgrimage called Lourdes, or to other places where the idea was copied. They went there because the clergy told them that they would get well if they did, if they had the water of Lourdes. Well now, only the name has really changed. In the nineteenth century the clergy would persuade people to go to Lourdes to get well, and more recently the medical profession have persuaded people to go to Karlsbad or Marienbad or Wiesbaden or some such place.

What did it all lead to? It really all came to this. The doctors would tell people: 'Well now, dear patients, your kidney system is not functioning properly. You need to drink as much of the waters at Wiesbaden or Karlsbad or Marienbad as possible,' — it all goes through the kidneys — 'and you have to push it through there.' So that for many people the state of health was such that during the winter they gave themselves up to their kidney functions, and it was the activity of the kidneys that would really think in them; during the summer they had need — for this really will not work unless there is a stimulus in mind and spirit, which they did not want, of course — to go to Karlsbad or Marienbad or to Wiesbaden, and there they would get their kidney system into a better condition again. As time went on, this business, where it was really always the abdomen for which people would take the cure, became a superstition.

Now you know what this was really about was that people should have developed an interest inwardly in activity, stimulus in mind and spirit. This is what they should have been looking for, for if there is no stimulus in mind and spirit at all the disorders which develop in the kidney region cannot be restored to order. And in the twentieth century the situation then was that all the people who should really have been thinking by means of their souls were merely thinking by means of their kidneys.

Gentlemen, a time will come when people will see more clearly, and the few who manage to keep a clear mind in the general confusion will say to themselves: 'What was it really, this great war at the beginning of the twentieth century? It was a kidney disease in the human race.'

You see, what matters is that we really discover the way things go together in reality. Then we'll know how to bring up young people, we'll know that it is quite unacceptable to teach them only the things they are being taught today. We'll know that we must use those wonderful years of youth, of childhood, to teach the young people something quite different. But the people of the nineteenth century were actually proud to say they knew nothing of soul and spirit, and the result was that this gigantic kidney disease developed which is still skulking about the world today.

At a future time people will ask: 'What clouded the minds of people at the beginning of the twentieth century? A kidney disease that went unnoticed.' This is what concerns us so deeply today. And we can decide to go in two directions. We can let things go on the way they are going now. The doctors will then have a great deal to do one day. People will be less and less able to use their common sense. They will come to think less and less of making sensible arrangements that will take them forward. The whole of the senseless way of going about things, which has really developed to a very high degree today, will reach its highest level. People will be weak, and the physicians will examine their urine. They'll find all kinds of nice things in there, you know — proteins, sugar, and so on. They will only discover that the kidneys are not functioning properly. For when you find all those things in the urine, the kidneys are not functioning properly. And they'll find: 'Strange, isn't it, that the world has never before produced as much sugar and protein as it does now!' But they won't know the real situation. At best some clever, crafty industrialist will get the idea of using the vast amount of sugar produced in his industry. So that is one direction.

The other direction is this. Let us stop talking about all the external arrangements and systems to begin with, and reform the people's life in mind and spirit, giving people decent ideas relating to the spirit. People will then discover how they should do things in outer terms so as to live properly. For it will only be if people have sensible ideas that we can hope they will be able to live the right kind of life in outer terms.

But, gentlemen, we'll not be able, of course, to achieve this by going on the way we have until now. It calls for a radical rethinking. And today's world will not get better by any kind of outer measures, but only if people begin to know something. You see, materialists imagine they know a lot about physical matter. But this is exactly what they know nothing about. This is the strange thing, that materialists do not know anything about physical matter. They will say for example: 'What has brought about this misery? Well, the misery is due to economic conditions.'

Well, you see, that is just like someone saying: What causes poverty? Poverty is caused by impoverishment. Just another word, isn't it? Economic misery is just another word for what we have today. It is just words, for people have created the economic misery, and man creates this because of the way he is. Today incredibly many people feel the urge to be racketeers, let us say. And all this is simply because the part of the human organism which is of a lower order and is setting the pace today should really be given a stimulus in mind and spirit. Materialists will merely say: 'Oh yes, this part of the organism which is of a lower order is important!' But we only realize why it is important through things we learn through mind and spirit. And so materialists are good at taking one's blood pressure, but they do not know what it means if the blood pressure is too high or too low, and that a low blood pressure means that the astral body and the I do not enter sufficiently into the physical body, whilst high blood pressure means that the astral body and the I enter too deeply into the physical body.

And today it is indeed the case that in the course of human history the blood pressure has very slowly and gradually grown too much, and people suffer from high blood pressure today. It really is the case that when a person wakes up today his blood pressure is too high; this then snatches at the astral body and the I, as it were. The result of this, of the blood pressure snatching at the astral body and the I, is that they go completely into the physical body. This has to be balanced out again by giving the person mental stimulus, so that he really takes some interest in things of the mind and spirit.

It is not enough to learn anthroposophical theories. If one only knows anthroposophical theories, it is merely the way people learned to read in the nineteenth century, the way they took up ideas in a superficial way. It should not be like this. The things we take in should be such that we make them our own inwardly.

You see, gentlemen, if you have been in stale air and go out into the open air, you take pleasure in this inwardly. And in the same way you should feel pleasure inwardly, experience interest, when you leave all the stuff that is called knowledge today and come into the fresh air of the soul, being told things of the spirit once more. Inner gladness, deep interest, is what we need for the life of the mind and spirit. And when people are full of interest the blood which has grown too heavy—the blood has grown too heavy in everyone today—will grow lighter again. The kidneys are made spiritual and the result will be that things will be better in the world when people want to know something again about the things that have been taken away from them for centuries. This is something one has to say over and over again, something I have to tell you in every possible way, for it is important for us to look the truth in the face and not let ourselves be blinded by science that is not science. I therefore wanted to add a few things today to the things I had told you on the previous occasions. Much can still be said about these things, but they will get clearer all the time.

We have to have a short break now in the series of talks. I have to go to England and will get someone to let you know when we can continue with this.

But what I wanted to make clear to you, especially at the end today, is how the great events in human history really have to do with what human beings are inwardly, and that this is the starting-point. Humanity therefore must first of all be enlightened, but enlightened about real things, not empty phrases. So this is what it is.

Druid wisdom. Mithraic sites. Roman Catholic ritual. Masonic rites. Ritual of the Christian Community

Gentlemen, it's been a long time since we were able to meet. Have you perhaps been able to think of something special, questions you'd like to discuss, during this time?

Member of the group: I would like to ask if the rite as it is celebrated today still has a connection with the world of the spirit, and how the rites of different nations relate to one another.

Rudolf Steiner: Well, gentlemen, here it will be interesting to consider the reason why a rite actually comes into existence, and what the intention is.

Perhaps I might just tell you something on this occasion which is of current interest because it has to do with my recent trip to Britain. It was really most appropriate that the course in Penmaenmawr[50] was given near an ancient mystery site. This was on the west coast of Britain, in Wales. There is an offshore island called Anglesey and there you still have ancient sites everywhere in the hills. They are in decay, and today one really only sees broken stones, I'd say, but if one knows one's anthroposophy one can certainly see what they once meant to people in that very place.

You see it would be just like going out into our hills here and finding such sites in them. Over there you find them everywhere, as it were, in the hills, and above all if a hill levels out at the top, so that you have level ground and even a slight depression. That is where those ancient sites would be. Today they are heaps of stones, but you can still see quite clearly what they looked like in the past. The smaller

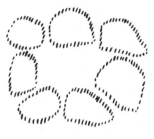

Fig. 29

ones consist of stones that were probably carried there once in the ice, and then dragged to the particular site where people wanted to have them. They were arranged in a kind of square, one beside the other, like this [Fig. 29]. Looking at them from the side, it would look like this. A large stone on top covered the others [Fig. 30]. The big mystery places would have similar stones [Fig. 31] placed in a circle, exactly 12 of them. The rite probably was at its height 3,000 or 4,000 years before our time, at a time when the area was only thinly populated, and there would be hardly anything except agriculture and animal husbandry. Writing and reading were quite unknown at the time when this rite was at its height. Writing and reading—they never even imagined that there might be such a thing.

Now we may ask what the significance was of that rite. Let me emphasize again that there was no reading and writing in those days. Now you know that when we want to

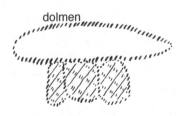

Fig. 30

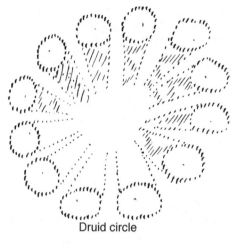

Druid circle

Fig. 31

get crops to grow in the field, to do really well, they have to be sown at particular times, and different things have to be done with them at particular times. And people also have to know the right times for getting their animals mated, and so on. This has to do with the way the earth relates to the whole of the cosmos around it, and I have told you about this on several occasions.

Now today people have their farmer's calendar and they'll look it up. It'll tell them what day of the year it is, and so they tend to forget that it is not a matter of arbitrary choice. You can't fix the dates whichever way you like, but have to fix them according to the movement of the stars, the position of the moon, and so on. Today's calendar makers calculate these things by following tradition. Calculations are made to show when this or that particular day will be. People are now working it out like this because at one time the days were calculated according to the position of the sun. You can still do it according to the sun today, but the people who generally observe these dates do not go by the position of the sun or of the stars but simply by the calendar, as it has been calculated.

In those earlier days that would have been unthinkable, for people could not read or write then. Such things only came later. So this takes us back 3,000 or 4,000 years, as I said. And reading and writing only came a little over 2,000 or 3,000 years ago in those regions. Those were early times, and the kind of reading and writing people had later on does not compare with what we have today, so you can't really say it existed then. At least the majority of the population did not know it in those days.

If you look at such a stone circle up on a hill you may think: The sun apparently — we know it is standing still, but you know we can put it like this because that is how things are, after all — the sun thus moves in orbit in cosmic space. It therefore casts a different shadow of this stone all the time, and you can follow this shadow all through the day. You can say that when the sun rises in the morning the shadow is there [*drawing on the board*], then it moves on a bit and the shadow is there, and so on. But the shadow also changes in the course of the year because the sun is always rising in a different place. It was like this in March, and a bit later on like this. And the wisdom of the learned person or the priest, if you like, the Druid priest who was appointed to observe such things in those times, lay in being able to judge this shadow. He would be able to know, therefore, that when the shadow reached this point here, this or that needed to be done in the fields. He was able to tell people this. He could see it from the position of the sun. Or if the shadow reached this point, let us say, the bull had to be taken around, the beasts had to be mated, for this had to be done on a particular day of the year. The priest would thus observe and know what needed to be done all through the year.

And so the whole of life was really governed by the

movements of the sun. Today people never think that they are doing the same thing, because they look in the calendar, as I told you. But in those days you had to go to the actual sources, you had to discover these things by considering the universe, as it were.

At any particular time, let us say in autumn, for example, it would be clearly established what had to be done in the fields, and the 'bull festival' would also be laid down for a particular time in the year from the things these people said. Then the bull would be taken round; at other times it would be kept away from the cows, and so on. The feasts of old were also fixed accordingly, and they would be very much in connection with these things. Today such an arrangement of stones would be called a Druid circle. This here [Fig. 30] is a dolmen or cromlech, with the stones characteristically standing like this, and covered at the top, so that the inside is in shade.

Now you see, gentlemen, people know, more or less, that the sunlight is sometimes more and sometimes less powerful, for they can feel it from the way they sweat or feel cold. What people do not know, however, is that the shade also varies, just as the light does. It varies in accord with the way the light varies. But people are not in the habit today of considering differences in a shadow. In those earlier times, people first of all developed the ability to tell the differences in a shadow. Within the shadow you see the spiritual aspect. The sun's rays have not only physical qualities but also spiritual qualities. And the Druid priest would observe the spiritual quality of the sun's rays in there, and it would depend on this if it was better to grow one particular plant in a particular country or another, for this depended on the spiritual quality that came down to the earth from the sun. The shadows also gave excellent opportunity to observe the moon influences. These play a particular role when it comes to mating farm animals, for example, so that the time for mating could be determined. And the whole year was really considered according to those observations made of the sun.

Now if we were to dig down underneath such a cromlech, we would find that it also served as a burial place. These stones were set up in places where people were also buried. The significance of this is that when a human being has left his body, that body has a composition which is different from everything else. The soul, the spirit, has dwelt in the body for a whole lifetime. When the body dissolves, the powers in it are different from those in the rest of the hills. And those powers would stream up and make it easier for people to see things rightly inside, in the shade. Those people still knew powers of nature that were very different from the powers people were to know later on.

And when one sees individual stones raised high up in some hilly regions—this is something one also sees in other parts of Britain; I saw it in Ilkley, for instance, where the first course was given during my visit to England[51]—with the site well chosen—one had a wide view over the area from up there—you'll find such signs there [Fig. 32], swastikas, a symbol used to create much mischief in Germany today. This swastika is now being worn by people who have no idea that it was once a sign used to indicate to people who came from a long way off that the people in that place saw

Fig. 32

not only with their physical eyes but also with the eye of the spirit. In my book *Knowledge of the Higher Worlds* I have described them as lotus flowers. The intention was to let people know they were able to see with these lotus flowers.

So you have a rite here which essentially consisted in people wanting to bring the spiritual element from the cosmos down to the earth for their social and life situations. You can still see it there today, and it makes the area extraordinarily interesting. These were the last of those ancient sites, places on the west coast to which people withdrew at the time, for after this, people came from the east and writing was introduced. That early form of writing was called runes. The runes were sticks that would be put together to form letters; very different therefore from today. And only then did Norse mythology develop, which is what we call it today—Odin, Thor and so on. This only came later, and it came because writing was transplanted to that region.

You need not be all that surprised to hear me talk of the shadow like this, for even an animal sees something in a shadow. Just watch the strange way a horse will behave when it is standing somewhere along a road at night, where there are lights, and looks at its shadow on a wall. One just has to know that an animal, a horse, does not see its shadow the way we do. Our eyes are set in such a way that they look ahead. The horse's eyes are set in such a way that they look to the side. Because of this the horse does not actually see the shadow itself, but perceives the spiritual element in the shadow. People will of course say the horse is afraid of its shadow. But the fact is that it does not see the shadow at all, but perceives the spiritual element in the shadow. And those primitive peoples also perceived differences in the shadow all the year round, just as we note differences in the sun's heat and in cold temperatures. So that was a rite which people had then. And you can realize from what I have told you that the rites which developed in ancient times were something that was really needed. They existed because people needed them. They took the place of all the things that could later be read, and at the same time it was a matter of communion between human beings and the gods. People did not pray so much, but they made these things known to others, and this then became part of life; it had a relationship to life, a significance in life.

Now to another rite, remnants of which you still find above all in Central Europe where you find sacred sites and specific images. The images show a bull, with a kind of rider on the bull wearing a Phrygian cap, a kind of revolutionary cap. This was later adopted from those origins. And down below in the same picture you'd see a kind of scorpion which is biting into the bull's genitals. Then one also sees the individual who is sitting on top thrusting a sword into the front part of the bull's body. And if it is like this [*drawing on the board*], with this rider up there, the scorpion here, there the thrusting sword, you see from it how the starry heavens are configured up above. Up there are the starry heavens. These rites were known as Mithraic rites. So the first ones were Druid rites, and what I am describing now are the Mithraic rites, as they were called. The Druid rites were on the west coast—one does also find them in other areas, but I have just been telling you of an area where I have been able to see this for myself. These other rites, the Mithraic rites, once spread from Asia across and along the whole of the Danube, through southern Russia as we know it today, Bulgaria, Hungary, Bavaria, the Odenwald, Black Forest areas, and so on. And this meant something quite specific. For you see, why did they have a bull just there? This is the first question we have to ask ourselves.

I have told you that the sun rises in a particular constellation in the zodiac in spring, today essentially in the

Fishes. The astronomers still give the Ram. This is wrong, however, for in reality it is the Fishes. For a long time, a period of 2,000 years, the sun would rise in the constellation of the Ram, and before that in the Bull. And people would then say to themselves: 'In the spring, when things begin to grow, the sun always rises in the Bull.' and they quite rightly connected the principle that above all has to do with growth in the human body—not in the head, but in the rest of the body—with the fact that the sun's rays change, and that behind this is the constellation of the Bull. And so they would say: 'If we want to refer to the animal human being, we have to draw a bull, with the actual human being, who is governed by his head, sitting on the bull.' The bull thus represents the lower, animal human being, and the one who is sitting up there, wearing his Phrygian cap, represents the higher human being. The whole is however really just one human being—lower human being and higher human being.

And the people would say to themselves: 'Oh, it is bad when the lower human being rules, when the human being gives himself up completely to his animal drives, only obeying his passions which come from the belly, from his sexuality and so on. The higher human being must govern the lower one.' And they would put it like this: 'This one, who rides on top, has the sword and thrusts it into the flanks of the lower human being. This means that the lower human being has to grow small compared to the higher human being. And then there is also the scorpion, biting into the genitals to show that if the lower human being is not made small by the higher one, lower human nature also harms itself, for the powers of outer nature come upon him and destroy him.' The image therefore showed the whole of this human destiny between the lower and the higher human being.

Above were the starry heavens. It is highly significant

that the starry heavens spread above. The sun rises in a particular point in the spring, in those days in the constellation of the Bull. But it moves on a little bit day by day. This movement happens in two ways. In the first place the spring point moves on. The following spring the sun will rise a little bit further along from the point where it rose the previous spring, so that 3,000 years ago it would have risen in the Ram, and even earlier than that in the Bull. Today it rises in the Fishes in spring. And so it gradually goes all the way round. In the course of 25,920 years the sun goes right round. But it also goes around within each year, so that it will not rise in the spring point the next day – it only rises there on 21 March – the next day it will have moved on a little, and so on. It also moves through all the constellations of the zodiac in the course of a year.

Now the people who served in the Mithraic rites had to observe when the lower human being, the animal human being, was more difficult to control – when the sun was in the Bull, that is, encouraging mainly the powers of growth. Yet when the sun was in the Virgin,[52] let us say, which would be in October – at that time more towards December, actually – the lower human being would not be so powerful, and less control would be needed. The people in general had no feeling for these things, but those who observed the Mithraic rites had to know them. And so the people who served in the Mithraic rites were able to say: 'It is more difficult to control the lower human being now that it is spring; and now again it is easier, for it is a particular time in winter.' And so the human being himself was used in those rites to get to know the seasons of the year, and of course the whole way the sun and moon would move through the zodiac. With the Druids, it was more the outer signs that were used, the shadows; here, in the Mithraic rites, it was more the effect on the human being which was used. And so the Mithraic service was also very much related to life.

All kinds of different rites thus existed. We have to understand of course that to observe the kind of thing the Druids once observed one needs to have quite specific regions on earth. You can still see this today. Living over there in Wales — the course of lectures took a fortnight — one always had rapid changes in the weather from small cloudbursts, I'd say, to sunshine and back again. It changes by the hour, so that the air there is quite different from the way it is here; it is always more full of water. If you have air like it is over there, where the Druids were, you can make such observations. You could not have made such observations in the regions where the Mithraic rite was more widespread, for there the climate would be different, and you had to take your observations more from the inner human being. People were more sensitive to such things then. And the rites therefore differed according to the region.

The Mithraic rites were common in the region of the Danube, in Bavaria and also in this part of Switzerland, though less so, even in earlier times, I think. It continued for a long time even when Christianity was coming to these regions. The last remnants were still to be found when Christianity had come to those regions, especially the Danube region. You still find these images in caves there, in the rocks. For those observations and rites were made and held in caves. They did not need the outer light of the sun but the stillness and quiet of a cave in the rocks. The spiritual influences of the sun and the stars go into those places as well.

Now that I have told you about two different rites you can see the meaning of ritual altogether. The Negroes still have their rites today. These are simpler, more primitive, but in their simple way they also show the desire to learn about the spiritual cosmos that surrounds us. At one particular time — this was about one and a half or two millennia ago—something developed from all the different rituals that were followed above all in Asia and Africa. They fused, as it were. Something was taken from one rite, something else from another, and the fusion of many different rites, above all the Egyptian, Persian rites, resulted in what you know as the Roman Catholic rite today. It is a fusion of all those things. You can see that it is a fusion if you look at the altar, for instance. You need not go very far and you'll see that today's altar is something like a tombstone. Even though there is no dead body beneath it, the form is that of a tombstone. In earlier times people knew that powers arise from a dead body, and this is still reflected in the shape of the altar today.

It is interesting to note that in Roman Catholic churches you also find a hint of the relationship to the sun and to the moon. You'll know that for particularly solemn celebrations the monstrance, the holy of holies, is placed on the altar [Fig. 33]. This, gentlemen, is in fact a sun, with the host, conceived as a sun, at the centre of the sun, and down below here the moon, a sign that this rite comes from a time when

Fig. 33

people sought to observe sun and moon directly, as I have shown when I told you of the Druid rites. This has been forgotten. When writing came and everything that goes with it, people no longer looked out into the vast spaces of nature. They then looked in a book, and the Gospels are of course also books. But a memorial remains in the sign of sun on moon which we see when the monstrance is placed on the altar.

It is therefore possible to show in every single detail that the Roman Catholic rite in particular goes back to the ancient rites that still related to the great universe. People have completely forgotten this, of course. The situation was that in the first three or four centuries after Christ people everywhere still knew a great deal about this real meaning of the rite, for the present rite was developed in Rome at that time and spread from there. It was made up of many different individual rites. In this part of Switzerland, too, and above all in the region of the Danube, the Mithraic rite was still known. One could see that it still related to the universe. In those early centuries, everything that still survived of the ancient rites was systematically eradicated, leaving only rites that did not show their relationship to the universe. And people look at the Roman Catholic rite today, you see, and it is considered most important that they actually do not understand, that they do not realize that it once related to the sun and the moon. For in ancient days religion and science were one, and art, too, was part of it.

A time did come, of course, when people said to themselves: 'Well, what is the point of it all? Surely it means nothing at all! The festivals, the seasons when particular things need to be done — they can be found in the calendar!' People therefore said it meant nothing. And the iconoclasts came, the image-breakers, Protestantism, the Protestant principle, going against ritual. Reflecting on this, we can now see why on the one hand everything once happened for people through their rites, and how on the other hand they all turned against ritual. At the time of the Druid rites — well, gentlemen, the enthusiasm people sometimes have for some movement or other today simply does not compare with the tremendous enthusiasm people had for their Druid rites in those days. They would have let themselves be stoned or beheaded for those Druid rites. The question is, why? Because they knew that one simply cannot live unless one has proper knowledge of what happens in the universe, one can't celebrate the bull festival at the right time, one can't sow one's grain, one's rye, at the right time.

Later it all became blurred, and then people said: 'But things must have a purpose in life!' Human attitudes to these things differ greatly at different times, and we can only understand this if we realize that things have been happening, such as the matter being completely forgotten, so that today we can only see how things once were from these symbols, as they are called. Understanding is at its weakest where you have symbols in a place, for you do not need symbols if you have the real thing. When an altar was built the way the Druids did in order to observe the sun itself, they would not put an image of the sun on it!

And it is this, for example, which has made certain rites, apart from the Roman Catholic ones, persist to the present day with hardly any change.

You see, this Druid rite was solely connected with agriculture and animal husbandry when it was at its height, for these made up people's lives then. Later on, skilled crafts or trades also developed in areas where until then people had lived solely from the agriculture and animal husbandry which had given their rite its full justification. Tilling the soil and looking after animals was all there was when the Druid cult had its flowering. People dressed in skins, and so on. Craft skills — there were no machines as yet — were such then that everything they made was made to meet a need. If a man had the time, he'd make something he needed to wear, or an object such as a knife made of very hard stone, for example, which he would work on, and so on. The important things were the crops and the animals, and for these, people wanted to know from their gods when they should do particular things. Gradually, however, trade skills became more important. Now you see, gentlemen, skilled trades do not relate as strongly to the starry heavens as do crops and animals. On the other hand, habits had developed, and so a kind of rite was also developed for crafts; it was taken from the ancient rites that related to the heavens.

One of the rites that has persisted and hardly changed at all is Freemasonry. It is all symbol, however. People really no longer know what these symbols refer to. Indeed, when civil engineering came in they applied the rites they habitually used for mason's work also to civil engineering. With architecture there is some point to it, if one wants to do really fine work. The designs are based on what the stars are saying, and so on, if one wants to do proper building work. And so Freemasonry developed. But when the rite developed people no longer knew the meaning of the individual symbols. And today it is all symbols, with people having no idea what they refer to, and saying the wildest things about them. I think it is fair to say that the more a rite is carefully maintained, the less do people know about things. And the most widely used rites today are really the ones where people understand least of all.

But you see, those earlier people used the rites for their life in the outside world. If we want to have rites again today — we are working on this, on a renewal of Christianity, and there are already some churches under Dr Rittelmeyer[53] in Germany — well, if you want to do this today it has to mean something a bit different from those ancient rites. For the ancient rites served an immediate purpose; today we simply know these things from calculations in ordinary astronomy—which particular day, 21 March, and so on. The ancients were not able to do that. They had to point to the shadow in their time, as I have described it for you. But today we need something different. What is needed today is that people altogether find a way again to understand anything whatsoever of the things that exist in the spiritual universe. No astronomy, nothing in the world will tell people today what is going on in the universe!

People fall into the greatest possible errors. They'll use telescopes to look at the world of the stars, for example, and they'll see a star when they look in a particular direction. And, gentlemen, if I move the telescope I'll see another star that is in another direction [*drawing on the board*]. On the other hand people calculate that the stars are so far away that one can no longer see this clearly but has to calculate in light years, which means the speed at which a ray of light travels.[54] They calculate the distance travelled by a light ray in a year. This is even more difficult to put in figures than paying for your midday meal with inflation money in Germany today—which is certainly difficult enough to put in figures! But the figure needed to say how fast a light ray moves, the distance it covers in a year, is thousands of millions. A star is so far away that the light would need so and so many light years. And so I turn my telescope in that direction, gentlemen, look into it and see the star. It needs 300,000 light years, let us say, to get here; the light needs that long. Another star may be a very long way off, taking perhaps 600,000 light years. When I look in that direction I am not at all seeing the star as it is now, but only the way it once was. And if I look there, what I see is actually not the reality. The star presents itself, but I am only seeing what it once was, because it took the light 300,000 years to get to me. So I am seeing an object which in reality is not there at all, having taken 300,000 years before it became visible! So you see, looking at the world through a telescope you simply do not see the starry heavens as they are! So that is one thing.

The other is this. People think when they see stars that there is something there. But the truth is that there is nothing there, for the ether actually comes to an end there where we see stars. This is not so with the sun and the moon — with the sun a little bit, but the moon not at all. With a star there is nothing there! There's a hole in the universe. It is indeed remarkable that this is exactly where we seem to be coming together with conventional science. When we established our institutes in Stuttgart,[55] I said that one of the first things we had to do was to show that nothing at all exists in the place where a star is, that a nothing is shining there. It is because there is something all around it there that we see a kind of light in the place where there is nothing. Now you know, we are really poor people with our research institutes, and the Americans are rich. And news has since come from America that in conventional science, too, it has been found that there is really nothing there in the places where the stars are.

Anthroposophy is thus actually working with the most advanced science. But it is easier to judge things with anthroposophy. You know, I am telling you this because you can see from it that people really do not know anything about the universe today. They judge things wrongly all the time. And why is that so?

You see, gentlemen, this is for a particular reason. Imagine this is a human head [*drawing*] and there's the brain. When someone perceives something on the outside, using his eye, for example, he takes note of it, using his brain to enable him to do so. But inside the brain is a small brain, right back there [Fig. 34]. This is built in quite a

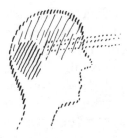

Fig. 34

different way from the big brain. If you cut through it, it is as if it was made up of leaves. And this is back there.

This small brain does not perceive anything that comes from the outside. We need the big brain – I've made it green here in my drawing – to get impressions of things outside. The small brain perceives nothing that comes from outside. But when someone deepens his inner life – I have shown how to do it in my books – this small brain begins to be particularly active and you get an inner feeling as if this small brain were getting bigger and bigger, as if it were growing. So it grows, and little by little you feel as if you were standing under a tree. This is why Orientals speak of Buddha under the Bodhi tree. He still experienced this small brain, called the cerebellum, as an organ of perception, and this is something we are rediscovering today. This small brain begins to be active if one does inner work as a human being. You do not perceive the material things that are outside, however, but the spiritual element. You begin to perceive the things of the spirit again with your cerebellum, and the laws and so on that belong to it. These must be part of the rites we create today. The inmost life of the human being needs to be made part of a ritual today because it is this inner part of the human being, this small brain which is separate from the big one, which is the organ that will take him out into the world of the spirit.

Today this way of developing a ritual out of the inmost life of the human being can at most only be a beginning. It was through the Druid rites that people knew how to garland the bull, set the time for the bull festival, walk the bull through the local village so that reproduction would be properly regulated, and if we develop a rite that will serve to develop perception in the spirit sustained by the cerebellum, we shall know what needs to be done in social life. Until then there can only be speculation, people will think things up, will do the kind of thing that is now being done in Russia. When it can be admitted that we must first of all know in the spirit what has to happen in the human world, because it flows from the universe, we will at last have a proper social science, and this will be something willed from the cosmic world that surrounds us.

That is how we must learn to think. And when one sees such things as the ruined stone monuments today, with only traces to show how things once were on Anglesey or in the other places on that coast, in Penmaenmawr where the course was held — yes when one finds such things one can see that much of what we need has been lost to humanity, and today we need new insights particularly when it comes to things of the spirit. We have to have new insights with which to work.

This is what I wanted to say in answer to your question. I think you can see from it that originally a rite was needed just as much as one needs a knife in everyday life, and that later on when it had become useless that it was actually wiped out; yet people would continue with it though they no longer understood it.

I have to go to Stuttgart again, but will be back in a few days. I'll ask them to tell you next week when we can meet again.

Role of protein, fats, carbohydrates and salts in nutrition. Effects of potato diet. Opponents of anthroposophy

Well, gentlemen, do we have anything on the programme today?

Member of the group: With regard to the food we eat, I wanted to ask if the situation with eating potatoes is different in other countries, a different situation, therefore, than the one that exists for Europeans, let us say.

Rudolf Steiner: Let us talk about the whole food situation again today, the way foods relate to the world of the spirit. As you know, the potato has only been introduced quite recently. I told you that people did not eat potatoes in Europe in earlier times, but other things, very much other things. This is, of course, a question we cannot be clear about unless we consider how the world of the spirit relates to nutrition altogether.

You'll remember — I did refer to these things before — people live on four kinds of products. The first is protein, which is really found in every food but in a characteristic, quite typical form in hen's eggs, we might say. We also eat fats, and again these are not limited to the animal fats we use as actual fats, for fats, too, are found in everything. You know that other products are processed to make foods rich in fat — milk into cheese, for example. The third kind of foods are products we call carbohydrates, and this is everything we have from the plant world, and to some extent of course also in other foods, but mainly in things like wheat, rye, lentils, beans, and also in potato, where it actually predominates. The last of the four things we need

for life are the salts. We usually only think of them as seasonings, but they are also very necessary to maintain life.
We mainly take our salts in the form of table salt, but all
foods actually contain salts. We may say, therefore, that in
order to live man needs to have protein, fats, carbohydrates
and salts.

Let me now tell you what these different food substances,
which we eat in different forms in a mixed diet, mean for
the human being. Let's begin with the salts.

Salts are really an extraordinarily important part of our
food, even if we take them only in small amounts, and they
are not just a seasoning. We don't just add salt to our food to
get a pleasantly savoury taste, perhaps. We add salt to our
food so that we'll be able to think. Salts must go as far as the
brain when we eat them, for only then will we be able to
think. Salts are therefore mainly connected with the principle we have in our thinking. If someone has an illness, for
example—and this is indeed an illness—where everything
that is salt in the food is deposited in the stomach or
intestines and does not go up to the brain in the blood, he
will grow feeble-minded, stupid. This is something of
which one has to take note.

Now you know we have to be clear in our minds that the
spirit exists; but to be able to play a role on earth the spirit
has to act in physical matter. And if we work with the science of the spirit we really must know how the spirit is
active in physical matter. Otherwise it would be just like
someone saying: 'To build machines is a material thing; but
we are spiritual people and don't want to have anything
material. So we don't want to buy iron or steel, but create
machines out of the spirit.' That is nonsense, of course. You
have to have the material. And when someone is prevented
from using the material substance and the salt is deposited
in the stomach and intestines rather than getting to the
brain through the blood, the individual will grow stupid.

The matter is not as simple as that, however. Human beings cannot use salt in the form in which it occurs in the natural world. So if you were to make a small hole in the skull — one could actually do this — and instil salts into the brain, this would be of no use at all, for the salt must first go to the stomach. By getting into the stomach and the intestines — for as you know, salt is already dissolved on the tongue — the salt is dissolved even more, very finely dissolved, getting more and more subtle. Because of the things human beings do to the salt, the salt is already in a subtle, non-material form when it reaches the brain. It is therefore not simply a matter of putting the salt directly into the brain. But someone who is unable to have the influences of salt in the brain will grow stupid.

Now let us look at carbohydrates. We eat them mainly when we eat peas, beans, wheat, rye or potatoes. Carbohydrates chiefly play a role in giving us our human form. If we did not eat carbohydrates we would see all kinds of distortions of the human form. We'd be such that the nose would not develop properly, if you like, or the ears. We'd not have this human form of ours. Carbohydrates play a role in making us outwardly appear as human beings. And if someone is organized in such a way that he does not take the carbohydrates up into the brain, so that once again they are deposited in the intestines and in the stomach, the individual goes to ruin. You'll then see such a person gradually collapsing on himself, growing weak, no longer able to maintain his form, as it were. The carbohydrates thus do their part so that we altogether have the right human form.

You see, we really need to get the right foods into the right places. Salts act mainly on the brain here in front. Carbohydrates act more on the back of the brain, on those layers there. And if someone is not able to digest enough carbohydrates and thus get them into those layers of the brain, you would soon also find that he's always hoarse, unable to speak clearly and distinctly. If you hear someone who used to speak perfectly well suddenly grow hoarse in his speech, you can say to yourself that something is wrong with his digestion. He cannot digest carbohydrates properly, they don't reach the right place in the brain. As a result his breathing is no longer the way it should be, nor is his speech. We are thus able to say that salts act mainly on our thinking. Carbohydrates act on our speech, for example, and everything connected with it. It is therefore necessary for us to have carbohydrates.

Now to the fats. Well you see, gentlemen, carbohydrates play a role in giving us form, but all they actually intend to do is to give us a figure and nothing else. They do not pad us out. We also need to be padded out. The fats do this. The fats therefore make sure, when the carbohydrates develop the figure, drawing a plan in the air, as it were, that this figure is also given substance. Fat thus serves to give us substance in the right way. And this shows itself in a very special way with fat.

You see, I told you before that the human being has an I, an astral body, an ether body and a physical body. Fat is, of course, deposited in the physical body, but the most important thing if the fat is to be deposited and remain alive — for we have to have living fat inside us — is the ether body. This ether body is most important for the depositing of fats. The astral body on the other hand is most important for sensation.

Now just think. When you are awake, your astral body is inside you, and when you sleep, it is outside. When someone is awake and the astral body is working in the ether body, the fat is worked all the time, and through it, everything in the body is lubricated. When we are asleep, so that the astral body is outside, fat is not worked but gets deposited. When we are awake the fat is used all the time to lubricate us; when we sleep it is deposited. We need both kinds of fat—fat that is deposited and fat that lubricates the body.

But if someone sleeps all the time—this was more common in the past; now it is getting more and more rare; someone who has a good pension, for example, and does nothing—fat is deposited also in the daytime, when he is 'awake' but really asleep. A potbelly develops and fat gets deposited everywhere! So you see, for fat to be properly deposited, the person must actually use up his fat by being alive, for it is produced all the time. The right way is for people to eat just as much as they use up. But if someone eats all the time and does not use any of it up, a potbelly will make its appearance.

Farmers know this instinctively, and they make use of this with their pigs. To fatten pigs one has to see to it, really, that the animals no longer lubricate their inner bodies at all but deposit everything they eat. And so their lifestyle has to be arranged accordingly.

It may of course also be that someone is not able to deposit fat properly, which means he is sick. People with a good pension are healthy in this respect; they deposit the fat. But it may also be that someone does not deposit carbohydrates and his speech grows hoarse. And so it may also be that the fats are not properly deposited but simply go away in the stools. In that case we have too little fat and cannot lubricate enough. Or if we have too little food altogether and have to go hungry, we cannot lubricate enough. Fat is the actual material we place in the body. So what happens if someone has to go hungry or his digestion is such that he cannot deposit the fat and it goes away in his stools? Such a person, who has no substance to his body, grows more and more spiritual. But a human being cannot grow spiritual in this way without being harmed. The spirit then burns up. The person will then not only grow thinner and thinner, but gases will develop in him and this will lead to delusions, as they are called, and the like, and a condition develops which is insanity due to starvation. It will always be destructive, destroying the body. If someone does not get enough fats, therefore, emaciation develops, we might call it 'consumption'; he fades away.

Now to protein. You see, protein has to be there from the very beginning, as it were. Protein is already there in the egg, before a creature comes into existence — a human being or an animal. We may thus say that protein is the substance which really creates, develops the human being. It is the original material, the basis. Everything else in the body has to develop from this. I think you can understand this? We may thus say the following. Protein has to be there from the very beginning if a human being is to develop. The mother has the protein in her womb in a small lump. The egg is fertilized, and on fertilization this protein is then able to develop into a human being, through the things I have described to you. But we need protein all the time, of course, and so our food must contain protein. If we have too little protein, or are unable to digest it properly, we would not only become emaciated from lack of protein — which would also kill us in due course — but if someone were to have no proper protein at all at one moment in his life, he'd have to die instantly. Protein is needed at the beginning, and it is also needed so that we may live at all. We are thus able to say that someone who is altogether unable to digest protein would have to die.

Let us now take a look at the individual foods. Looking at the salts, we find a connection above all with the front part of the brain. That is where salts are deposited. Carbo-hydrates are deposited a bit further back and are respon-sible for our human form. Fats are deposited even further back and from there fill out the body, for the fats do not go into the body directly but move from the blood into the head, and it is only from there that they are taken for use in the body. Everything goes through the head, even the protein.

There is a big difference, however, when it comes to the carbohydrates. Looking at things like lentils, beans, peas, rye or wheat, you can say that these carbohydrates come from fruits. For in wheat we have a fruit of the earth. Lentils—that, too, is a fruit. Fruits have the characteristic that they are digested in the stomach and intestines and only send their powers to the head. We all know that lentils and beans are digested in the intestines, because of the particular state we get into when we eat lentils and beans. All of it—rye, wheat, lentils, beans—is digested in the intestines. Fruits thus have the special characteristic that they are fully digested in the intestines.

We cannot eat the fruit of potatoes, however. If we were to eat the fruit of potatoes we would actually be taking poison, a fatal poison. So the situation is that the potato does not permit us to eat it the way we eat lentils, beans, peas and so on, or grains like rye and wheat. So what do we eat of the potato? Something which is down below—the tuber. And tubers are the part of all plants—roots and so on—that is digested least in the intestines. Fruits are digested in the intestines. But we can't eat the fruit of potato plants. The tuber we eat is not a proper root but a thickened stem. So when we eat potato it gets into the stomach, into the intestines. There it cannot be digested right away but now goes up undigested with the blood. Instead of it getting up there nicely like rye and wheat which are then immediately sent down into the body, the potato first needs to be digested up there in the brain. So if we eat good rye bread or wheaten bread, we digest it properly in the stomach and intestines and don't ask our head to take care of their digestion. The head can immediately see to it that they are distributed in the body. But if we eat potato bread, or just potatoes, we find that the head must first work to digest the potato.

Now if the head has to be used to digest potatoes, it can no longer think, for it needs its energies to be able to think, and the lower body must provide the energy needed for digestion instead. And if someone eats too much potato — which has been increasingly the case since the potato came to Europe and became an important food here — the head is gradually less and less available for thinking, and the individual progressively loses the ability to think with his middle head; he will then only think with the front of his head. But this front part of the head, which depends on the salts, causes him more and more to be only a person of materialistic rationality. The situation is, therefore, that thinking has indeed grown less and less in Europe from the moment when potatoes became a staple food.

We have to be clear in our minds that powers others than those that exist on earth also play a role in creating the human being. This is something I have been telling you all the time, that man is created out of the whole environment, that he is created by sun, moon and stars. Now when he eats potatoes he uses only his middle head to digest them. He closes himself off from the surrounding world, and no longer acknowledges it. He'll then say: 'It's all twaddle what people say about the cosmos, about a spiritual element coming down from the cosmos.' And we may thus say that excessive potato consumption has played a considerable role in driving humanity into materialism in more recent times.

Now the situation is, of course, that it is mainly people of insufficient means who have to depend on potatoes, for potatoes were cheap for a time. And well-to-do people can buy more of the foods that influence the front part of the head, that is, add more savour and salt to their dishes. Seasonings act on the front of the head just as salts do. And the result is that these people become entirely rational, and the others will easily follow those with rational minds because they are no longer able to use their heads to think. And so the potato does have quite a special connection with the mind and spirit. It has really made human minds materialistic.

Now if we consider the different bodies of man, we have to say that the physical body initially originates in protein. Protein has a connection with the birth and death of the physical human being. The ether body has its main field in the fats, the astral body in the carbohydrates, and it is only the I which has the salts for its field.

We are therefore able to say that sentience in us — you see, it is not the physical body which feels something if I slap my hand and feel something, for in that case everything physical would have sentience — it is the astral body. I push the flesh back, the muscle back, and because of this the flesh in the muscle is pushed out of the astral body and I have a sensation in my astral body. All inner sensation, inner response, happens in the astral body. The astral body has to depend on being able to work properly, however. As I told you, if the astral body also sleeps during the day and is not able to work properly, a potbelly develops — fat. And if someone only does intellectual work in his head, using his rational mind, fat is deposited in that case as well. But the astral body, which is also active in our speech, needs carbohydrates in the whole body and not only up there in the head. The astral body has to move our legs, the astral body has to move our hands, it needs carbohydrates in every part of the body. When I give it rye or wheat carbohydrates, the energies go into the whole body. If I merely give it potatoes, the energies remain up there in the head and the individual grows emaciated, weak, with his astral body unable to work properly. It is the spiritual principle, therefore, which grows feeble and gets more and more sleepy in us if we are unable to get carbohydrates into ourselves that go to every part of us. This cannot happen if people live on potatoes only, for the potato gives so much work to the head that nothing is left over for the body.

Now we may ask: 'What is done in science?' Well, analyses are made to establish how much carbon, oxygen, nitrogen, hydrogen and other things a protein contains — these are the main elements to be found in it. So it is found that a protein contains so and so much carbon, so and so much hydrogen, in per cent, with different percentages found in fat and different ones again in carbohydrates. But people have no idea as to the significance of these elements. They only know the percentages. But this will get us nowhere. The nutrients are simply in a different way inside potato than they are in rye and wheat, and one has to know that when we eat a flower or a fruit this is digested in the intestines, whilst a root is digested in the head.

Otherwise one also can't make use of them in medicine. Someone who is able to think in a proper medical way will know that a tea made of flowers or seed, or of fruit, will act mainly on the intestines. Roots boiled in water, which is then offered as a tea, can have a medicinal effect in the head. If we eat the roots, this has a material effect on the head. This is particularly important to know.

We can also take this further and say: 'Yes, but if someone on a diet of potatoes does not only grow emaciated so that he can no longer move his hands and feet, but also reaches a point where the things that contribute to reproduction are no longer active, then we have an even worse situation.' Let us assume, therefore, that potato gains so much the upper hand that this influences the female reproductive organs, making them feeble and inactive. Well, gentlemen, we do not descend from our ancestors only, for the soul and spirit part of our nature comes from the world of the spirit and unites with the part that comes from our ancestors. Let us take a look at this. I'll draw it quite big, a little bit enlarged [*drawing on the board*].

We can say that the human being develops from the egg cell. This is a much enlarged drawing of it. The male seed penetrates into it, and then all kinds of star-shaped forms develop in there. Cells divide and gradually the human body develops. But there can be no human body unless the element of spirit and soul which comes from the world of the spirit connects with all this.

If the situation is one where the mother or the father has eaten too much of a potato diet, the embryo which develops will be of a kind where the head has to do much work. So if you look at the embryo of someone whose father and mother eat the right kind of diet, it looks more or less like this [*another drawing*]. But if you look at one where the parent's diet contained too many potatoes, the situation is like this. You see, everything else is little developed in the embryo, only the round sphere of the head; that is the main thing in the embryo, and it is the most developed part. The element of spirit and soul must then enter into the head. And when the element of spirit and soul enters into the head it has to work with that head. When still in the mother's body, the element of spirit and soul works mainly on the head.

Now if this element of spirit and soul finds the kind of situation in the head that one gets if the mother eats rye and wheat, the spirit and soul is able to work properly in there. For the flower heads in which the rye and wheat grains and so on develop rise above the soil, and then the spiritual element comes close to the plant, and the spiritual element then has an affinity. So if the element of spirit and soul finds something that comes from fruits in the mother's body it finds it easy to work. But if it finds a child's head in the mother's body that is developing mainly on the basis of a potato diet, it cannot get at it. You see, the potato goes down into the soil, it is even covered by the soil; it is dug up, for it grows in darkness and has no relationship to the spiritual element. The spirit cannot get to it, and the result is that the embryo then looks like this [*drawing*] — I am caricaturing it a little bit. A huge watery head is born, a hydrocephalus. For if the spirit does not get there, the physical will just grow. A watery head develops. If the spirit does get to it, it keeps the water down; the spirit then works in the material substance and the head develops properly. You can therefore say that the enormous watery heads often seen in embryos are due to inadequate nutrition, mainly again to potato. And the situation is then that not only is the human being himself emaciated, but he is born in a way where his spirit and soul are not properly inside the physical body.

But you see, gentlemen, the situation is like this. Man does consist of physical body, ether body, astral body and I; but they are not the same at every stage in life. In children up to the seventh year of life the ether body, astral body and I are such that they must really go right inside; they must first of all enter wholly into the physical body. The second teeth develop when the ether body enters fully into the physical body. Sexual maturity is reached when the astral body enters wholly into the physical body. So if you have such a head, where the element of spirit and soul cannot enter properly into the physical human being in the womb because of a diet of potatoes, problems also arise with the things that should develop in the 14th, 15th year of life. The individual will then go through the whole of his life as if he did not have a body at all, as if it were feeble, washed-out. People are not strong enough for life when they are born under the influence of a potato diet.

You see, gentlemen, these are tremendously important things. You just have to say to yourselves that social conditions depend on many more things than people generally tell us about today. Social conditions also depend on making the right use of our fields and not growing more potatoes than people can cope with and still grow strong.

Social science therefore means that one also has to do a proper study of the natural world. This is certainly necessary. It is not enough just to talk about added value, capital, and so on; this will do no good on its own. For just imagine Communism were to succeed in eradicating all capital, with the Communists in sole charge of everything. Well, if they have adopted the bourgeois way of not putting the fields to proper use, and if they do not know that it is more harmful to fill the stomach with potatoes than with rye or wheat, then nothing will be any good. This is what we have to consider. We do not need people talking all the time about one thing or another, but genuine knowledge, seeing how the spirit can be active in matter.

You see, it is because of this that anthroposophy has to battle on two fronts all the time, as it were, without wanting to do so. Why? Well, today's scientists only consider physical matter, and only the percentages of things — how much carbon, oxygen, nitrogen, hydrogen are found in protein, and so on. But this does not tell one anything about matter. Material science does not let us know about matter because you can only get to know matter if you know how the spirit is at work in it. What good is it for someone to say: 'I want to get to know about a watch. Right, I'll try and be clear in my mind about this watch. It is made of silver. The silver in my watch has been mined there and there. It was then taken to this or that city in trains. There it was delivered to the merchants, and so on. The watch face is of porcelain. Porcelain comes from there and there, was taken to this or that city,' and so on. He knows nothing at all about his watch! You'll only know about it if you know what the watchmaker did to make it. And it is not even important, if you want to understand why a watch works, to know how the silver was mined. What matters is that one knows how it works, how the watchmaker made the cogwheels, and so on.

And when it comes to the health and sickness of people, it is essentially quite immaterial to know in an abstract way how much carbon, oxygen, nitrogen, hydrogen, protein, fat, carbohydrates and salts are in the foods. For human health and sickness it is basically important to know specifically how it is with the potato. It feeds us as little in mind and spirit as it does in body. Basically the things written about it are quite unnecessary. For other purposes you need knowledge. For those other purposes one may well know about silver mines, and so on, but this kind of knowledge is unimportant when it comes to understanding human health and sickness. Yet people do not even realize where their knowledge is inadequate. And when one wants to add what is missing, doing so out of anthroposophy, people will fight against it. And that is how the front has developed where we fight materialism. Materialists say that in anthroposophy people want to explain everything from fantasy. Scientists who are against anthroposophy object to it being a science of the spirit. This, then, is the one front.

The other one, gentlemen, comes from the side of theology, the representatives of religion, and so on. On the one hand people are always told that the soul goes to heaven. And they do, of course, talk about the way people get to heaven by means of prayer, the sacraments, and so on. Well and good. But when someone is in a position in the physical world where he actually does not inhabit his body properly, so that he cannot relate to life on earth in a proper way, he'll find it extraordinarily difficult to get his bearings after death. This is something they do not tell him. It is indeed necessary for us to be practical people in life and know how to work with physical matter. We can say, therefore, that people are told all kinds of things about religion and theology today, but all this is not enough to make a person really strong in earthly life, so strong that he will later gain his bearings, being thus prepared. For prayer without real knowledge, for example, will actually distract people from the things they need to know for a healthy life. You're unlikely ever to hear from a pulpit what people should do where a diet of potatoes or wheat is concerned, so as to be strong. Most Protestant or Roman Catholic clergy wouldn't think of telling their congregations the situation regarding eating rye and wheat for their health. They'd consider it of no importance. They'd say it was not holy, for to be holy means to pray or talk about the Gospels and similar things.

But the divine is at work not only where prayers have been said, or people have talked about the Gospels, but in the whole of nature. There, too, the spirit is at work. If someone does not let spirituality enter into his head because he keeps it too busy with potatoes, the situation is that he will be able to pray. Well and good. But if he eats too many potatoes his prayer will serve no purpose, for he will be distracted from the things of the spirit. But people don't notice this. Nor do they notice that God did not find the earth as a lump of clay one day and make all things of it, but that the divine principle is truly at work in everything, in every detail, and must be sought there. If you do that, however, the theologians and religious people will call you materialists!

We are therefore called fantasy-led spiritualists by people who work in science, and materialists by the theologians. Which shows the value people put on things. Just as it was in 1908 when people said they were against anthroposophy because it was Jesuitical. It was said that anthroposophists were actually being delivered into the hands of the Jesuits by their leaders. Things have changed since. Now the Jesuits say anthroposophists are delivered into the hands of the Freemasons. You see, that's how things are always done. But it is not what matters. What matters is that one truly gains knowledge that can equally well tell us why a watery head, as hydrocephalus, develops in the mother's womb, rather than one that is properly developed.

You'll say, gentlemen, that one does not see many people with hydrocephalus around. Of course not, for other forces then counteract it and when the head is born it is no longer as big as it was in the embryo. But it is no longer able to take in anything but potatoes and water. It may even grow small in the process and yet be a watery head. The important thing is that heads have been too large in the maternal womb ever since potatoes became part of the diet. They are pushed together later, but it is exactly this pushing together before they are born that causes harm, for they will then not be able to take in the right things, but solely and only materialistic things. When the individual is born, you no longer see the watery head if you just look at the size. Now of course, hydrocephalus in the usual sense depends on the size, but here it is above all a question of whether water is acting in the right way, or something else is able to act. And it is just as important to know this as it is to know all the other things presented to mankind through science on the one hand and theology and religion on the other. But it is certainly necessary that one looks at the matter carefully and properly.

You see, how do people actually treat anthroposophy? Some time ago a congress was held in Berlin of people who called themselves 'non-anthroposophists who know anthroposophy'. They say they are not anthroposophists but know anthroposophy. One man who spoke a lot at the conference was a Dr Gösch, who used to be here once, but has left our ranks. He spoke to clergy, to people who teach at theological faculties and professors. And today, you see, people are everywhere giving lectures based on the things Dr Gösch has told them. Now you'll say these people — teaching staff, professors — were convinced from what Dr

Gösch told them that anthroposophy is extremely harmful. But please, gentlemen, consider what today's clergy, professors and teachers of theology generally have in their heads, and listen now to what Dr Gösch told them. He said anthroposophy was particularly harmful because anthroposophists were being deluded. Mrs Steiner and Dr Steiner really intended to split off a piece of the earth, separate it from the earth, and create their own planet, to create a planetary world colony in the universe with all the anthroposophists! This is what he told those enlightened people. You can imagine that not one of them would really believe this, but they pretend that those words have convinced them that anthroposophy is indeed harmful.

Now just think what a crazy business this is! Those enlightened people do not only attend that meeting, but the next day, or the day after, they are attending all kinds of other meetings, where all kinds of destinies are decided. And they are no brighter there than they are at other meetings. This is something to reflect on, what kind of people actually govern the world today. But please understand that their opposition to anthroposophy is indeed opposition to the truth. They do not want it to be known what all this is really about, the things one learns about the human being. They say: 'Anthroposophy is full of secrets.' Well, gentlemen, how can it be anything but full of secrets? Of course it is full of secrets, but no more so than you have secrets when someone has stolen something and hidden it; it will then be a secret until it is discovered. And in the same way anthroposophy is full of secrets, because these things have been hidden in science and the rest of academic life. And it is because of this, of course, that anthroposophy is such a mysterious business today. But things cease to be a mystery the moment they are discovered. There is no intention of being mysterious in anthroposophy, but rather to bring to light the things which others have been keeping secret.

I have to go to Vienna now and I'll ask them to tell you when we'll be able to continue.

Translator's note

This being the last of the four volumes of discussions with
the workers I have been asked to translate, I'd like to say a
big Thank You to the Kingston/Surbiton study group who
kindly read each talk aloud in our group meetings so that I
was able to hear them, make changes where the flow of the
words came to a halt, and so on. We enjoyed reading and
discussing them amongst us.

   I have added a list of German names and terms that
appear in the text, with indications as to how they may be
pronounced. Reading the lectures aloud, in a group, for
instance, people often feel they would like to pronounce the
words properly, and I hope this may be a help.

Burle	boorle
Erbsmehl	airps male
Falb	falp
Fürth	firt
Gösch	goesh (oe as u in burn)
Heilbronn	hilebron
Karlsbad	carls but
Marienbad	mah ree en but
Natur	netour
Neue Freie Presse	noye frye presse
Nürnberg	nirnbirg
Odenwald	ohdnvalt
Prater	prahta
Richard Traugott	soft ch in Richard, like the h in huge trowgot
Rittelmeyer	riddle myer

Schleich	shlyh (last h as in huge)
Schopenhauer	shohpn hour (h on hour sounded as h)
Tübingen	tibingen
Wiesbaden	vees bahdn
Zahn	tsun
Zaun, Zäune	tsoun, tsoyne

Notes

The lectures in this volume were taken down in shorthand by stenographer Helene Finkh (1883–1960), who then also made fair copies of them. The original shorthand records were completely reviewed with new fair copies made for the 1979 German edition. Changes in the text compared to the first edition and lectures published singly are due to this.

The original drawings had been made on black paper put on to the blackboards and have been preserved. They have been published in Vol. XXVI of *Wandtafelzeichnungen zum Vortragswerk*, Dornach: Rudolf Steiner Verlag 1994. ISBN 3-7274-4100 (series), 3-7274-4126-7 (Vol. XXVI).

The original works of Rudolf Steiner are identified by their number in the Collected Works (*Gesamtausgabe*, GA).

1 See lecture given on 3 March 1923 in GA 349 (translation not available).
2 See lecture given on 18 April 1923 in *From Limestone to Lucifer*. Tr. A. Meuss. London: Rudolf Steiner Press 1999.
3 See lecture given on 21 April 1923 in the above volume.
4 See note 2.
5 See lecture given on 17 March 1923 in the above volume.
6 Steiner, R., *Towards Social Renewal* (GA 23). Tr. F. T. Smith. London: Rudolf Steiner Press 1977.
7 The text here refers to the *solfatara* (volatiles) at Pozzuoli, a half extinct volcano by the Bay of Naples, with a crater that is 770 metres in diameter. The hot sulphurous vapours continually rising from countless cracks (*fumaroli*) there increase greatly in volume if a burning piece of paper or torch is brought to the *fumaroli* vents.
8 Rudolf Falb (1838–1903), Austrian writer. His theories are set

out in two of his publications: *Grundzüge einer Theorie der Erdbeben und Vulkanausbrüche* (1870) and *Das Wetter und der Mond* (2. Aufl. 1892).

9   See lectures given on 9 and 13 September 1922 in *The Human Being in Body, Soul and Spirit. Our Relationship to the Earth*. Tr. J. Reuter, rev. S. Seiler. Hudson and London: Anthroposophic Press and Rudolf Steiner Press 1989.

10   See lecture of 30 May in this volume.

11   See lecture given on 21 February in *From Limestone to Lucifer* (as in note 1).

12   A few sentences are missing here. To show the 'really interesting thing', Rudolf Steiner probably described a set-up that would look something like this:

I   incandescent lamp
C   condensor lens
S   slit
F   sodium flame
L   imaging lens
P   prism

Using this arrangement, it is possible to see the yellow absorption line in the yellow part of the continuous spectrum of the incandescent lamp of which Rudolf Steiner then spoke. The drawing on the board was only a very rough sketch.

13   In 1859, Bunsen and Kirchhoff discovered spectral analysis.

14   See note 11.

15   Geissler tubes, after Heinrich Geissler (1815–79), glassblower and mechanic.

16   Often quoted in alchemical literature and said to have been composed by Basilius Valentinus, said to have been a Bene-dictine monk at St Peter's monastery in Erfurt, Germany, around 1413. A version of it is published in *Gesammelte Schriften des Basilius Valentinus*, Hamburg 1740.

17   This incident was more fully described in a lecture Rudolf Steiner gave in Berlin on 20 April 1915. Published in Steiner, R., *Destinies of Individuals and of Nations* (GA 157). Tr. A. Meuss. London: Rudolf Steiner Press 1984. The story was

originally published in G. H. v. Schubert, Die Symbolik des Traumes, 3. verb. u. verm. Aufl. Leipzig, pages 10 and 11, as follows:

> Erasmus Francisci dreamt ... when he was a young man that someone who even in his dream called him by a familiar first name wanted to shoot him dead but that he was saved by his aunt who grabbed the barrel and pulled it aside. In the middle of the day he told the dream, jokingly, to his aunt in whose house he was staying. She took the matter more seriously, however, and asked him not to go out that day, all the more so since a child had recently been shot dead by someone who was careless. To encourage the young man to stay at home, she gave him the key to the room above his, where fruit was stored. The young man went to his room, having had a brief conversation first with the servant who was on the side of the passage directly opposite to his room, cleaning some rifles that had been lent out and only just returned. At that moment he escaped the imminent danger of which his dream had warned him, for the person who wanted to shoot him in the dream had had the same first name as the manservant. The young man had barely sat down at his desk, reading for a few moments a book that he normally enjoyed, when his hand and eyes fell on the key his aunt had given him. This drew him away irresistibly from his book and to the room where the apples were kept. He had only just moved from his seat when the rifle, unbeknownst to the servant loaded with two bullets for a wolf hunt, went off and the whole charge hit the wall immediately above the chair. If the chair had not just been moved, it would inevitably have struck the young man right in the middle of his chest. In this strange case, therefore, the dream had without doubt saved the life of someone who later became a most useful and learned man.

18 George Stephenson (1781–1848), English railway engineer who constructed the first locomotive in 1814. Stephenson

was engineer for the construction of the Stockton & Darlington mineral railway which opened in October 1825.

19   See Hagen, R., *Die erste deutsche Eisenbahn*, 1885, S. 45.

20   Karl Ferdinand Friedrich von Nagler (1770–1846), who developed the modern postal services.

21   Cromwell F. Varley (1828–83), electrical engineer and inventor of an early kind of telephone. The passage which follows comes from Carl du Prel, *Die monistische Seelenlehre. Ein Beitrag zur Lösung des Menschenrätsels*, Leipzig 1888, S. 195:

> Varley, a member of the Royal Society in London, electrical advisor to the Atlantic Cable Society, tells of an even more complicated case, and it is truly helpful that we have a witness who really counts in this peculiar case. He once went to the country with his wife to visit his sister-in-law — for the last time, it was feared, for she suffered from heart disease. During the night, Varley had a nightmare and could not move a muscle. Whilst in this state, he saw his sister-in-law's double stand by his bed, for he knew the lady was in a closed room. She said: 'You'll have to die unless you move!' Varley tried, in vain, and she went on to say: 'If you submit yourself to me, I'll give you a fright, and you'll then be able to move.' He resisted at first, for he wanted to learn more about her presence in the spirit, and when he finally agreed, his heart had ceased to beat. Her efforts to give him a fright proved unsuccessful at first; but when she called out: 'Oh, Cromwell, I am dying!' he woke from his paralysed state. He found the doors closed and made a note of the time. In the morning the sister-in-law, who had been told nothing of all this, told of the whole event as of a terrible dream she had had. (*Berichte der dialektischen Gesellschaft II*, 108)

22   Schleich, Carl Ludwig (1859–1922), *Vom Schaltwerk der Gedanken*, Berlin 1916, S. 261. See also R. Steiner, *Spiritual Science and Medicine* (GA 312). Tr. not known. London: Rudolf Steiner Publishing Co. 1948, 3rd lecture.

23   Lodge, Sir Oliver Joseph (1851–1940). See his book *Raymond*; see also R. Steiner, *Cosmic and Human Metamorphoses* (in GA 175), lecture of 6 February 1917. Tr. H. Collison. London: Anthroposophical Publishing Co. 1926.

24   The story was published in Carl du Prel's book (see note 20), page 194 f.:

> Professor Perty tells the story like this: 'One afternoon in August 1853, Miss Sophie Swoboda—she was 20 at the time—lay down on the sofa in her mother's room because she had a severe headache, and she finally went to sleep. It then seemed to her that she was quietly leaving the room; she awoke. Sophie now felt quite weightless and free from pain; she rose quickly to hurry after her mother into the third room and tell her that there had been this change for the better. Her mother was sitting at her knitting, and opposite her sat Sophie's father, reading aloud from Bonaventura's (Schelling's) *Mystische Nächte*. Sophie stood beside the two of them, waiting for a break in the reading to tell her story, but her parents took no notice of her, in spite of the fact that they would look up every now and then and talk to each other about the text they were reading. Sophie, feeling put out by this, withdrew into a window alcove and listened to the text. Before long her mother got up, saying: "Sophie's not well, and that worries me; I must go and see how she is." Sophie quickly went up to her to reassure her, but her mother did not look at her but went straight to the door and to the first room. Sophie, wanting to make herself noticed, wanted to surprise her with a kiss as she came up behind her. But her mother, seriously concerned, went quickly up to the sofa where Sophie had lain down before, calling out to her sister, who had come in by another door: "How pale she looks!" Sophie now looked in the same direction and was greatly surprised to see herself lying on the sofa, her face pale as death and her eyes closed. Her mother and sister were much concerned, bending over her, calling her by name,

and this made Sophie go up close, so that they might finally see her. At that very moment she felt herself flung on the sofa with great suddenness. She opened her eyes with great difficulty and much effort and then her mother and sister helped her to sit up. When Sophie had recovered a little, she told her parents of her experience and they were not a little surprised to hear her quote the passages her father had read and the views her parents had expressed, some of it word for word. She had, after all, been three rooms away, with the door closed.' (*Psychische Studien* 1979, 294)

25   Julius Robert Mayer (1814–78), German physician and physicist. Established the law of conservation of energy in 1842, and the mechanical heat equivalent in 1851.

26   Mammoths.

27   See lecture of 2 June 1923 in this volume.

28   Christopher Columbus (1451–1506).

29   Nicolaus Copernicus (1473–1543). His theory, first developed in 1507, was published in 1543.

30   Robert Hamerling (1830–89). The event described by Rudolf Steiner has been published in an essay by Hamerling entitled 'Was mir bei einer Hellseherin begegnete' (Hamerlings sämtliche Werke in sechzehn Bänden, hg. v. Michael M. Rabenlechner, Leipzig o. J., 16. Bd, S. 67 ff, bes. S. 70–73).

31   See note 7.

32   Christian Thomasius (1655–1728), philosopher and lawyer, the first university teacher to give lectures in German at Leipzig University in 1687.

33   Dr P. Gruner, professor of theoretical physics. *Die Neuorientierung der Physik*, vice-chancellor's address at the 87th anniversary of Bern University on 26 November 1921; Bern 1922.

34   Steiner, R., *The Philosophy of Spiritual Activity. A Philosophy of Freedom* (GA 4). Tr. R. Stebbing. London: Rudolf Steiner Press 1989.

35   Immanuel Kant (1724–1804).

36 Friedrich Nietzsche (1844–1900).

37 Eduard Bernstein (1850–1932), German socialist theoretician who developed revisionism as a moderate approach to socialism in the 1890s, being against revolution.

38 August Bebel (1840–1913), founded the Social Democratic Party in Germany with Liebknecht in 1869.

39 The report was published in the *Basler Nachrichten* of 5 July 1923. It referred to the essay on 'Traumpsychologie' by Richard Traugott published in the bimonthly journal *Natur* (Heft 11/12 v. 1./15./März, H. 14 v. 15. April u. H. 17 v. 1. Juni 1923).

40 E.g. *Der Traum, psychologisch und kulturgeschichtlich betrachtet.* Würzburg 1913.

41 *Pierers Konversations-Lexikon*, 7. Aufl., 12 Bände, Berlin 1888–93. The sentence reads: 'He (Drake) was for a long time wrongly said to have introduced the potato to Europe, with a monument set up for him in Offenburg.' (4. Band, Spalte 859)

42 Karl Hansen, b. 1833, Danish hypnotist, emigrated to Australia in 1853, where he gave performances as a mesmerist. Later he made hypnotism widely known with performances in the Scandinavian countries, Germany and so on, though he did not contribute to the scientific investigation of hypnotism.

43 Aristotle (382–322 BC)

44 Augustin Smetana (1814–51), canon regular of the Holy Cross and suppl. professor of philosophy in Prague. The full story is given in *Geschichte eines Excummunicirten. Eine Selbstbiographie von Augustin Smetana. Aus dessen Nachlasse herausgegeben ... von Alfred Meissner*, Leipzig 1863.

45 Arthur Schopenhauer (1788–1860), German philosopher. See his *The World as Will and Idea* (1819, final version 1859, 2 vols).

46 German for conscience is *Gewissen,* and to be certain of something is *gewiss sein.* Translator.

47 British reference works on the origin of words say 'conscience' means to 'know together', and therefore also

'together with oneself', 'privity of knowledge', 'inward thought'. This may, of course, be arguing from hindsight. Translator.

48 In 1879, Leo XIII declared Thomas Aquinas to have been the first teacher of the Roman Catholic Church.

49 Steiner, R., *Knowledge of the Higher Worlds, How is it Achieved?* (GA 10). Tr. D. S. Osmond, C. Davy. London: Rudolf Steiner Press 1976. Also as *How to Know Higher Worlds. A Modern Path of Initiation.* Tr. C. Bamford. Hudson: Anthroposophic Press 1994.

50 See Steiner, R., *The Evolution of Consciousness. As Revealed through Initiation Knowledge.* Penmaenmawr. Thirteen lectures. Tr. V. E. Watkin, C. Davy. London: Rudolf Steiner Press 1966.

51 See Steiner, R., *A Modern Art of Education* (GA 307). Tr. J. Darrell. L13 by G. Adams. London: Rudolf Steiner Press 1970.

52 The reference to the sun in the Virgin in this passage is puzzling. When the Bull stood at the spring equinox the Virgin was adjacent to the summer solstice, then occupied by the Lion. The Scorpion stood at the autumn equinox and the Waterman at the winter solstice. It would make more sense, therefore, if the passage read 'Yet when the sun stood in the Waterman ...' (which it would have done in December). Three of these zodiacal regions are reflected in the Mithras myth — the Bull, the Scorpion and the Man (Waterman) on the bull's back. The Lion represented a grade of initiation in the mysteries of Mithras while the sun in the Waterman has always been a symbol of resurrection and rebirth. Since Steiner was not in a position to check the transcript of these lectures for accuracy himself, it is important that attention should be drawn to what appear to be errors of fact. Editor.

53 Friedrich Rittelmeyer, PhD (1872–1938), German Protestant pastor; well-known preacher at Nuremberg from 1902 to 1916, later at the Neue Kirche in Berlin; co-founder and first leader of the Christian Community when this was founded in 1922 (movement for religious renewal).

54 The distance light travels in a year (at a rate of *c*. 300,000 km/s) is approximately 9.46×10^{12} km.

55 Der Kommende Tag Scientific Institute (including a biological department), and Der Kommende Tag Institute of Clinical Medicine.

FROM COMETS TO COCAINE...

Answers to Questions

Rudolf Steiner

Nicotine and alcohol; the causes and timing of illness; pregnancy; vegetarian and meat diets; the human ear, eye and hair colour; influenza, hay fever, haemophilia; planets and metals; mental illness; the ice age; the thyroid gland and hormones; beavers, wasps and bees; the nose, smell and taste; jaundice, smallpox and rabies, and much more!

ISBN 1 85584 088 X; 320 pages; £14.95

FROM LIMESTONE TO LUCIFER...

Answers to Questions

Rudolf Steiner

Technology; the living earth; natural healing powers; colour and sickness; rainbows; whooping cough and pleurisy; seances; sleep and sleeplessness; dreams; reincarnation; life after death; the physical, ether and astral bodies and the 'I'; the two Jesus children; Ahriman and Lucifer; the death, resurrection and ascension of Christ; Dante and Copernicus, and much more!

ISBN 1 85584 097 9; 256 pages; £12.95